Stephanie Cain Van D'Elden

Peter Suchenwirt and Heraldic Poetry

Verlag Karl M. Halosar
Wien 1976

PT 1656
S82Z8

ISBN 3-900 269-06-8
©Verlag Karl M. Halosar, A-1040 Wien.
Druck: Offsetschnelldruck A. Riegelnik

PETER SUCHENWIRT AND HERALDIC POETRY

Stephanie Cain Van D'Elden

ERRATA

Abbreviations, Zeile 5 für Neimeyer lese Niemeyer
Seite 22, Zeile 11 für persuit lese pursuit
Seite 35, Zeile 10 für become lese becomes
Seite 62, Zeile 3 für den lese dem
Seite 62, Zeile 3 für drea lese drey
Seite 75, Zeile 1 für gules, lese (gules,
Seite 117, Zeile 17 für sines lese shines
Seite 119, Zeile 17 für durch lese "durch
Seite 121, Zeile 6 für were lese was
Seite 124, Zeile 28 für Gutherie lese Guthrie
Seite 125, Zeile 36 für Pälastina lese Palästina
Seite 126, Zeile 33 für Hugo II lese Hugo III
Seite 141, Zeile 25 für on lese of
Seite 144, Zeile 32 für Phanberg lese Phfanberg
Seite 145, Zeile 34 für whould lese should
Seite 146, Zeile 15 für for lese of
Seite 148, Zeile 6 für Garaert lese Geraert
Seite 148, Zeile 9 für Neuft lese Nueft
Seite 149, Zeile 5 für Neuft lese Nueft
Seite 149, Zeile 28 für Neuft lese Nueft
Seite 155, Zeile 28 für were lese where
Seite 157, Zeile 6 für maurading lese marauding
Seite 160, Zeile 31 für armies, lese armies and
Seite 166, Zeile 23 für a lese as
Seite 181, Zeile 34 für terms. lese terms,
Seite 208, Zeile 16 für courses lese sources
Seite 215, Zeile 28 für to lese for virtue
Seite 216, Zeile 20 für Aristotles lese Aristotle
Seite 216, Zeile 36 für füursten lese fürsten
Seite 239, Zeile 11 für snonymous lese synonymous
Seite 254, Zeile 9 für unedirte lese unedierte
Seite 266, Zeile 3 für 34 lese 43
Seite 266, Zeile 10 füge hinzu pp. 123-132.
Seite 270, Zeile 36 für baben-bergisch- lese babenbergisch-
Seite 276, Zeile 7 für Goerg lese Georg
Seite 277, Zeile 20 für Templeordens lese Templerordens
Seite 277, Zeile 36 für 47 lese 43.
Seite 280, Zeile 2 für beytrag lese Beytrag
Seite 280, Zeile 8 für Moten lese Moyen
Seite 281, Zeile 10 für 301 lese 310
Seite 283, Zeile 22 füge hinzu 1970.
Seite 287, Zeile 10 für Schöen- lese Schön-
Seite 287, Zeile 19 für 8.3.lese 8,3
Seite 288, Zeile 26a nach 203, füge hinzu see Suchenwirt VII
Seite 291, Zeile 18a für Garaert lese Geraert
Seite 291, Zeile 10b für Gutherie lese Guthrie
Seite 292, Zeile 10a für Neuft lese Nueft
Seite 292, Zeile 20a für Eral lese Earl
Seite 292, Zeile 3b für 138 lese 139
Seite 292, Zeile 15b für 161 lese 261

CONTENTS

PREFACE

The justification of this book lies, I think, in the fact that it is the only work so far to attempt an evaluation of Peter Suchenwirt as a heraldic poet, to trace the development of German heraldic poetry of the Middle Ages to the end of the fourteenth century, and to compare it to the same genre in other literatures of that period. My interest in the subject matter began with my doctoral dissertation which was written under the guidance of Professor Evelyn S. Firchow of the University of Minnesota, for whose many helpful suggestions I am most grateful. Although this book represents a substantial revision of my dissertation I would be remiss if I did not extend thanks to the members of my committee, among whom Professors M. Alison Stones, Gerhard Weiss, and Ronald Akehurst were especially helpful with constructive suggestions, as was my husband, Professor Karl H. Van D'Elden of Hamline University.

During the preparation of the final version I received many useful suggestions from Professor Otto Höfler and Dr. Manfred Zips of the University of Vienna. Throughout the entire project I relied on numerous occasions on the gracious assistance of Mr. Hans Blosen of the University of Aarhus whose forthcoming edition of Peter Suchenwirt will greatly enhance the body of knowledge concerning this unique poet.

The libraries of the Universities of Minnesota and Vienna generously supported my research, and without the gracious help of the Frankfurt and Berlin offices of IBM Deutschland GmbH and IBM Österreich the preparation of the final copy would have been far more difficult.

Regarding the bibliography I have tried to steer a middle course between giving too much and too little. If I have erred by supplying too many titles, no harm will have been done. The same applies to the index in which I attempted to list the most important items, especially names and places. The glossary of heraldic terms is designed for readers with a limited knowledge of heraldry and in the hope that it may facilitate coping with the numerous variants of the same terms.

ABBREVIATIONS

ADB	*Allgemeine Deutsche Biographie.* Berlin: Duncker and Humblot. 1875-1912; rpt. 1967-1971.
AfdA	*Anzeiger für deutsches Altertum und deutsche Literatur.*
ATB	Altdeutsche Textbibliothek. Halle/Tübingen: Max Neimeyer, 1881 ff.
DTM	Deutsche Texte des Mittelalters. Berlin: Deutsche Akademie der Wissenschaften, 1904 ff.
DVLG	*Deutsche Vierteljahrsschrift für Literaturwissenschaft und Geisteswissenschaft.*
GAG	Göppinger Arbeiten zur Germanistik.
GRM	*Germanisch-Romanische Monatsschrift.*
MF	*Des Minnesangs Frühling.* Ed. Karl Lachmann, Moriż Haupt, and Friedrich Vogt. 34th ed. rev. by Carl von Krauś. Stuttgart: S. Hirzel, 1967.
MGH	Monumenta Germaniae historica.
MIÖG	*Mitteilungen des Instituts für österreichische Geschichtsforschung.*
MSB	*München, Sitzungsberichte der Akademie der Wissenschaften, Phil.-hist. Klasse.*
MLN	*Modern Language Notes.*
NDB	*Neue Deutsche Biographie.* Berlin: Dunker and Humblot, 1853 ff.
PBB	*Beiträge zur Geschichte der deutschen Sprache und Literatur.*
RL	*Reallexikon der deutschen Literaturgeschichte.* Ed. Paul Merker and Wolfgang Stammler. 1st. ed. 4 vols. 1925-1931; 2nd ed. Klaus Kanzog, Werner Kohlschmidt, and Wolfgang Mohr. Berlin: Walter de Gruyter, 1958 ff.
SAH	*Schweizer Archiv für Heraldik.* Also known as *Archives héraldiques Suisses* and *Archivio Araldico Svizzero.*
SLV	Bibliothek des Litterarischen Vereins in Stuttgart. Stuttgart and Tübingen: H. Laupp.
VL	*Die deutsche Literatur des Mittelalters. Verfasserlexikon.* Ed. Wolfgang Stammler and Karl Langosch. 5 vols. Berlin: Walter de Gruyter, 1933-1955.

WSB	Wien, Sitzungsberichte der Akademie der Wissenschaften, Phil.-hist. Klasse.
ZfdA	Zeitschrift für deutsches Altertum und deutsche Literatur.
ZfdPh	Zeitschrift für deutsche Philologie.
ZfdU	Zeitschrift für den deutschen Unterricht.

INTRODUCTION

It is difficult today to ascertain precisely how prevalent heraldic poetry was in the fourteenth century when Peter Suchenwirt flourished. Although documentation is erratic, the persistent interest in heraldry from the twelfth century through the sixteenth century, indeed up to modern times, suggests that it was an obvious topic for popular poetry. On the other hand, Otfried Weber takes the position that heraldic poetry was not deemed worthy of preservation since it was considered only occasional poetry.[1] He postulates a vast corpus of heraldic poetry in the broad sense, i.e. any work with reference or allusions to heraldry; he maintains that heraldic poetry narrowly defined as *Ehrenreden* or laudatory addresses was also popular but that much has been lost. While disregarding "lost literature," the examples discussed here are representative of heraldic poetry of the time. Furthermore, they reveal much about the late Middle Ages—history, customs, politics, and people including heralds.

Among the literary genres listed in the most recent literary histories is *Herolds- und Wappendichtung* which Hans Rupprich[2] loosely defines as a description of arms combined with an *Ehrenrede*. After praise of the famous deeds of the hero being honored, the poet provides a professional description of the arms and the armor, especially the shield and helmet. The general term *Ehrenrede* was first coined by Alois Primisser, the editor of Peter Suchenwirt's[3] works, and was applied solely to Suchenwirt's poems honoring famous Austrian nobles. These were poems which followed a strict formula. They begin with an introduction with a formal expression of humility, then continue with general praise of the hero, description of his specific deeds, repetition of general praise, prayer for intercession of his soul (if the hero was already deceased), description of his coat of arms, both shield and helmet, name of the hero with a short closing prayer. Obvious prototypes of the *Ehrenrede* such as death laments and other addresses of praise which were popular

among the Greeks, Romans, and early settlers of Northern
Europe are not considered *Ehrenreden* per se since they do not
adhere to the strictly defined formula.

The most distinctive elements of the *Ehrenrede* are the
specific enumeration of the hero's deeds (which makes the
Ehrenrede individual and personal) and the description of the
hero's arms. It will be shown that the *Ehrenrede* as defined
here appears fully developed only in the works of Peter
Suchenwirt, a herald in the service of the Dukes of Austria,
and the herald known as Gelre from Gelders[4] on the Lower
Rhine. While the highly formularized *Ehrenrede* may be isolated,
a precise definition of the broader term heraldic poetry and
the heraldic poem *(Wappengedicht)* remains elusive; heraldic
poetry is frequently defined in terms of Peter Suchenwirt and
Gelre, and Suchenwirt is always described as the prime example
of a German heraldic poet. The terms heraldic poetry, heraldic
poem and poet, and *Ehrenrede* need to be examined in the light
of the social, cultural, historical, and literary climate
which produced them. For example, to define a heraldic poem
narrowly in terms of Suchenwirt's *Ehrenreden* is to isolate a
genre of poetry which has far-reaching historical origins.
Rupprich and his predecessors tend to dismiss earlier works
by Heinrich von Veldeke, Hartmann von Aue, and Wolfram von
Eschenbach who also included coats of arms as integral parts
of their works; their works are not considered true heraldic
poetry *(keine eigentliche Wappendichtung)*.[5] Even Konrad von
Würzburg, who in the middle of the thirteenth century described the armor and arms of knights participating in an
imaginary tournament at Nantes, is not considered a true
heraldic poet because his descriptions are not those of a
professional herald. Rupprich maintains that the true heraldic poets, successors of the *Spielleute,* are *Reimsprecher* who
appear in the service of noblemen at tournaments where they
call out the name of their masters and recite the meaning
of various coats of arms.

It is obvious that interest in heraldry was high in the
Middle Ages: many heraldic books, heraldic treatises, and
references and allusions to heraldry in literary works attest

to this fact. However, there are very few extant examples of
Ehrenreden which are similar to Suchenwirt's. Should heraldic
poetry then be defined narrowly as *Ehrenreden* according to
Peter Suchenwirt's model or broadly as all works containing
heraldic material?

The purpose here is to examine heraldic poetry of the
fourteenth century and especially the poetry of its chief
German exponent, Peter Suchenwirt, to determine whether a
broad or a narrow definition of the genre should be adopted.
First it is important to understand the role of heraldry and
the state of heraldry in the fourteenth century. Heraldry
was becoming more regulated and formal and the symbolic
reasons for selecting heraldic charges was becoming less
vital. Since the narrow definition of heraldic poetry seems
to require a herald as author, the role of heralds needs to
be examined to ascertain whether they are indeed suited to
this task and whether writing heraldic poetry was considered
to be one of their duties. There was a change in the roles
of heralds--from *Spielleute* to ambassadors and confidential
advisers, from criers at tournaments to the organizers of
tournaments--to positions of responsibility and authority.
Although there is much evidence that they compiled heraldic
books, there is less evidence that they also wrote poetry.

The immediate prototypes for fourteenth century heraldic
poetry include the death lament tradition, political-historical
songs which sometimes contain heraldic allusions and always
contain biographical information about heroes--axiomatic to
the *Ehrenrede*--and finally the subgenre of heraldic poetry
which may be called "tournament and siege poems." The heraldic
poet, the composer of *Ehrenreden*, must have been familiar with
these prototypes and with their diverse components including
history, biography, politics, heraldry, the art of tournaments and warfare.

In order to place Suchenwirt's work in its proper
chronological perspective, these prototypes must be considered first, and they are, therefore, discussed in detail
in PART ONE. While others have mentioned the relationship

between Suchenwirt and his predecessors, the contents of his works have not previously been examined in detail to support this theory.

The heraldic poet Peter Suchenwirt, who is discussed in PART TWO, performed several roles--those of herald, historian, and political commentator--in the composition of his *Ehrenreden*. In addition, the second major heraldic poet of the fourteenth century, the Netherlandic herald Gelre, will be discussed in relationship to heraldic poetry in general and to the Austrian herald.Suchenwirt in particular.

An examination of the roles performed by these poets may lead to a definition and an understanding of the nature of heraldic poetry, *Ehrenreden,* and the heraldic poet--especially Peter Suchenwirt.

PART ONE: HERALDIC POETRY

I. THE ORIGIN AND SYMBOLISM OF HERALDRY

In the Middle Ages heraldry maintained an all encompassing position touching upon virtually every element of society. Its importance was not questioned; its significance was understood by all. Evidence of heraldry appeared on the battlefield, at tournaments, on armor, weapons, shields, and flags, on the horses' bardings, on tents, in the crest, badge, and device, in the livery, in the battle cry, in military, ecclesiastical, and domestic architecture, on tapestries, illuminations, seals, jewelry, and clothing. A knowledge of heraldry formed part of a gentleman's education, and was recognized by the people in popular political songs. In England heraldry was regulated by Visitations, i.e. tours of inspection conducted by heralds, that is officers of arms, once every generation from 1413 to 1686.[6] Such systematic regulation of heraldry did not develop on a wide scale in Germany because of the myriad political divisions. As early as the fourteenth century, however, there is documentation of the existence of concern that two knights should not bear the same arms (see pp. 21, 75). Long after tournaments and armor ceased to be important the social and genealogical impact of heraldry remained vigorously alive.

The importance of heraldry in the lives of everyone in the Middle Ages quite naturally leads to the question of its origin. Every scholar writing on the subject of heraldry has been plagued by this problem, and since it has consumed so much time of the scholars and non-scholars, it is appropriate here to examine several theories of the origin of heraldry. One school of thought places an exact date upon the origin of coats of arms "aus dem dringenden Bedürfnis nach einer weit sichtbaren Kennzeichnung,...als praktische Notwendigkeit."[7] A date in the twelfth century is generally accepted in the theory that heraldry is the direct result of the crusades and the need for "cognizance" among armored knights. Donald Lindsay Galbreath suggests three possibilities for the origin of coats of arms:

1. the derivation of arms from family and city signs of the classical past,

2. the takeover and adoption of arms through the Crusaders from the Orientals, and

3. the most recently postulated connection with Germanic runes.[8]

Eliminating all vestiges of heraldry before the twelfth century, other scholars define coats of arms narrowly; for example, according to Johann Christian Siebenkees a coat of arms

1. must be regular, not arbitrary or haphazard,

2. must be permanent, perpetual, and unchangeable, a family sign, and hereditary,

3. must be a sign of special superiority, an honor or privilege.[9]

Furthermore, Siebenkees maintains that the essence or core of heraldry is Germanic in origin.

Anthony Wagner upholds the same position when he defines "true heraldry...as the systematic use of hereditary devices centred on the shield."[10] He maintains that "contrary to . popular belief, most Coats of Arms have no known meaning. Their primary purpose was and is to be distinctive, not significant, and it is certain that many designs have been fixed upon for no better reason than that they happen not to have been used before. But," he continues, "this only makes more interesting these cases in which a definite reason for the adoption of a coat is known or inferred."[11] Furthermore he claims:

> The elaborate researches of Smith Ellis and others have brought to light nothing that can safely be called heraldic (in our sense) of earlier date than this [second quarter of the twelfth century], unless it be the strikingly similar system of family devices prevalent in Athens in the sixth and fifth centuries before Christ; which, however, died away without posterity or traceable connexion with the heraldry of the Middle Ages.[12]

Thus this theory eliminates characters or signs which serve as religious or profane subjects such as Mercury's serpent staff, Neptune's trident, or Apollo's lyre. The shields and helmets of the Egyptians, the flags and coins of Greek city-states, the Roman eagle, the bear of the Goths, the olive branch of peace, rings for engagements are not considered heraldic.

A second approach to the origin of arms is to postulate a preheraldic time out of which heraldry suddenly developed.[13] Accordingly, evidence of heraldry before the twelfth century is designated preheraldic. This approach allows one to discuss the fascinating "preheraldic" precedents such a flags, shields, and coins of antiquity, the pictorial account of the shields on the Bayeux Tapestry, and eye-witness accounts of the First Crusade without having to label them as heraldry, then to continue with post twelfth century examples.

Finally, Otto Höfler[14] takes a broader evolutionary position which encompasses all the other theories. He states that the criteria for "true" heraldry postulated by Siebenkees and others do not occur simultaneously which greatly increases the difficulty of establishing an exact date. Some would place the hour of birth of heraldry in 1127 when Henry I of England presented his future son-in-law, Geoffrey of Anjou, with a lion's shield. Others see "true" heraldry in the shields of the Bayeux Tapestry, shortly after 1066, certainly before 1082. Quite a difference! Thus if one concedes that the distinction between preheraldry and heraldry did not occur at a specific point in time, that it evolved slowly over a number of years, even centuries, then it is also logical to assume that the forms themselves evolved slowly over the years. If one discards the notion of a radical break between preheraldic and heraldic times, then one can look for possible continuities and connections between the two periods.[15]

Heraldic symbolism presents a similar problem for examination as exemplified by the following discussion of animal and figure charges selected for symbolic reasons. The boar, for example, appears as the heraldic symbol of numerous European noble families. Théodore de Renesse[16] counted no fewer than 913 families who either have a whole boar, a boar's head, or boar's tusks in their coats of arms. These include such names as Eber, Everswyn, Swynskop, Swyneshead, Pigg, and Hogg. Warriors' helmets with boar's figures appear in Sweden

as early as the seventh century; the heraldic helmet of Lord
Basset of Drayton (†1390) includes a boar's head growing out
of the helmet--the closed visor acts as a mask.[17]

In the case of Henry the Lion or Richard the Lionhearted
no one doubts the symbolic character of the name. When
Walther von der Vogelweide greeted Emperor Otto IV

> Ir tragt zwei keisers ellen: 13,2,7
> des aren tugent des lewen kraft,
> die sint des herren zeichen an dem schilte,[18]

he was referring not only to the Emperor's coat of arms which
included the half eagle and three lions, but Walther was more
importantly pointing out the fact that this man had a share
of the very being of the eagle, the king of the birds, and
of the lion, the king of the beasts.

There must be a basic symbolic reason (Höfler calls it
a *Wesens-Beziehung*) for the selection of animals or figures to
designate families, individuals or races. This choice does
not seem to be arbitrary. Nor does it seem to stem from
purely practical purposes of recognition (such as signs chosen
by firms--the Mercedes' star or the peace symbol) since
hundreds of families wear the boar in their arms and research
indicates that relatively few animals out of many possibilities have been chosen for coats of arms.

The relationship between a knight and his arms was very
close; a famous knight honored his arms, and famous arms
could bring fame and honor to their bearers. Descriptions
of arms frequently include the formula "als (sam) er (es)
lebete," thus closely identifying the bearer with the coat of
arms.[19] Similarly the practice of naming a sword and assign-
ing to it a personality dates back to early Germanic times.[20]
In prehistoric times animals were chosen to bring the wearer
protection and help. Coats of arms may be insulted, e.g.
the vilification of the banner of Leopold V of Austria in
1191 by the order of Richard the Lionhearted at Acre, an
action which had serious political consequences. When
heraldic symbols are employed as family names which no longer
express or even symbolize any innate being and merely function
as distinguishing marks they are deprived of their meaning

and can lose their power just as their bearers lose their
power; thus the boar, the dog, the eagle, and the lion may
be reduced to mere labels.

The best evidence regarding the symbolic meaning of
animals, figures, and colors comes from medieval nature
treatises, epic poems, official rolls and documents, and
from heraldic treatises.

Thomasin von Zirclaria includes a very instructive
chapter on heraldic symbolism and heraldic language in his
Wälscher Gast (ca. 1216). Although Thomasin is primarily
interested in the allegory and symbolism involved in the
choice of arms and does not present a reliable set of rules,
this work represents the oldest treatise representative of
the spirit of the thirteenth century:

> Swer an sîm schilde vüeren solde   10425
> rôsen, ob er danne wolde
> die bluomen gar ûz dem gevilde
> ouch vüeren an dem schilde,
> des diuhte mich gar ze vil.
> daz selbe ich iu sagen wil,
> swer die sunnen vüeren solde,
> ob diuhte daz er vüeren wolde
> die sterne und dar zuo den mân
> und den himel, ez wær seltsân:
> sîn wære halt gar ze vil....
> swaz er vüeret amme schilde,   10447
> ist ob er vrum ûfme gevilde,
> ich vertragez deste baz,
> ir sult mir wol gelouben daz....
> swer den eber vüeren sol   10457
> an sîme gewæfen, hüete wol
> daz er nin vüere ein swînherte gar,
> wan daz stüend übel, daz ist wâr.[21]

The epic poets were often quite explicit in explaining
the motives behind the choice of particular coats of arms.
Wolfram von Eschenbach was especially concerned with knighthood, with heraldry, and with providing his hero with good
credentials. To the Parzival story of Chrétien de Troyes he
prefixed two books of his own, containing the story of
Parzival's father, Gahmuret of Anjou. Gahmuret rejects the
family arms, choosing for himself an anchor cut out of ermine.
But Wolfram tells his audience that this anchor never struck
ground, either on land or in port:[22]

> sîn anker heten niht bekort   14,28
> ganzes lands noch landes ort,
> dane wârn si ninder în geslagen:
> der hêrre muose fürbaz tragen
> disen wâpenlîchen last
> in manegiu land, der werde gast,
> Nâch dem anker disiu mâl,
> wand er deheiner slahte twâl
> hete ninder noch gebite.
> wie vil er lande durchrite
> und in schiffen embefüere?[23]

At the tournament at Kanvoleis King Kaylet of Spain, bearing
an ostrich as his crest and a dragon's head on his shield,
begged Gahmuret's help against King Hardise of Gascony.
Gahmuret replied: "Does your ostrich still stand there without
a nest? Drive your dragon's head against his demi-griffin.
If he charges against me, my anchor will strike ground in him."

> stêt dîn strûz noch sunder nest?   68,7
> du solt dîn sarapandratest
> gein sînem halben grîfen tragn.
> mîn anker vaste wirt geslagn
> durch lenden in sîns poinders hurt.

Wolfram pursues this theme of an anchor seeking anchorage
until Gahmuret inherits the crown of Anjou upon the death of
his older brother. At a tournament in Valois he meets a
knight wearing the sable panther of Anjou inverted, signifying the death of the heir. Gahmuret exclaims that his anchor
has struck ground at last:

> ich sol mîns vater wâpen tragn: 99,13
> sîn lant mîn anker hât beslagn.
> der anker ist ein recken zil:
> den trage und nem nu swer der wil.

In the case of Heinrich von dem Türlin (ca. 1220) the
motive involved in the choice of arms includes a humorous
twist:

> Er vuorte ûf sînem schilde   9812
> Von swarz ein rûhe bern klâ
> (Der schilt was gar anderswâ
> An dem velde von golde)
> Dâ bî man wizzen solde,
> Daz er was wilder denne ein ber.[24]

The rough black claw on the shield indicates to all that he
was wilder than a bear.

It is typical for the late Middle Ages that many
contemporaries saw the origin of coats of arms in biblical

lore. A Welsh book of arms by John Trevor (1557) entitled
Llyfr Arfau illustrates this biblical approach:

> Arms were first borne after the time of the Flood, when the
> heavenly four coloured arc appeared, which is called the rain-
> bow, and which is visible against the sun through a dark cloud.
> And these four colours are produced from the four substances
> from which are made all created things, namely, fire, air, water,
> and earth; the red colour from the fire, the ruddy colour from
> the sky, green from water, and dusty black from the earth.[25]

The earliest treatises on heraldry were not only
concerned with the origins of arms but also with the intrinsic
symbolic value of the colors and figures. For example, Trevor
asks why red is "ordained to a prince more than white or black
or blue or golden colour?" The answer is "because this colour
represents cruelty, and a prince ought to be cruel towards his
enemies, and it behooves him to punish disorder. And every
cruel wild animal that lives on flesh and blood of other
animals hates and fears this colour. This colour, too, is
borne by the kings of England in their arms...."[26]

Hartmann von Aue in *Erec* defends his use of a single
color, red, for a coat of arms:

> sîn ros was grôz unde hô,   9015
> starc rôt zundervar:
> der varwe was sîn schilt gar:
> sîn wâpenroc alsam was,
> er selbe rôt, als ich ez las,
> gewâfent nach sînem muote.
> ich wæne sîn herze bluote
> swenne er niht ze vehtenne envant;
> sô mordic was sîn hant.[27]

The same symbolic rationale lies behind the choice of
animals for coats of arms. Perhaps the most popular animal
in Germanic heraldry is the eagle. Scholars of the Middle
Ages especially praised the keen sight, the power of rejuvenation, and the generosity of the eagle. The aspect of
rejuvenation is emphasized in the German version of the
Physiologus from the twelfth century entitled "Von Tieren unde
Fogelen:"

> es zelt Phisiologus des Aren geslehte sus.
> so der Ar alt wirdet, so swærent im die vederen, die
>   ougen im tunchelent.
> so suochet er an den stunden einen chochen brunnen
> unde vliuget von dem brunnen uf zuo dem sunnen.

da brennet er sine vedere, in den brunne vellet er nidere,
der im da zuo ist worden chunt, daz tuot er danne dri stunt.
so wirt er gejunget unde darnach gesehent.[28]

The poets especially praised the generosity of the eagle,
for this was one of the most admired knightly virtues--fortune
without generosity was considered worthless. Heinrich von
Veldeke writes in *Eneide* (1184-1186):

ein adelar sînes goedes   12619
end ein lêwe sînes moedes.[29]

The virtuous scribe in the *Sängerkrieg* on the Wartburg maintains:

sô weiz ich einen derst von kindes jugent   3,7
ob im ein adelar.
zuo allen zîten ist mit hôhen vlügen er gewesen
darzuo hât er gein vînden wol eins vrechen lewen muot.[30]

The eagle was not a suitable symbol for the poor knight who
could not afford to be generous and who would have been
ridiculed had he sported an eagle in his arms. Thomasin von
Zirclaria explains:

Swen diu milte ist an geborn,   13997
ist er arm, er hât verlorn
sîner brieve insigel gar.
dâ von geschiht, daz ist wâr,
daz man dem brieve geloubet niht
dâ manz insigel an niht siht.[31]

On the other hand, a rich knight who did not practice generosity could bring dishonor to his arms as seen in the
Jüngere Titurel by Albrecht von Scharffenberg (1272):

ich nenne ir nicht besunder, wan Artus den wirt von
    disem lande.   1861,4
Der adelar ist gezweiet an siten von nature.
mit grozer milte er heiet der vogel, vil doch wirt
    etslichem sure,
swelchen er begrifet mit den fůzen.
er trit ie uf den nehsten und let di andern alle
    hungers buzen.
Nu was der eren blůme Artus in solcher milte.
sim hohen adel ze růme fůrt er den adelar an sinem schilte
halp vor her dan, daz ander teil enpernde,
der snabel trůc die milte, die fůze waren vogel todes wernde.[32]

These are only a few examples from medieval authors
proclaiming and explaining the symbolic reasoning involved in
heraldry. By the fourteenth century the symbolic reasoning

behind each coat of arms may have been forgotten, but nevertheless the coats of arms were still important to the entire
concept of knighthood. A knight without arms was not a knight.
Arms continued to bring honor to a family and could still be
dishonored or insulted. The very act of identifying a man
with his arms was a method of honoring a man. King Richard II
impaled his own royal arms with the arms, as he called them,
of St. Edward, the Confessor, a gold cross and five martlets
on a blue field (azure, a cross patonce between five martlets
or).[33] These arms were certainly never borne by St. Edward,
but in Richard's time it would have been inconceivable for
a king not to have arms. In this same spirit arms were
assigned to Moses, Solomon, Alexander the Great, King Arthur,
and Charlemagne, among others. This is the main reason why
Peter Suchenwirt carefully blazons the shield and helmets of
the knights he honors in his *Ehrenreden*.

The broadly defined heraldic poetry of earlier centuries,
in which the symbolic nature of the arms is all important,
thus gives way to the narrowly defined heraldic poetry of the
Ehrenreden, in which the arms are inherently important in a
matter-of-fact way and their very existence confers honor
upon the bearer. Thus the social-historical change, that is,
the fact that arms are no longer selected for symbolic
reasons and that the symbolism intrinsic to older arms is
forgotten, is reflected in a literary change in which the
focus of attention shifts from imaginary epic heroes to the
true heroes of the age.

II. HERALDS

In the twelfth and thirteenth centuries wandering poets, clerics, and minor nobility generally wrote romances about imaginary heroes bearing symbolic coats of arms. But as early as 1250 Konrad von Würzburg wrote about real heroes at an imaginary tournament at Nantes. By the fourteenth century heralds such as Peter Suchenwirt, Gelre, and the Chandos Herald wrote of the deeds of true heroes with real coats of arms. The literary shift in focus from imaginary coats of arms and imaginary heroes to real ones suggests not only a change in public demand but also in the position of the authors of popular literary works. The heralds of the four-teenth century are closely related to the wandering poets of earlier times; however, they now emerge as literary figures of somewhat higher social stature and increased responsi-bilities.

Although the term "herald" has early Germanic etymo-logical origins,[34] it appears to have been reintroduced into German from the French *hiraut* or English *herald*. The first reference to a herald in French literature[35] is in *Le chevalier de la charrete* by Chrêtien de Troyes, written between 1164 and 1174. In this episode the herald, contrary to what was expected of him, fails to recognize the disguised Lancelot. But this, of course, is part of the story:

```
Lanceloz trestoz desarmez      5533
s'estoit sor ce lit acostez.
La ou il jut si povremant,
a tant ez vos un garnemant,
un hyraut d'armes, an chemise,
qui an la taverne avoit mise
sa cote avoec sa chauceüre,
et vint nuz piez grant aleüre,
desafublez contre le vant;
l'escu trova a l'uis devant,
si l'esgarda; mes ne pot estre
qu'il coneüst lui ne son mestre,
ne set qui porter le devoit.[36]
```

The term "herald" is not found in German literature and German documents prior to the fourteenth century, possi-bly because heralds played a very lowly and unimportant role or, more likely, because they were given other titles. The

forerunners of heralds in Germany were a class whom the poets
called *farende liute*. They appear in literary works from 1180
on in connection with battles, tournaments, and festivals.
An early example is found in *Erec* by Hartmann von Aue (ca.
1195):

```
swaz der diete dar kam        2166
diu guot umbe êre nam,
der entete man eines niht rât.
den gelimph varndez volc hât,
swâ man einem vil gît
und dem andern niht, des hât er nît
und vluochet der hôchzît.37
```

"Sie nehmen Gut um Ehre," that is: they praise the name of
the generous, but one should not arouse their envy. If they
believe they are receiving less compensation than others,
they will spread evil talk throughout the land--they curse
the festive occasion.

Just how dangerous it was to incur the displeasure of
these people is described by the poet known as "Der Unverzagte:"

```
Swen gernde liute gerne suochent, der ist eren riche:   III,8,1
swen gernde liute schiuwent, der ist maniger tugende vri.
Swen gernde liute gerne an sent, der lebet gar wirdikliche;
swen gernde liute ungerne sent dem won(e)t schande bi.
Swen gernde liute minnent, der ist gerne an triuwen stæte;
swen gernde liute hazzent, seht, der pflit vil valscher ræte.
swen gernde liute prisent, der ist sæliklîche geborn:
swen gernde liute vluochent, der hat triuwe unde ere unt
    wirdikeit verlorn.38
```

He who treats *farende liute* well, will be rewarded, but he who
curses them will lose all courtly virtues and will be shamed.

The broad term *farende liute* included a number of sub-
classes: 1) *die garzûne*, 2) *die crogierer*, 3) *die spilliute*. The
documentary evidence pertaining to the status and remuneration
of these sub-classes is confusing and often conflicting.
Apparently the *garzûne* and *crogierer* were a step above the
spilliute and fulfilled the duties which later accrued to the
heralds.[39] The name *garzûne* clearly comes from French *garçon*.
Eilhart von Oberge translates this directly from French in
his *Tristan:*

```
do geschûfen die jungelinge    8228
an al iren gebêrin
```

> und mit cleidern, als sie wêren
> zwêne varende knappen:
> zwô rôte korze knappen
> trûgen die garzûne
> in wâren die schapperûne
> von gelwem fritschâle.[40]

In *Wigamur* (before 1230) *garzaun* is translated as *pot*, i.e.

messenger:

> Mit schoner kurthaseye   4682
> Naygt sich gen menigelichen der garzaun;
> Scharlach rot und prawn
> Was sein mantel gehalbiert,
> Mit zendal gefüttert.
> Der pot also dannen lieff.[41]

Thus the loanword *garzûne* and the translation *varender knappe* or *bot* appear together and are synonyms, describing those who fulfill the same duties and obligations as the later heralds.[42]

About the same time the term *crogierer (crôjierære, grogirer)* is used for the same position. The differences between the *garzûne* and the *crogierer* are unclear, but Gustav Seyler believes that the *garzûne* stood one step higher.[43] Thus in *Biterolf*:

> vil manic crôjierære sprach 11884
> nâch site âner herren lant.
> man pruovte ir helm unde ir rant.
> dar zuo ir ritterlîchen muot.[44]

And in *Willehalm* by Rudolf von Ems (ca. 1230):

> Die grogirer da liefen,   6747
> Grogierende si riefen
> ,Wara war! wer kumet da?'[45]

The entire class of *farende liute* belonged to those without rights, to the propertyless. In the *Sachsenspiegel* in a chapter entitled "Von aller lûte weregelde und bûze; wer âne weregelt sî" one finds:

> Spillûten und alle den, die sich zu eigen geben, den gibt
> man zu bûze den schaten eines mannes. Kemphen unde iren
> kinderen den gibt man zu bûze den blic von eime kamphschilde
> gein die sunnen.[46]

The shadow of a man or the reflection *(Blick)* from a battle shield turned towards the sun, in other words: there was no punishment for killing one of these people.

Towards the end of the thirteenth century the terms *garzûne* and *crogierer* tend to disappear to be replaced by the *knappen von den wâpen (knaben von den wâpen, wappenknaben, knechte von*

den wapene, chnappen von den wappen, etc.). Konrad von Würzburg
writes in his *Turnier von Nantes:*

> ein cnappe von den wâpen reit   952
> des mâles dâ croijierende
> und mangen schilt brüevierende;[47]

and in *Engelhard:*

> und swaz der ritter ûz erwelt   2752
> rosse dâ bejagete
> diu gap der unverzagete
> den knaben von den wâpen.[48]

In the middle of the fourteenth century Peter Suchenwirt
writes in connection with Burgrave Albert of Nuremberg:

> Ir chnappen von den wappen hört,   VII,11
> Tzung unde munt mit lieb erpört,
> Dy von den wappen tichtens phlegen,
> Nicht lat mit willen underwegen.[49]

These individuals appear in North German documents as *knapen
von den wâpen,* variously spelled: a document from the monastery
Broda from 1230, recorded in the *Mecklenburgische Jahrbücher,* was
witnessed by "Hans und Gerezlaw broder, knapen, van wopen,
heten Hauelberg." The editor of the *Mecklenburgische Jahrbücher,*
perhaps confused by the punctuation, claims he does not know
where the town "Wopen" is located. In a document from the
Großherzogliche Archiv in Schwerin from 1392 a "Henneke Wedele
en knape van wapene" is mentioned. Syffred von Bydenfeld
calls himself "ein Knappe von deme Wapene" in a document
from 1332.[50]

    In the thirteenth century during the reign of Rudolf of
Habsburg the title *herold* was not used in Germany; however,
a certain Meister Rûmelant wrote a poem about an evil
character with the name "Heralt" who praised bad men and
damned good men. Seyler maintains that Meister Rûmelant
copied the poem from an English original and misunderstood
"heralt" for a person's name; clearly it stood for typical
members of the class of *farende liute* who were always willing
to write songs of praise for monetary rewards.[51] Meister
Rûmelant's poem reads as follows:

> Heralt ein singer was genant, des muot was so verkeret,   IV,25,1
> der sank den bœsen herren lob, unt schalt die guoten.
> Do man des wart gewar, da sprach man: „swer nu ist geuneret,
> der mak sich lobes in Haraldes don vermuoten."

> Der triuwe und ere in herzen truok mit allen guoten dingen,
> den man er schalt;
> dem al diu menge laster sprach, des lop begund' er singen
> des pflak Heralt:
> noch weiz ich den, er enschlichet nimmer also lise
> er enbezzer sich, sin lop kumt in Haraldes wise.[52]

As a title *herold (erald)* was first used in German by
Peter Suchenwirt in the fourteenth century. In the poem
describing the Prussian crusade of Duke Albert III of Austria
in 1377, Suchenwirt writes:

> Eralden und gernde leüt   IV,139
> Des fursten mild al da erfrewt:
> Lerdez! -- man ruft in vrewden gail.

Suchenwirt describes an earlier campaign to Prussia in
connection with Leutold von Stadeck:

> Gen Praizzen durch des gelauben er,   XV,115
> Da man sach tzwene chünig her,
> Vil Pehem und vil Unger
> Mit in vil helde iunger,
> Fürsten, grafen, freyen,
> Der namen hört man chreyen
> Von den eralden, persewant,
> Der wappen volger Tribliant,
> Man sach, da wer der geste vil
> Auz vremden landen ane tzil.

Suchenwirt himself claims to belong to the class of *farende
liute*, to be *ein gernder man,* in his poem "Von dem Phenning:"

> Ich rait allain in fremdew lant,   XXIX,1
> Daz ich den edeln würd bechant,
> Durich notdurft meinez leibs nar
> Nam ich der pideben herren war,
> Als gerndem orden wol antzimpt,
> Der güt durich got, durich ere nympt
> Und chunst beschaidenleichen phligt,
> Der pideben herren ere wigt
> Für die pösen wirdichleich....
> Ich sprach: „Ich nym durich er güt   22
> Und pin tze recht ein gernder man,
> Und sag, waz ich gewizzen chan
> Von den pideben gütes."

Thus the terms *herold, knappen von den wâpen,* and *farende liute*
continue to be used simultaneously and interchangeably. For
example, the Bavarian herald Johann Holandt (ca. 1420) calls
himself alternately *Ernholt* and *Khnab der waffen:*

> Ich Johann Holandt,   1
> Ein Ernholt weit erkhannt,...
> ...darumb ich bin   16
> Ein Khnab der waffen, des Adels Khindt.[53]

Heralds, no matter what they were called, first appear in connection with tournaments. The heralds are sent as messengers by their masters to announce the time and date of a tournament and to invite prospective participants. At the tournament judges are chosen from among the older and experienced knights not taking part; for example, in *Partonopier und Meliur* (11. 13486-13566) by Konrad von Würzburg seven judges are selected. The heralds who are experienced and knowledgeable in the art of heraldry then serve as advisors and couriers for the judges. They have the following duties:

1. to announce the commencement of the tournament

2. to examine the weapons and coats of arms before and during the tournament to insure that no ineligible individuals take part

3. to comment during the tournament on especially artistic thrusts, and afterwards to write songs of praise (?)

4. to call out various battle cries *(Waffenschrei)* such as "wîcha wiche," "warâ wer," "sûsâ," "hurtâ hurt," "ahî," etc.

5. to maintain a schedule of events

6. to summon the knights to church or to battle

7. to give the signal when the tournament is over, "den frideban ruofen"

8. to proclaim the decisions of the judges.

Broken armor, weapons, and other valuables left on the tournament field fell into legal possession of the heralds.

The task of verifying coats of arms *(prüfen, prüfieren, later blasnieren)* was called *Helmschau*. Heralds bring the helmets to be examined. A herald stands with a staff in hand to inspect the helmets and to push away those which are ineligible. This process of elimination is described by Marx Wirsung in connection with a tournament at Augsburg in 1518:

> Als man die helm und klainetern wolt anfahen zů beschawen ward dazů verordnet Jörg Schwabland / dozumal der weyt erfarnest herold im Reich von dem man weßt zu sagen...und so die zeit kumpt das man turnieren so / und nänlich an der herberg ist / sol ain yeder der newer genoß ist und turniern wil zů seinem turnier vogt geen under den er gehört und sich lassen einschreiben / dabey sollen drey herold sein....[54]

The strictness of the *Helmschau* is indicated by a report written in a letter from Heinrich von Vippach, an official on the Wartburg, to Duke Wilhelm zu Sachsen referring to a tournament at Eisenach in 1480. A certain Gotz von Ende was not permitted entrance and could not understand why: both he and Gotz Wolffestorff were wearing the same arms:

> ...er Gotz vom Ende sy geschlagen worden, er wisse aber nicht warum. Werde ich durch ander(e) bericht(et), dass er vom Ende und Gotz Wolffestorff myt worthen Gotz sich yrß woppen halben begriffen haben, also daß sy eyn helmzeichen allewege gefordt haben, sundern er Gotz vom Ende habe synem wolff itzt ein kron uffgesatzt, daß vor nyaner gewest ist. Dy den(n) durch dy zu den helmen geschickten, dy helm zu theylen, dem wolff abgenomen, also dass er sy nicht hat dorffen foren; auch dass er Gotz vom Ende gereht hadt, dass er Gotzen Wolffisdorf nicht zugehore; hierumb lassen sich dy michs bericht(et) haben dungken, dass Gotz Wolffesdorf ern Gotzen vom Ende das zugeschickt habe, dass er geschlagen worden sey. Auch haben sy den genanten Gotzen Wolffesdorff yn tornir nicht wolt(en) rite(n) lass(en).[55]

From a literary point of view the poems of the herald Peter Suchenwirt are most informative regarding the duties of heralds. *Frau Minne* declares, in the poem "Von der Mynn slaff," she will hold a tournament. First she must find a · man *(chnappen)* who can differentiate among coats of arms:

> „Und hiet wir einen chnappen,   XXX,169
> Dem underschaid der wappen
> Wær mit namen wol bechant,
> Der solt verchunden in di lant
> Den türnay in dew Vräudenaw."

Suchenwirt names himself, replying:

> „Vraw, so nemt den Suechenwirt,   XXX,177
> Der red mit worten schon florirt,
> Den vindet man in Österreich
> Pey den fürsten tugentleich."

The Chauvency tournament of 1285, *Tournoi de Chauvency,* by Jacques Bretel clearly emphasizes that heralds were expected to recognize the combatants. The kings of heralds were very occupied by inquiries regarding the identity of various knights; the knights could only be distinguished by their arms, since their faces were obscured by closed helmets. The heralds were quite proud of their skill. In one episode the author calls out the name of a certain knight of Hainault, whereupon a herald questions who "the devil" made him so proficient at *hiraudie:*

> Li chevaliers qui s'aprestoit   470
> Contre lui, fu de vers Hainnaut.
> Adont escrïent cis hiraut.
> Chascunz huia en son latin,
> Et je crioie 'Bazentin'
> Que je ciuda que ce fust cil.
> --'Dïable vos fait si soutil',
> Dist uns hiraus, 'en hiraudie'.[56]

Since Bretel makes many derogatory remarks about heralds, he is not considered to have been a herald himself;[57] he says heralds are boorish and deceitful and greedy in their persuit of booty after tournaments.

ˑA poem of the late thirteenth century, "Li contes des hiraus," by Baudouin de Condé satirizes the life of heralds. The author reminisces about the olden days when heralds roamed the countryside frequenting tournaments from Denmark to Ireland to Flanders. But now, Baudouin claims, they have abandoned their rags as well as their *hiraudie* and attempt to imitate knights:

> Or ont cangiet tout cel abit   513
> Li mal glout, qui tempres labit!
> Il ont mis jus les hiraudies
> Et viestent les cotes hardies
> Et les robes as chevaliers.
> Trop les ont en haus escaliers
> Montés et d'orguel enaigris
> Li chevalier, qui vair et gris
> Lor dounent par lor negligence.[58]

Documents do not always distinguish between heralds and minstrels, but frequently they indicate rivalry between the two professions; thus, for example, the author of *Karlmeinet* (ca. 1320) identifies minstrels with *spilliute* who are familiar with heraldry and who sing of adventures from years past:

> Ouch quamen dar me dan vere   A287,11
> Hundert mynistrere,
> De wir nennen speleman,
> Ind van wapen sprechen kan.
> Sulche konden singen
> Van ouenturen ind dingen,
> De geschagen in alden iaren.[59]

Documents from the fourteenth century indicate an advance in the status of heralds marked by the increased importance of their duties: heralds are sent out to ask for

a parley; frequently they are entrusted with important letters;
in 1339 the herald of the Duke of Gelders, Gelre, was sent to
the King of France with a verbal challenge to battle which,
being accepted, "se parti li hiraux et prist congiet au roy
et as seigneurs qui li donnèrent grans dons et biaux draps,
et s'en revint en l'ost des Englès et recorda tout ce que
vous avês oy."[60] Hereafter heralds are regularly sent with
letters to foreign sovereigns, and with instructions to, or
in the retinue of, ambassadors.[61] Detailed information
regarding the role of heralds is found in Jean Froissart's
Chronicles . He recognizes, for example, his obligation to
"aucuns rois d'armes et leurs mareschaus qui par droit sont
et doient estre juste inquisiteur et raporteur de tels
besongnes"[62] for knowledge pertaining to feats of arms during
the war between England and France. Elsewhere he relates the
incident in which March, king of arms, brought news of the
peace of 1394 to Richard II, "sicomme le hérault nommé Marche
ou le Roy Marche me dist depuis à grant loisir en chevauchant
aveuc luy ens ou royaulme d'Angleterre."[63]

The importance of heralds is emphasized by their
activities at the Council of Constance from 1414 to 1418.
Ulrich Richental writes in his chronicle:

> Item recht herolten von allen küngrichen, die der küng waupen
> trügend und ir bottschaft wurben und iro herren er und wirdikait
> ußsprachen, si wärind cristan oder ains anders globen, die mir
> och diß sach seitend und ich ir och ettlichen zu huß lüd und
> sy fragt.[64]

Ulrich Richental invited the heralds into his house to report
about their various activities involving the Council. Further:

> ...so ist nun och ze wissen, wie menger fürst und herr, der nit
> zegegen was, sin gewiß bottschaft ze Costentz hatt, baide mit
> briefen, mit erbern lüten und ir ettlich durch ir herolt und ir
> pfifer und spillüt, die der fürsten und herren waupen anschlugen
> und ir lob uß saitend.[65]

Altogether there were twenty-four heralds with their servants
at the Council: "Recht herolten der küng: XXIIII mit ir
knechten."

For their diplomatic activities a knowledge of foreign
languages was useful for heralds. The Bavarian herald
Johann Holandt (ca. 1420) claimed:

> Ich Johann Holandt,   1
> Ein Ernholt weit erkhannt,
> Von sechs sprachen, die ich khan,
> Latein, Teutsch und Polan,
> Frantzösisch und Enngelisch,
> Darneben guet Ungerisch.[66]

The public demanded knowledge from heralds which could only have been gained through extensive travels. A true herald should have at least traveled as far as India, the land of Prester John. Occasionally heralds felt called upon to cover up their ignorance and lack of experience by fantastic elaborations of their supposed travels. Hans Rosenplüt attests to this in his song honoring Duke Albert of Bavaria:

> Ich hab durich sucht drew Iman   49
> Der hochmechtig priester Johan
> Und auch der gross kam von Kathey
> Und das kunigreich von Barbarey
> Und das keyserthum von Trebisunda
> Bey den allen ich keinen finden kunda
> Als ir mir ein habt vorgemelt.[67]

The profession of heralds was divided into three classes or ranks corresponding somewhat to those in the trade guilds. The lowest class were runners or messengers who did not necessarily come from the nobility. They served for three years either on horseback or on foot before they were eligible to become pursuivants. The pursuivant then had to serve another seven years before becoming a herald "wenn er die Heralderey als Meister verstand."[68] A king of heralds or king of arms loosely commanded the heralds in his district.

The office of king of heralds was probably associated with a fixed allegiance. By the fourteenth century there is evidence of ceremonies of creation and coronation of kings of heralds performed by a sovereign or his deputy. There were similar oaths and initiation ceremonies for the lower ranks of pursuivant and herald in which the initiate was invested with a tabard or escutcheon showing his master's arms.

The first record of the coronation of an English king of arms was chronicled by Froissart. He relates that after his coronation at Westminster in 1377, Richard II "fist che jour quatre contes et neuf chevaliers...et fist Camdos le hirault roy d'armes d'Engleterre."[69] It was the duty of the king of arms to survey and record the bearings and descent

of the armigerous persons in their provinces and to correct
arms irregularly used. In due course they began to devise
arms for other persons of sufficient standing to bear them,
and by the middle of the fifteenth century they were actually
granting arms. Occasionally in the fifteenth century, and
with some regularity in the following two centuries, the
heralds made periodical circuits of various parts of the
country, under the authority of Royal Commissions, to inquire
into all matters connected with the bearing of arms, geneal-
ogies and similar subjects, to correct arms unlawfully borne
or usurped, to collect information, and to draw up authori-
tative records. The earliest of these Visitations took place
in 1413 (see p. 6).[70]

German documents indicate a "kingdom" of heralds
comprising the archbishopric of Mainz; in 1358 Archbishop
Adolf named his piper and servant Brachte to be "Künige
farender Lute durch alle unser Erzbisthum und Lant."[71]
Similar kingdoms existed in the Palatinate on the Rhine, in
Alsace, around Zurich, in Bavaria, and in Austria. Seyler
maintains that the poet known as the König vom Odenwald was a
king of arms in the fourteenth century.[72] Documentary evidence
for these kings of arms is quite sparse, but from the reign of
Emperor Frederick III there are several grants of kingship.
In Neustadt on June 13, 1466 Frederick made Panthaleon, called
Sidoni, king of arms for the Roman Empire:

> Wir haben angesehen solich erberkeit vnd vernuft die vnser vnd des
> reichs lieber getrewer Panthaleon genannt Sidoni des hochgebornen
> Johansen herczogen zu Medina vnd Sidonia vnsers lieben oheims vnd
> fürsten erhalt an im hat auch die getrewen vleissigen dinste die
> er vns vnd dem heiligen reich getan hat vnd hinfür wol tun mag vnd
> sol in kunftig zeit vnd in darumb mit wolbedachtem mute rechter
> wissen vnd dem vorgenanten vnserm lieben oheim vnd fürsten zu eren
> geuallen vnd von sunderlichn vnsern kaiserlichn gnaden zu unserm
> vnd des heiligen reichs künig der wappen erhabt gewirdigt vnd ge-
> macht vnd darczu den vorgenannten namen Sydoni den hinfür zu haben
> zu gebrauchen vnd also genennet zu werden gnediclich confirmirt
> vnd bestett.[73]

It was customary for heralds to be given professional
names such as Suchenwirt (*suche den Wirt*), Suchensinn (*suche den
Sinn*), Lob-den-frumen (*lobe den Tüchtigen*), Irrgang, Sorgnicht, etc.
Traditionally, heralds were also given the name of the country,

the name of the master or of his castle. The herald of the
Roman Emperor (established since the time of Sigismund) was
known as "Romreich," that is *römisches Reich.* Eberhard
Windeck writes in his contemporary chronicle of King Sigismund
the following:

> ...Do sandte der konig seinen herolt Romreich zu dem konig
> von Polande mit Imme doraus zu reden....[74]

Under the Emperors Frederick III and Maximilian I the imperial
herald was still called "Romreich." Emperor Charles V made a
change in 1521 when he crowned Caspar Sturm king of arms,
bestowing upon him the professional name "Teutschland:"

> ...den genanten Caspar Sturm zu vnserm keyserlichen Erenholden
> auffgenommen vnd verordnet, vnd ym den namen Teutschland geschöpft
> vnd gegeben haben.[75]

The costumes of the heralds seem to have made a distinct
impression upon the poets of the Middle Ages. The following
passages from *Wigalois* by Wirnt von Gravenberg (ca. 1212) are
typical descriptions of heralds found in epic poetry:

> nu kom gên im geloufen her   1416
> ûf dem wege ein garzûn.
> der truoc einen schappern
> gesniten von fritschâle:
> mit rôtem zendâle
> was er gefurrieret.
> sîn huot der was gezieret
> mit bluomen und mit loube....
> hantschuohe wîse   1428
> hêt er an den henden.
> den stap begunde er wenden
> nâch der garzûne site.[76]

The *garzûn* came into view wearing a coat of expensive material
trimmed with fur, a fancy hat, white gloves, carrying the
typical herald's staff.

Besides the descriptive passages there are numerous
illustrations of heralds dating from the fourteenth century;
it seems to have been common practice for a herald to include
a portrait of himself in his *Wappenbuch.* The short heraldic coat
(Wappenrock) or tabard was embroidered with the coat of arms of
the herald's master. The herald is frequently depicted with a
staff in his hand; the king of arms with a crown on his head
and a necklace around his neck. In a document from November
26, 1592 the herald Hans von Nadelwitz zu Bersdorf is described

as follows:

> Der Heroldt ist mit einem weissen doppeltafften Rock so ihme
> biss an die Knie gangen, angezogen gewesen, darüber ein rothes
> Leviten-Kleid, *in Forma* einer Kassel, so ihm ein wenig unter
> die Gürtelstadt gangen, von dergleichen Zeug, so wohl einen
> rothen Huth, *in Forma* einer Mützen, darüber eime weisse Binde,
> so was herunter fliegend gehangen, auf dem Leviten-Kleid ist
> hinten und forne, des Röm. Reichs Adler auf einem Tuch abgemahlet
> gewesen, in des Adlers Hertz des Königreichs Böheim Wappen, als
> ein weisser Löwe, in des Löwen Hertz des Marggraffthums Ober
> Lausitz Wappen, als mit vergoldeten Zinnen, über den Zinnen
> im blauen Felde ein weisser Hund.

> Der Herold hat einen Stab, so gelb und blau gewesen in seiner
> Hand geführet. Nach besatzter Ehren-Taffel sind die Trommeten
> aufgeblasen, und Heer-Drummeln aufgeschlagen, und unter dem
> Blasen die Parten durch den Herold aufgeführet worden.[77]

One of the earliest illustrations of a herald is that
of Gelre who lived in the middle of the fourteenth century.
His tabard shows the arms of the Gelders family: a red lion
with golden claws and forked tail on a blue field (azure, an
armed lion gules, queue-forché or). The picture, which
concludes his *Wapenboeck,* seems to indicate the termination of
his service as herald since he is holding a broken necklace
in his hands.

It was part of the duty of the herald to recognize
the arms of those within his master's sphere of activity. By
the end of the thirteenth century it seems that the herald
was engaged in making written and painted records of arms
according to a systematic plan. There is some question as
to whether the heralds themselves compiled these records,
known in English as "rolls of arms," in French as *armorials,*
and in German as *Wappenbücher,* or whether this task was performed
by clerks. However, there is early evidence of a herald's
participation in the work of copying rolls; in Vienna there
is a copy of the so-called *Compiègne Roll* of 1278 which was
copied about 1405 by a king of arms known as Beijeren (see
p. 78).

Heraldic books or rolls may contain emblazoned (i.e.
painted) shields, blazoned coats of arms (i.e. not painted
but described in technical heraldic language), or both. In
some cases the blazon is a poetic expansion of standard
heraldic language. Heraldic books or rolls may furthermore

be divided into several different classes or types:
illustrative, occasional, general, and local.[78] The
illustrative heraldic books were probably not products of
heralds since they consist merely of illustrations or
decorations in the margins of chronicles, cartularies,
liturgical books, account books, song books, etc. Occasional
rolls give the arms of those present on a particular occasion
such as a battle, siege, or tournament. General rolls and
heraldic books begin typically with the blazons of the arms
of Prester John, the King of Jerusalem, the Emperor of Rome,
continúe with foreign rulers, and conclude with local rulers
and nobility. The arms in local books or rolls are either
grouped by localities or belong to only one locality.

The *Clipearium Theutonicorum*, the oldest general heraldic
book of Germany was not compiled by a herald but rather by
the Zurich canon and choir-master Conrad von Mure between
1242 and 1249.[79] Written in Latin leonine verses it includes
seventy-three descriptions of coats of arms arranged according
to the rank of the bearer.[80] It begins with the Roman Emperor,
followed by the kings of France and Spain, dukes, counts and
lesser nobility. Where Conrad did not know the arms he
invented them; he also accorded arms to heathen princes known from
literature. The blazon is sometimes inexact and incomplete
and it is possible that the work was written with reference
to a roll of arms; this would explain the mistakes and missing
arms.

The black eagle on a gold field, the arms of the Roman
Emperor are blazoned as follows:

> Rex romanorum siquid veri mea prefert   1
> Vox, aquilam nigro forme croceo clipea fert.

Conrad made up a coat of arms for the King of Hungary, a
white horse with saddle and bridle on a red field:

> Albus equus rubeo clipeo regis solet esse   4
> Ungarici. Nec equo frenum nec sella deesse.

William of Orlens, the hero glorified by Wolfram von
Eschenbach and Rudolf von Ems, wears a blue shield with a
golden star:

> Orlens Wilhelmi clipeo qui blavus habetur   50
> Aut de lasurio nitet, aurea stella vedetur.

Generally the blazons are accurate with special attention drawn to the exact tinctures.

One of the most important German local heraldic books is the *Zurich Roll* (Zentralbibliothek Zurich, Schweizer Landes-museum)[81] compiled about 1325-1345. It includes the coats of arms of families from German Switzerland, Alsace, Baden, and the area of Lake Constance. To some extent they are arranged according to family branches. The roll is on a narrow long piece of parchment 400.5 cm long, 12.5 cm wide with shields in two registers on both sides. Part of the original roll is missing, but there is a copy from the nineteenth century containing the missing portion. The entire roll contains 559 coats of arms, shields and helmets, and twenty-eight banners of bishops. The arms are identified but not blazoned.

However, the best example of a heraldic book organized by localities is the *Wapenboeck* (1334-1372, Brussels, Royal Library MS 15652-56)) by Gelre,[82] herald of the dukes of Gelres. This *Wapenboeck* includes over 1,800 painted coats of arms as well as poetic blazons. It is the work of an accomplished artist who was completely familiar with the entire art of heraldry. It is arranged on a regional plan and was compiled by a king of arms, a combination which Wagner suggests is "not merely fortuitious, but that from early times it was a recognized part of a King of Arms' duty to have knowledge of the arms of persons within his sphere of activity, and that by the end of the thirteenth century it would already be natural for him to fulfil this duty by making written and painted records on a systematic plan."[83]

Since it appears that one of the duties of a herald was to compile books of arms, either pictorial or verbal, it is certainly possible that the herald Peter Suchenwirt also compiled such a book; however, none of the Suchenwirt texts extant are illustrated, although his *Ehrenreden* include poetic blazons of coats of arms. These *Ehrenreden* are very similar to those of the herald Gelre from whom are extant both illustrated poems as well as a heraldic book without blazon.

The limited evidence points to the compilation of

heraldic books by heralds but is insufficient to prove that
the heralds' duties included the composition of heraldic
poetry. On the other hand, the close connection between
heralds and *farende liute,* the wandering poets, suggests that
heralds may have been capable of such heraldic composition.

THE DEATH LAMENT TRADITION

As stated in the introduction the term *Ehrenrede* is in effect a narrow definition of heraldic poetry. These laudatory addresses have their most obvious origins in the long tradition of the death lament. The purpose of both the death lament and the *Ehrenrede* was to honor an individual hero, in the case of the death lament a deceased hero, in the case of the *Ehrenrede* either a deceased or a living hero. Certain themes and certain structures are common to the death laments from the earliest Germanic tradition up to the fully developed *Ehrenreden* of the fourteenth century.

The transformation from the old heathen German world to the Christian German world is especially clear in the development of the death lament.[84] Christianity expediated the dying out of the heathen choral death lament; church decrees against this practice were promulgated. Christianity also promoted the cultivation of the individual lament through a relaxation of the spiritual life. The individual lament appears in various forms; it develops through individualizing reflection to a mellowing of the human soul to the courtly lament.

Leopold Heinemann[85] attempts to illustrate that the classical Roman lament with its strict structure 1) name, 2) lament, 3) eulogy, 4) good wishes for the dead, not only influenced the medieval Latin laments (including those of the most different metrical forms) and the Middle Latin epics and ballads, but also the German lyric lament poets; for one finds throughout the German lament the same three elements: 1) lament, 2) eulogy, 3) intercession. The Middle Latin laments and the Middle High German are merely imitations of earlier times in both form and content.

A turning point in the development of the lament comes in the works of Heinrich von Veldeke who introduces the element of courtliness and the concept of *mâze*, courtly moderation. The expression of pain is no longer suppressed through one's own nature but through the tenets of *mâze*. The

outward gestures are mellowed. This mellowing is found also
in Hartmann von Aue, Ulrich von Zatzikhoven and Wolfram von
Eschenbach. One of the main characteristics of the typical
courtly lament is reflection. Although the courtly laments
include such stock praises as: "ouwê, daz ich ie wart
geborn!;" "ouwê, daz ich dich ie gesach!;" "des muoz mîn
herze fröude lân!;" "daz wil ich immer klagen!" their content
gradually becomes more personally related to a specific
individual. The old Germanic spirit though in a somewhat
milder form, mellowed by the introduction of Christian
elements, appears again in the *Nibelungenlied* in the form of
wildness of pain and absence of *mâze* reminiscent of pre-
courtly times. The laments interspersed in the Middle High
German epic seem to reflect the older form of laudatory song
which included the method of death instead of a Christian
prayer for intercession. One of the first and often imitated
examples is the lament of Alexander for his dying enemy Darius.
The *Rolandslied* , Eilhart's *Tristan,* Heinrich's *Eneide, Athis
und Prophilias,* Herbort's *Trojanerkrieg,* Hartmann's *Erec* and *Iwein,*
Wolfram's *Parzival* and *Willehalm* all include such individual
laments.

Thus Richard Leicher recognizes a three stage
development of the death lament:[86]

1. The old heathen stage: *Beowulf,* the *Elder Edda,
   Hildebrandslied,* and, with some mellowing, the
   Nibelungenlied representing its last remnants.

2. The early Christian stage: *Heliand,* Otfrid's *Evan-
   gelienbuch, Wiener Genesis,* Frau Ava; *Alexanderlied,
   Rolandslied,* Eilhart's *Tristan, Graf Rudolf,* and (a late
   appearance) Herbort.

3. The courtly-Christian stage: Heinrich von Veldeke,
   Hartmann von Aue, Ulrich von Zatzikhoven, Wolfram
   von Eschenbach.

Similarly, Heinemann[87] has isolated what he considers
to be sixteen pure examples of death laments in Middle High
German, all of which include the three parts: lament, eulogy,
intercession. They can be traced directly back to the Latin
death laments of the classical times and the early Middle Ages
and are even recognizable in old Latin epitaphs. He maintains
that of the epic death laments only two follow this model:

Charlemagne's lament over the death of Roland and Laudine's
lament over the death of King Ascalon.[88] Whereas the epics
are abundant with laments, they vary markedly from this
tripartite form. Heinemann explains this difference through
the innate disparity in the genres of epic and lyric; the
single lyric is a personal expression of grief by the mourner
even if this person is not the poet himself (e.g. Reinmar's
widow--*MF* 167,31; Hartmann--*MF* 217,14). On the other hand,
in the epic the lament must fit into the outline or framework
of the entire work as part of the action not personalized by
the poet. The poet has full reign to express sorrow in many
different ways, but very few epic poets followed a specific
scheme--much less a tripartite one. The epic poets tell of
the sorrow and pain of the followers, describe the moment the
news of the death arrived, etc. but never include intercession.
The central idea of all descriptive individual laments is the
personal need and the destitution, loneliness of the entire
world after the death of the hero. This often appears in the
stylistic form of rhetorical questions. A good example is ·
the lament for Leopold VI by the population found in Jansen
Enikel's *Fürstenbuch* [89] where the lamenting questions follow one
another anaphorically twenty times in forty-five lines.

This stylistic technique is employed by Peter Suchenwirt
only once--in the lament for the Empress of Bavaria. Otfried
Weber[90] maintains Suchenwirt needed a model for his only
lament dedicated to a female, and, not finding a lyric counter-
part, turned to the epic where women were often lamented.
Generally, however, the lyrical death lament remains limited
to men (mainly princes and colleagues of poets). Although
the descriptive manner of the poem honoring the Empress of
Bavaria corresponds closely to that of the epic, its
structure is modeled on that of the lyric death lament:
lament (II,1-27), eulogy (II,28-67), intercession (II,68-92).

Christian influence provided another development in the
content of the lament. During the so-called Ottonian
renaissance Priest Otloh warned against the lament and against
ancient literature because it did not aid the Christian in his
"hour of death." Thus the warning against the world and its

pleasures becomes a major theme in the lament, the idea of
memento mori, of vanity, etc. The world is a tree under which
man pauses to rest, but he oversleeps and forgets the goal
of his journey *(St. Gall Memento mori)*. The Bamberg canon Ezzo
described the cross as the mast of a ship which carries man
homeward over the dangerous sea of the world. He who travels
in this ship has no fear of death, death is merely entrance
to his goal. But woe to him who is devoured by the world:
he succumbs to the death of the soul, a death from which there
is no redemption. The questioning of the usefulness of one's
life is not new; Ovid asked the same questions before the
birth of Christ, as have many others before him.

These same tones echo in courtly poetry next to heroic
sounds from the Germanic past. There is a dichotomy of
purpose. The knight takes over the role of the hero, but his
goals are different. The Middle High German death lament
thus includes a suggestion of *memento mori* but at the same
time the earthly deeds of the knight are described. The idea
of *êre* prevails, i.e. earthly fame, but nevertheless this is
merely the proper way to act on earth, and heavenly rewards
are more important. For this reason the prayer for the soul
of the deceased becomes increasingly important. The Christian
memento mori and the heroic *memento vivere* often mingle with one
another in a peculiar manner.

The individualization process, propounded by Leicher,[91]
becomes diffused in later German death laments; sometimes it
appears to be dependent upon the ability of the individual
poet. Thus many good epic poets were able to present an
individual lament in the third person, expressing both the
personality of the lamenter and the deceased. Similarly,
mediocre poets composed lyrical laments which could be
applied to almost anyone.

A typical representative of the *Minnesang* lament
tradition is Meister Rûmelant. His poems are short, one or
two strophes. The laments include the usual motifs: lament,
eulogy, and prayer for intercession. The deeds and virtues
of the deceased are praised in general terms which could
apply to any knight. *Milte* or generosity is the most valued

virtue. In several instances Rûmelant seems to praise *milte*
simply because he as a poet profits from the generosity of
his patron. The name of the deceased is generally mentioned
near the conclusion of the first strophe. In the lament
honoring the murdered Marner (murdered before 1287, probably
before 1273)[92] the idea of *memento mori* is strong:

> todes kunft uns allen   I,9,5
> willich ist bereit.

The middle part of the poem contains longer lines and the
climax; the moderate expression of lament become passionate,
almost a curse:

> Schentlicher mort der wart noch nie begangen   I,9,13
> an eime kranken, blinden, alten manne,
> dem selber nach dem tode mohte erlangen.
> die morder sin die sten(t) ze Gotes banne.

The lines are shortened, and the poem concludes with a prayer
to the Virgin Mary to intercede with her son:

> Kristes muoter, sueze   I,9,17
> maget, gedenke,
> waz er dines lobes grueze
> schone mit gelenke
> manigem kunde schallen diner wirdikeit!

The actual laudatory part of the poem is concentrated in
these last lines where the poet expresses outrage over the
dastardly murder and sympathy with the sacrifice. There is
nothing about sadness or "loss of art" *(Verlust der Kunst)* as
generally found in laments to artist colleagues. During his
life Marner was made fun of and criticized by Meister Rûmelant
for his poetic arrogance.

In the poem to Count Gunzelin of Schwerin (†1274)
Rûmelant again praises the *milte* which was a source of joy to
the poet:

> Vil vröude ich wilen was gewon   VIII,10,5
> bi im, da bin ich leider von
> gescheiden truriklichen abe.

Again the Virgin Mary is called upon to intercede with her
son:

> bit im din kint genædik sin,   VIII,10,13
> dem uz erwelten vriunde min:
> daz was der grabe Gunzelin,
> der werde, wise von Zwerin,
> den man durch sine tugende verne erkande.

This lament, according to Ludwig Ferdinand Clauss,[93] which exhibits such personal sentiment, cannot have been an official lament but rather must have originated from the poet's own personal feeling. The entire mood is affectionate and simple.

Walther von der Vogelweide wrote a famous lament in honor of his teacher and artistic rival Reinmar der Alte (✝ before 1214). The lament opens with elegiac observation reminiscent of Ovid's lament for Tibullus. It is unrealistic to postulate that Walther was familiar with or even directly influenced by Ovid, but he did recognize the same spiritual forces:

> Owe daz wisheit unde jugent   12,1,1
> des mannes schoene noch sin tugent
> niht erben sol, so ie der lip erstirbet![94]

Walther's poem consists of two strophes, the first of which seems to be aimed at the mourning public; the poet is merely the spokesman for a large group of mourners. The lament flows out of a general elegiac reflection and concerns the loss of art, which is not viewed by the poet himself in the first person, but with the eyes of a "wise man:"

> Daz mac wol klagen ein wiser man,   12,1,4
> der sich des schaden versinnen kan,
> Reinmar, waz guoter kunst an dir verdirbet.

Since Reinmar put his artistic ability to the praise of women, they have the most reason to lament. They are entreated to honor his memory in prayer:

> „so wol dir, wip, wie reine ein nam!", du hetest also
>   gestriten   12,1,11
> an ir lop daz elliu wip dir genaden solten biten.

In the second strophe Walther expresses his personal sentiments:

> Deswar, Reinmar, du riuwes mich   12,2,1
> michels harter danne ich dich,
> ob du lebtes und ich waer erstorben.

Even though there may have been some misunderstanding between the two poets, probably based on envy on the part of the older Reinmar, Walther does not allow this to disturb him nor to take away from the praise of Reinmar's art. Nevertheless the lament is pointed towards the poet and not the man:

> Ich wilz bi minen triuwen sagen,   12,2,4
> dich selben wolt ich lützel klagen:
> ich klage din edelen kunst, dat sist verdorben.

The highest praise he can deliver is to describe Reinmar as
the augmenter of joy:

> Du kundest al der werlte fröide meren.   12,2,7

Walther expresses his pure and noble intention when he regrets
that he cannot accompany Reinmar to the other life although
he himself does not expect to live very much longer:

> ...min singen ist niht lanc.   12,2,12

The poem concludes with thanksgiving and prayer.

This poem had far reaching influence on the Middle High
German death lament, most of which did not reach such superb
quality. Typically authors of laments address the choir, God,
or the Virgin Mary in prayer, the murderer in a curse, but
seldom do they address the deceased. Other laments of this
period (except those by Reinmar von Brennenberg) do not use
the *du*-form.

Laments written by the *Minnesänger* differ markedly in length
and specific content from those of the fourteenth century. In the
fourteenth century there are several laments, mostly anonymous,
which are remarkably similar to those of Peter Suchenwirt and
which represent the final stage in the development from the
death lament to the *Ehrenrede*.

The death of Duke Johann I of Brabant (1260-1294) is
mourned by an unknown poet in a death lament from the *Würzburg
Songbook* (Munich, University Library Cod. MS 731) of the fourteenth century.[95] There is no reference to Johann's poetic
accomplishments since they were not widely known in his homeland; on the other hand, his knightly exploits were famous.
The lament begins in allegorical fashion similar to many of
the poems by Suchenwirt: the poet meets a hermit while deer
hunting ; they discuss the deterioration of courtly love and
knighthood as expressed in customs, costumes, demeanor, and
song. They praise the good old days when knights rode out in
service of ladies. Among others the hermit praises Diepold
of Pfirt, Friedrich Klet of Utenheim, Count Rudolf of Nidau,
Count Werner of Honberg (see pp. 43-44), Konrad Wernher of

Hadstatt, Walther Spender, Count Johann of Spannheim (see pp. 82-83),
Johannes of Klingenberg, and Heinrich Ronauwer. After describing a degenerate knight, the hermit assures the poet that
Duke Johann of Brabant is not to be counted among the
decadent. Although the name Johann of Brabant appears most
often, there is really very little in the lament about him.
His deeds and his fame are described in very general terms
similar to the accounts in the earlier *Minnesänger* laments.
However, the poem is 395 lines long in comparison to the
single or double strophes of the earlier poems. The length,
the allegorical elements, and the frequent reference to coats
of arms (but no description of arms) place the "Klagegedicht
auf Herzog Johannes von Brabant" clearly in a new tradition
of death lament which finally culminates in the poems of
Peter Suchenwirt.

A similar death lament--this one also anonymous--is
that honoring a duchess of Carinthia and Tyrol, who was born
Countess of Savoy (Donaueschingen, Fürstenberg Library MS 69).
This poem is so general that it is difficult to determine
exactly which duchess is being honored. It is probably
Beatrix, the wife of Henry V, Duke of Carinthia and Count of
Tyrol who died in 1331 and who was the father of Margaretha
Maultasch.[96]

The poem begins in the usual allegorical manner. The
singer mounts his horse one morning and rides into the
mountains. Suddenly he hears two lamenting voices. When he
approaches, he sees two women dressed in mourning. He
describes their beauty and their clothes, their wailing
gestures, and their lament. From scrolls written with
golden letters hanging from their clothes he recognizes one
as Knighthood and the other as Joy. When he speaks to them,
they not only continue their lament, but they also describe
to him the suffering which is caused by the burial of the
duchess; they commence their lament anew until they are
exhausted from pain and suffering and sink into unconscious-
ness. The singer runs to a stream where he picks fresh grass
with which to revive the unconscious women. Then upon his
request they identify the deceased, whom they are so painfully

and sorrowfully mourning. Unsuccessfully he tries to
persuade them to moderate their weeping, the cause of which
they cannot alter. They explain that they have decided to
build a dwelling in this wilderness and to spend the rest of
their days in mourning for the deceased duchess and in prayer
for her departed soul. They refuse his courtly offer to
remain with them and serve them. They thank him and send him
back into the world with the mission to report to all those
who inquire about Joy and Knighthood that they have buried
themselves for ever in the wilderness.

To be sure the duchess is honored in a very gratifying
manner. The exaggeration of sorrow as well as the gestures
and fainting are somewhat reminiscent of the French tradition.
The allegory and the personification of virtues place this
poem also clearly in the Suchenwirt tradition.

From the East Franconian poet Lupold Hornburg five
poems are preserved in the *Würzburg Songbook* (Munich, University
Library Cod. MS 731) of Michael de Leone:[97] four are political
poems, one of the four may be called an *Ehrenrede*, and the fifth
poem is a *Meistergesang* in Marner's tone. In the political
poems Lupold discusses the people and problems of his day;
some of these events overlap those described by Suchenwirt--
especially those in connection with Albert II and Louis the
Bavarian. But it is the *Ehrenrede* which corresponds most
closely to Suchenwirt's works both in form and in content.

Although very little is known about Lupold's life, he
does identify himself in each of his songs and calls himself
a "knappe." There is a document referring to a gift made to
the Church in 1316 in Rothenburg ob der Tauber in memory of
the deceased daughter of a Lupold Horenburg, very possibly
the poet. The poems, on the other hand, are rather simple
to date: according to Konrad Zwierzina[98] numbers I-IV fall
between the years 1347 and 1348, number V being written a
few years later. In the second poem, "Die Rede von des
Ryches clage," Lupold states that he was present at the
assembly of princes held in Passau in July 1348. From the
content of the poems it appears that Lupold tried to make his

living as a political poet in the service of the opponents of
Emperor Charles IV although in the case of the Passau assembly
he seems to have temporarily veered to the other side. He
probably worked in Würzburg under the patronage of Michael
de Leone.

Otfried Weber identified the fourth poem, "Ein
derbermeliche clage," as the earliest preserved German
example before   Peter Suchenwirt of its type--namely a
"Leichen- und Ehrenrede"--a panegyric written in honor of
the knight Freiherr Konrad III of Schlüsselberg. The
Schlüsselberg family was among the most powerful and wealthy
in Franconia. Konrad was a follower of Emperor Louis the
Bavarian and served as one of his privy councilors. He was
wounded in the battles of Gamelsdorf (1313) and Mühldorf
(1322). In 1328 he accompanied the Emperor to Italy. Although
Konrad never wavered in his loyalty to the Emperor, ultimately
he was abominably *(lesterlich)* abandoned by the Emperor. Disputes
arose between the Bishops of Würzburg and Bamberg and the towns
of Würzburg, Windsheim, and Rothenburg. The towns allied
themselves with Konrad von Schlüsselberg, the bishops with
the burgraves of Nuremberg and Heinrich von Henneberg. Konrad
was killed on September 14, 1347 on the walls of his castle
Neideck by a shot from a besieging catapult. He died without
heirs and his foes quarreled for years over his great wealth.
"Ein derbermeliche clage" may have been composed for Konrad's
funeral, making it the first of Lupold's extant poems.

Lupold, a citizen of Rothenburg, naturally takes the
part of Konrad and presents him as a model of a true nobleman;
he bitterly criticizes the Emperor for his desertion of this
staunch and loyal knight. Not suprisingly Lupold falls back
on the example of the death lament. Weber[99] analyzes the
features as follows: it begins with an emphatic formula of
humility (1-7), leads from a short declaration of lament to
the main section, a detailed praise of the knight which is
presented in three parts: first a general eulogy (11-13), then
his accomplishments as a knight (14), then finally praise of
his manly virtues and the renewed lament that death caused
such a life to end (31-40). The next section proclaims the

name--also together with praise--mentions the coat of arms
and gives the battle cry *(krey)* of the hero (41-55). Finally
Lupold concludes with an intercession for the mercy of God
for the deceased as well as for himself whom he names.

Lupold is clearly on the side of Konrad against the
bishops of Würzburg. It is probably not merely empty talk
when he begins:

> Sit die warheit nieman tar   IV,1
> Gekunden leider offenbar,
> Er muzz. des libes angest han.

He continues with a few words about the coat of arms, but
unlike Suchenwirt, Lupold does not include a specific
description, for he claims that a "bürgerlicher Knappe" does
not have the authority to do so (presumably a herald is
required):

> Ey, kond ich von den woppen   IV,5
> Gegriffen vnd getöppen
> Reht als ein blinder mit dem stabe,
> So wolt ich vngefuger knabe
> Ein rede kunden vnde sagen,
> Vnd einen biderwen herren clagen.

However, he seems to be aware of the convention of describing
a coat of arms in an *Ehrenrede:*[100]

> Sine wöppen laz ich ligen,   IV,51
> Sie sint im in sin grab gedygen;
> Vnd bit da vür altissimo,
> Das sin krey ge also:
> „Ey sluzzelnberg!"--die werde kry-
> Zu himel dort den selen by.

Lupold begins the eulogy: "Der was ein rehter pantyr helt"
(he used the same praise for Duke Albert II of Austria in
number II "Dyse rede ist von des Ryches clage" line 353).
Konrad carried "den fanen mit dem adelarn," the imperial flag
and twice gave his blood for the Empire:

> Den fanen mit dem adelarn   IV,14
> Furt im der vnverdrozzen,
> Vnd höt sin blut vergozzen
> Wol uber zwir by dem Rich.

But the Emperor deserted him and allowed him to be killed:

> Den lye ein keyser lesterlich   IV,18
> Beliben in den nöten,
> Vnd wider reht ertöten.

In a world of lies and quarrels Konrad was a man of truth.

And with disdain Lupold continues:

> Darumb er auch erworfen wart   IV,26
> Mit einem bliden steine
> Zu nidek, der vil Reyne
> Müst sterben vmb sin eigen gut.
> Das selten nu kein herre tůt:
> Der luge, e er ein dorf verlůr,
> Vnd der ez liez an sine kůr.
> Daz tet der werde herre niht:
> Der sayte sleht die vademriht
> Dem keiser als dem herren,
> Den minnern als den merren,
> Den Richen als den armen.

Then the solemn mention of Konrad's name and the prayer of intercession: the heavenly eagle should give him eternal reward in St. George's host (which is preferable to the imperial eagle which did not protect him):

> An sante yorgenritters schar,   IV,57
> Da der himel adelar
> Dir gebe den eweclichen solt!

The poet names himself: "Des bit ich, langer luppolt," and prays for himself: may I also deserve that they ask mercy for me too as one does for this knight:

> Ob ich darumbe sterbe,   IV,63
> Daz ich doch hie erwerbe,
> Daz man spreche sunder spot:
> „Nu gnade im vnser herregot!"
> Als man tůt disem herren.

Lupold's lament represents a development beyond the two anonymous laments discussed above (which cannot be dated with accuracy). In fact it corresponds most closely to Suchenwirt's *Ehrenreden* which will be discussed later. The only distinction between a lament *(Klagelied)* and a heraldic poem *(Wappengedicht)* such as Suchenwirt's appears to be the inclusion of a description of a coat of arms in the narrowest sense. There are, however, a couple of anonymous contemporary poems which do deserve to be called heraldic death laments.

The lament honoring Count William of Holland in the Berlin *Tristan* manuscript (Berlin, MS Germ. Quart. 284)[101] contains the same standard motifs (allegory with woods, hermits, etc., eulogy, and finally the name of the deceased) as the laments, but it also contains a description of William's arms.

There is some question regarding the identity of Count
William since the historical material in the poem is limited.
It is probably William IV who actually ruled the four
countries of Holland, Zeeland, Friesland, and Hennegau;[102]
he is identified as "der herre van vier landen" (line 424).
The quartered coat of arms is described in very general terms,
indicating perhaps that the poet was not a professional
herald: for Holland the red lion in a golden field; the same
for Zeeland but only half a lion on top, beneath blue and
silver wavy stripes; for Hennegau the black lion on a golden
field; for Friesland two golden lions on a blue field.

The contents of the lament are extremely general: the
poet walks into the woods to a fountain with nightingales and
meets the mourning sister of *Frau Ere*. While resting in the
clover he is approached by six beautiful ladies dressed
alike: *Truwe, Milde, Manheyt, Demuyt, Warheyt, Stede*. They take him
to *Frau Ere* where he introduces himself as a Syrian Sarazen
astronomer. From the disturbance of the stars (it is now
night) he recognizes the death of the count, an Aquitainian,
who must be Count William of Holland. (The first Carolingian
count of Holland was Dietrich of Aquitaine.) After the
description of the quartered shield with the arms of the four
countries, there is a short prayer for the soul of the deceased.

A second heraldic death lament, a more likely prototype
of Peter Suchenwirt's *Ehrenreden*, is the lament in honor of
Count Werner of Honberg found in a late fourteenth century
manuscript (Donaueschingen, Fürstenberg Library MS 104) and
published by Laßberg in his *Lieder-Saal*.[103] The allegory is very
similar to Suchenwirt's: the poet meets three mourners, *Frau
Ehre, Minne*, and *Mannheit*, on a green meadow. *Frau Ehre* is doubled
up in pain; when she regains consciousness, she begins to
tear at her hair and dress, bemoaning her great loss. She
is interrupted by *Minne* who expresses her sorrowful sentiments
in similar tones. The deceased's virtues and great deeds
are alluded to in very general terms. Then *Mannheit* takes over
and describes the death and funeral of the hero--how the
sword and shield were inverted towards the earth, how his
banner with his coat of arms and the swan's head helmet

were buried with him.[104] All three proclaim the virtues of
Count Werner of Honberg, mentioned by name for the first time
in line 178, over those of all other knights of his time.
Mannheit concludes the lament with the request to knights,
ladies, and maidens to pray to God and Mary that they might
break the bonds hindering Werner's delicate soul on its way
to heaven.

The description of the arms--two black eagles on a
gold field--does not appear to be as professional as
Suchenwirt's, but perhaps it is more integrated into the poem:

```
Beschechen nach dem willen min      113
Owe der liechten waffen sin
Wie sach ich dü verkeren
Den schilt dem so vil eren
In mangen landen ist beschächen
Den müsz ich vor mir ligen sechen
Er waz von liechtem gold fin
Das ich so recht claren schin
Von kainer farw nie gesach
Wie daz mir nit myn hertz veriach
Do ich die aren baide
Sach vff dez goldez haide
Hangen gen dez schiltes rant
So swartz wart nie kol noch brant
Als sy von zobel waren
Nach lüftes flug gebaren.
```

Laßberg claims that the poem refers to the last Count
of Honberg because of the funeral description with the
inverted shields and swords,[105] but the last count was only
eight years old when he died. The few details in the
allegorical poem point more accurately to his father, Werner
the *Minnesänger*, who lived from 1284 to 1320. There are
numerous documents referring to this Werner of Honberg, son
of Count Ludwig the Brave and Countess Elisabeth of Raprechtswyl.[106]

These poems correspond very closely to Suchenwirt's
death laments which do not fit the *Ehrenrede* formula. The
laments honoring the Duchess of Carinthia and Tyrol, Werner
of Honberg, and Count William of Holland do not exhibit the
same sharp division of contents as do the poems of Lupold
and Suchenwirt, but nevertheless the second and third
correspond quite closely. The "Klagegedicht auf Herzog
Johannes von Brabant" is not an *Ehrenrede;* according to

Joseph Seemüller it is simply mislabeled by its editor. It
should be called "Klage auf den Verfall ritterlicher Sitten."[107]
Johann of Brabant is merely named among others as an example
of true knighthood. On the other hand, the poem is related to
the *Ehrenrede* since it stems from the same poetic and intellectual climate, praising and lamenting both living and dead
knights. It is interesting to note that the form of adventure
was chosen; in the manuscript this poem is entitled "ein
abentür." Suchenwirt employs the same form in his *Ehrenrede*
honoring Ulrich of Pfannberg (XI) and in his poem "Daz ist
der getrew rat" (XXXIII).

The lament most similar to Suchenwirt's, composed by
Lupold Hornburg, lacks the professional blazonry for which
Suchenwirt is best known. Lupold names the deceased at the
beginning of the poem in the lament section and again after
the eulogy, whereas Suchenwirt always names his hero in
connection with the coat of arms at the conclusion of the
poem. Weber considers this difference a significant improvement on Suchenwirt's part.[108] Another difference, innovation
by Suchenwirt, seems to be the explicit account of the hero's
deeds: Lupold selects only choice events. Weber vacillates in
his opinion: on the one hand he claims originality and
improvement in individual parts of Suchenwirt's works, and on
the other hand he discounts originality, claiming that
Suchenwirt copied from models which are now lost. Seemüller
and Primisser view Suchenwirt's poems as great innovations,
creating a new genre of the *Ehrenrede*. Seemüller rejects the
tradition inherited from the *Minnesänger:* "Das Lied- oder
spruchartige Klagegedicht kommt hier nicht in Betracht."[109]

Suchenwirt's *Ehrenreden* include the three individual
parts typical of a death lament, but also other elements
which are less typical and more specifically his own. The
confirmation of the death of the hero is broadened through a
lament in which the poet tells how unqualified he is to the
task (more specific and developed than in Lupold's poem).
The section of eulogy is divided into three sub-parts:
general praise of the hero's personality characteristics, a

detailed description of his successful deeds which includes
a short summarizing eulogy of the knightly courage and
bravery of the hero. Finally Suchenwirt concludes with a
plea for intercession for the mercy of God, or more commonly
for the intercession of the Virgin Mary. Up to this point
the *Ehrenrede* resembles the lyrical individual lament. It
only departs from this in the detailed description of deeds
and the blazon of the coat of arms.

It appears that Suchenwirt's *Ehrenreden* fall completely
within the long tradition of the death lament. The tripartite
division of motifs can be traced back to classical times. The
allegorical introductions are in keeping with the tastes of
the fourteenth century and are mirrored in the laments
honoring Duke Johann of Brabant, the Duchess of Carinthia and
Tyrol, Count William of Holland, and Count Werner of Honberg.
The enumeration of specific deeds, unlike general descriptions
found in earlier laments, is similar to that of Lupold
Hornburg. And finally there is even precedence in heraldic
blazonry, witness the poems honoring Count William of Holland
and Count Werner of Honberg. Nevertheless, since these other
poems appear quite isolated in single manuscripts, it seems
quite clear that Suchenwirt represents a milestone in the
development of the death lament. The fact that Suchenwirt
wrote twenty-two death laments and *Ehrenreden* of similar form
and content indicates that he was aware of a tradition, if
not a genre. Suchenwirt's deviation from the standard
fourteenth century lament represents not only his adaptation
to the changing times, but it also devolved from his concepts
of the role of a herald. His particular form of poetry
directly reflects his self-image and his self-consciousness
as a herald at the court of Duke Albert III of Austria.

Besides the lament there are several other traditions which play a part in Suchenwirt's *Ehrenreden* and in his other poems: political and historical poetry as well as heraldic poetry written in connection with tournaments and sieges. For the purpose of establishing prototypes for Suchenwirt's poems it is not necessary to distinguish in detail between political and historical poetry. Suchenwirt's *Ehrenreden*, dealing with historical-biographical material, could be classified as historical and his so-called occasional poems, dealing with major political problems of the day (which are now of historical interest), could be termed political. Erich Seemann simplifies the question of definition by employing the term "geschichtlich-politisches Lied."[110] He claims that since man is possessed of a primitive, instinctive urge to sing, it is perfectly natural to sing historical-political songs.[111] From the beginning of time men sang of their leaders, of battles, disputes, about robbers, fires, floods, crop failures, and adventures. It is possible that when Tacitus wrote in *De Germania* of old songs "quod unum apud illos memoriae et annalium genus est"[112] he was referring to such songs.

There are a considerable number of poems in the vernacular which deal with battles--the *Ludwigslied* , the Anglo-Saxon poems on the battles of Maldon and Brunanburgh, the chansons of Roland and William of Orange, and the *Nibelungenlied*. The Latin tradition is also quite considerable including both panegyric and censure of a ruler, celebrating the deeds of the ruler as well as historical events.

As a genre political poetry came into its own with the Provençal *sirventes* which according to Emil Levy "handelt von Politik, von Krieg, und Kreuzfahrt, von den Fehlern der Geistlichen und den Sünden der Reichen...."[113] Friedrich Diez[114] divided political *sirventes* into *Kampflied, Aufruf, Lobgesang,* and *Rügelied,* establishing the basic categories, two of which depend on events, two on personalities. Karen W.

Klein defines political poetry very narrowly excluding "moral reflections, thoughts about friendship, generalizations about virtue, didactic and gnomic statements...nonspecific general criticism of kings as rulers, of the abuses of the Church, especially simony, of the wining, dining, and whoring of the clergy, of the precarious state of the world;" in other words "a political poem is one devoted entirely to a political event or public figure or both"[115] which has a unity holding the strophes together. Suchenwirt's *Ehrenreden* as well as many of his other poems meet her definition of political poetry even though they encompass elements which she precisely excludes. She concentrates her examination on Bertran de Born (flourished 1180-1195) and Walther von der Vogelweide (flourished 1190-1230) who not only fit the definition but also epitomize the genre. Although their poems include criticism, this criticism is frequently coupled with counsel meant to influence the ruler to change his policy; they are intended also for the wider audience of the court supporters of the particular ruler.

The German tradition after Walther von der Vogelweide includes other *Minnesänger* such as Ulrich von Singenberg, Reinmar von Zweter, Bruder Wernher, Der Marner, Meister Friedrich von Sunnenburg, Meister Sigeher, Meister Rûmelant, Der Unverzagte, Der wilde Alexander, Regenbogen, Prince Wizlav III of Rügen, Heinrich von Meissen (Frauenlob), Hugo III von Montfort, and Oswald von Wolkenstein. Only the last two are contemporary with Suchenwirt; Hugo von Montfort and Suchenwirt accompanied Duke Albert III of Austria on his famous campaign to Prussia described in Suchenwirt's poem "Von hertzog Albrechts ritterschaft" (IV).[116]

The relationship between the poet and his patron is especially important in the composition of political poetry since this poetry is essentially partisan. The poet composed his poetry expressly for his patron to praise, counsel, criticize, and to publicize him. He propagandized his patron's various causes, denounced his enemies, and rallied his allies.

Where a number of scholars have characterized the

political *sirventes* as a type of medieval newspaper,[117] Karen
Klein maintains that such comparisons distort the significance
of the poems. Although the poets do publicize the figures and
events they write about, they do not do this for what would
today be a "newspaper" type of audience. This poetry was not
popular poetry, but rather designed for a small elite audience.
Furthermore she claims that the poems are not reportorial
articles, that they must be examined aesthetically and not for
the amount of news or information they provide. This is true
to a certain extent; political poetry was not designed to
persuade the masses. Nevertheless the wandering minstrel
provided continuous news for medieval courts. Later in the
Middle Ages came a new awareness of the potentiality of the
propaganda value of poetry and of its use to publicize events
as well as a new self-consciousness on the part of the poet.
There was a change in the audience from strictly court circles
to a wider middle class urban environment. The poets also
became more professional in their outlook. They themselves
reflect about the tasks which they have to perform according
to their office. At the end of the fourteenth century
Suchenwirt summarizes the tasks as follows:

> Durich notdurft meinez leibs nar   XXIX,3
> Nam ich der pideben herren war,
> Als gerndem orden wol antzimpt,
> Der güt durich got, durich ere nympt
> Und chunst beschaidenleichen phligt,
> Der pideben herren ere wigt
> Für die pösen wirdichleich.

It is his duty to praise good, to condemn evil, and to pursue
his duty to the best of his ability.

There was also a broadening of the scope of political
poetry. The extent of the empire described in the *Anno-Lied*
as "von Tenemarc unz in Apuliam, van Kerlingin unz an
Vngerin,"[118] and by Walther as "von der Elbe unz an den Rin
und her wider unz an Ungerlant"[119] is similarly limited by
Suchenwirt: "von Leyfflant in Tuschkane, von dem Rein in
Ungerland." Suchenwirt completes his definition by a
systematic recounting of noble spiritual and bourgeois realms
which form a total political geography: an impressive

manifestation of a new political consciousness of space in terms of centers and areas rather than national boundaries. Even conflicts in Northern Italy do not occur "abroad" as far as he is concerned. Regarding politics he sees the greatest danger in internal strife; the fate of the Duchy of Brunswick is for him the prime historical example.

The poem "Von der fürsten chrieg und von des reiches steten" (XXXVII) from the year 1387 contains a differentiating political diagnosis from a lofty perspective: princes and cities are recognized as rightful political powers. They must keep peace among one another because they both depend upon the peasant who supplies them with food, for famine exacerbates the social tension between poor and rich and a revolt of the proletariat threatens every legitimate authority. Up to this point the poem evaluates the interplay of political forces objectively. Then, however, Suchenwirt insists that to find salvation in a sacred imperial establishment King Wenceslaus must have himself crowned in Rome and, as returning Emperor of peace, create justice and order in the Empire.

Suchenwirt relates the papal schism to the European split into groups with the Empire, England, Poland, and Scandinavia on the one side, and with Provence, France, and the Iberian kingdoms on the other side; its solution is again based more on historical theology than on the realities of politics: instead of the disorder created by the existence of two popes and the absence of an emperor the balance must once again be restored by one emperor and by one pope (XXXV).

Suchenwirt's attitude towards history and politics will be examined in more detail below. A look at several contemporary political-historical poems will illustrate the general cultural climate in which he worked. There was much overlap of poets, heroes, and events. Even methods of portrayal such as heraldic animals battling allegorically in place of their masters were common to the time and to the genre. Suchenwirt and the Chandos Herald describe the siege of Calais and the battle of Poitiers from the partisan perspective of their respective heroes. Suchenwirt relates the battle of Sempach

from the Austrian point of view while Halbsuter later on presents
the Swiss version. Heraldic blazon is a common element in
this genre. Extant examples of political-historical poetry
from the fourteenth century are not numerous; what does exist
strongly suggests a unified literary and intellectual tradition
which had evolved gradually over the past few centuries.

A major example of a political-historical poem is the
Vie et gestes du Prince Noir, a chronicle-poem describing the life
of Edward, the Black Prince of England (1330-1376), written
in French verse by the Chandos Herald,[120] the domestic herald
of Sir John Chandos, a devoted friend and follower of the
Black Prince. The poem was composed about 1385-86, nine
years after the Prince's death, to commemorate the leading
events in the life of "the most nobel Edward who never
turned craven,"[121] and to eulogize his valiant feats of arms
and his piety. The author never attempts to be impartial in
his praise of the hero: for example, in the introduction he
compares the Black Prince to Clarus, Julius Caesar, and King
Arthur:

> Ore me laisse Dieux avenir, 47
> Car je voil mettre m'estudie
> A faire et recorder la vie
> Du plus vaillant prince du mounde,
> Si come il tourne à le reounde,
> Ne qui fut puis les temps Claruz,
> Jule Cesaire ne Artuz...[122]

The poem is one of the most valuable sources on certain
episodes in the Hundred Years War; it is the sole source for
information regarding the years 1366 and 1367. The poem
commences with a description of Edward III's French campaign
of 1346, culminating in the battle of Crêcy, and followed by
the capture of Calais. The author includes details of the
plot for the recovery of Calais at the end of 1349; then he
gives a detailed and valuable account of the victory of
Poitiers. Historically the most important part of the poem
records the events of which the author was an eye-witness:
the Spanish Campaign of the Black Prince on behalf of Don
Pedro of Castile and the battle of Najera. The author
briefly summarizes the disastrous conclusion of the Prince's

government of Gascony and of the war which led to the loss
of almost all the possessions acquired at Brétigny. Finally
the close of the Prince's career and his dying moments are
related with considerable detail. At the end of the poem is
a versified list of those who were the chief officers of the
Prince in Aquitaine and a copy of the epitaph on his tomb
in Trinity Chapel in Canterbury Cathedral.

Since dates are not suitable to poetic form, there are
few dates included and some of these are incorrect. Nevertheless other details appear to be accurate.

The author writes very briefly on the battle at Crécy
since he was not an eye-witness although his employer
participated. He merely enumerates the participants and
mentions the valiant actions of the Prince:

> Là fut lui Prince de bountez,   323
> Qui en l'avant-garde restoit.
> Si vaillamment soi gouvernoit
> Que merveille fut a véir.
> A paine lessoit envaïr
> Nul hom, tant fut hardyz ne fortz.

The English won the battle, but one king, King John of Bohemia,
one duke, eight counts, and more than sixty bannerets were slain.

The King of England and his army besieged the town of
Calais for eighteen months until it surrendered. But after the
King returned to England the town of Calais was treacherously
sold to the French. In the ensuing battle the Black Prince
fought valiantly and saved his father:

> Et luy noble Prince, son filtz,   428
> Qui moult fut vaillant et hardyz,
> Là combati si vaillamment,
> Qu'il rescout veritablement
> Par force son piere, le roy...
> Car plusours gentz recordex ont   447
> Que le roy éust esté pris
> N'eut esté le Prince, son filtz.
> Mais sa puissance et sa hautesse
> Et sa très-párfite proesse
> Rescout illoec le roy, son piere.

Although it is possible, even likely, that Chandos
Herald and Froissart communicated with each other abroad,
it is unlikely that Chandos Herald is indebted to Froissart
for any of his facts.[123] It is interesting to compare

Froissart's account with that of the Chandos Herald as well
as the references in Peter Suchenwirt's *Ehrenreden*. Chandos
Herald and Suchenwirt were writing poetry, not history, for
the purpose of honoring specific heroes, the Black Prince
and Hans von Traun. On the other hand, none of the three
could be considered an objective writer according to modern
standards.

The battle of Poitiers took place on September 19, 1356.
According to Suchenwirt's version the King of England honored
Hans von Traun with the charge of bearing the English standard.
Suchenwirt describes the battle with much animation. The
hostile armies advanced on foot, the archers forming the
vanguard.

> Nyemant da dan andern pat   XVIII,262
> Umb veyal noch umb rosen,
> Tzärtleichez freüntleich chosen
> Mit hertzenliebe daz was auz.

Many a knight was forced to swallow iron and steel, like an
ostrich, that is to overcome in death the sensations inflicted
by the spear and javelin. The battlefield echoed with the ·
sound of clashing swords, clubs, and battle-axes:

> Di her tzæsambe rukchten   XVIII,271
> Und in einander drukchten,
> Cholben, hakchen, scharffe swert,
> Da mit vil manger wart gewert
> Des todes gar an seinen dankch.

Each side attempted to bolster up its courage with a battle
cry:

> Di Frantzois schriern „nater dam!"   XVIII,279
> Daz spricht: unser fraw mit nam;
> Der Engelischen chrey erhal:
> „Sand Jors! sand Jors!" gar ane tzal,
> Das spricht: sand Jörg, und was ir chrey.

Hans von Traun rushed forward to encounter the standard-
bearer of France:

> Der des chüniges panyr trüg   XVIII,294
> Von Franchreich, den traf er gericht
> Mit einem stich durch daz gesicht,
> Davon di panyr nider gie,
> Di man nymmermer auf lie
> Chomen an ir rechte stat.

Hans planted his foot upon the staff. Then the King of France
was taken captive and the battle was won. Chandos Herald

describes the same scene:

> Là véissez à l'encontrer   1302
> Ces grosses launces abaisser
> Et bouter de chescune part.

When his followers wished to abandon the struggle, the Black
Prince cried out encouragement:

> "Avant, seigniour, fait-il, pur Dieu!   1337
> Gaignons ceste place et cest lieu,
> S 'avons counte de notre honour."

Finally King John was taken prisoner with Philip, his son,
and many others. The English rejoiced shouting "Guyane!
Saint George!"

Froissart described the battle in much more detail
than either one of the poems. The English shouted "St. George
Giane!" more to confuse the enemy than to encourage themselves.
Then Sir John Chandos implored the Prince: "Sire, sire,
chevauciés avant: la journee est vostre, Diex sera hui en
vostre main " (V,440). The Prince called to his banner-bearer:
"Chevauciés avant, baniere, ou nom de Dieu et da saint Jorge"
(V,441). Soon they were in the midst of the battle. Froissart
does not mention the name of the banner bearer (was it really
Hans von Traun?). The day ended in a rout for the French
although many deeds of valor were performed. According to
this version the King of France and his son surrendered in a
none too glorious manner to the Black Prince. Froissart sums
up the losses:[124]

> Et fu là morte, sicom on recordoit adont pour le temps, toute
> li fleur de le chevalerie de France: de quoi li novles royaumes
> de France fu durement afoiblis, et en grant misère et tribulation
> eschéi, ensi que vous orés recorder chi-après. Avoecques le roy
> et son jone fil monsigneur Phelippe, eut pris XVII contes, sans
> les barons, les chavaliers et les escuiers, et y eut mors entre
> V^c et VII^c chevaliers et escuiers, et VI^m hommes, uns qu'autres
> (V,458).

Since the English found that their prisoners were twice as
numerous as they themselves, they decided to ransom most of
them on the spot. Froissart, Suchenwirt, and Chandos Herald
relate the supper given by the Prince of Wales for his
prisoner, the King of France. The Prince is praised in these
accounts for his gracious and courtly attitude toward the
King: the Prince of Wales insisted he was unworthy to be

seated at the same table of so mighty a prince and so brave
a soldier as the King of France:

> ...et servoit toudis li princees au-devant de la table dou
> roy et par tout les autres tables ossi, si humblement qu'il
> pooit; ne oncques ne se vot seoir à le table dou roy, pour
> pryère que li roys l'en fesist, ains disoit toudis qu'il
> n'estoit mies encorres si souffissans qu'il appertenist à
> lui de seoir à le table de si grant prince et de si vaillant
> homme (V,461).

Chandos Herald portrays a similar picture:

> Là fut devant luy amenez   1414
> Lui roy Johan, c'est veritez.
> Lui Prince moult la festoia,
> Qui Dampne-Dieu en gracia;
> Et pur le roy plus honourer
> Lui voet aider à desarmer;
> Mais luy roy Johan lui ad dit:
> "Beaux dous cosyns, pur Dieu mercit
> Laissez: il n'appartient à moy;
> Dar par la foy que jeo vous doi,
> Plus avez ce jour de huy honour
> Qu'onques n'éust prince à un jour."
> Dont dist li Prince: "Sire douls,
> Dieux l'ad fait, et non mye nous:
> Si l'en devons remercier,
> Et de bon coer vers lui prier
> Qu'il nous voille ottroier sa gloire
> Et pardoner ceste victoire."
> Ensi ambedeux devisoient
> Doucement ensemble parloient.

The account regarding Hans von Traun is not recorded by
Froissart: according to Suchenwirt Hans von Traun was rewarded
for his bravery as standard-bearer by being given the place of
honor between the captured King of France and the Black Prince.
He was also given a pension of one hundred marks for the rest
of his life:

> Tzwischen di chünig tugentleich   XVIII,311
> Satzt man den degen mütes reich
> Durch sein manhait, merchet daz.
> Er sprach: „Nie wirdichleicher saz
> Mein geslächt, daz ich ew sag,
> Als ich hewt sitz an disem tag."--

At this point Froissart breaks off his account. However,
Froissart does describe a similar situation in which James
d'Audelée was declared the bravest and best of the day on the
side of the victors. For this he was rewarded by a yearly
pension of five hundred marks. One could almost assume that

James d'Audelêe and Johann von Traun are one and the same,
but there are other records of James d'Audelêe who remained
in the service of England until he died in 1369 as *sénéchal*
of Poitou in France.[125]

There is, however, a Sir Hans Trouer listed among the
Black Prince's German bachelors who was given a reward of one
hundred marks for life at the conclusion of the campaign to
Guienne--for good service in Guienne and especially at the
battle of Poitiers. Sir Trouer, "a knight of Almain," was
awarded several other gifts to help defray expenses of
returning to his own country.[126] Surely this is the same
brave knight described by Suchenwirt at Poitiers and whom
Froissart simply overlooked as one of many foreigners.

Obviously the various battles, sieges, truces, and
heroic deeds of the Hundred Years War were popular subject
matter for poetry.[127] The equally partisan attitude of
Suchenwirt, the Chandos Herald, and Froissart suggests that
this was the accepted method of recounting historical and
political events. Suchenwirt's *Ehrenreden,* each one dealing
with a single hero, have much in common with the *Vie et gestes
du Prince Noir* which is much longer and more monumental in scope.
The principal difference is perhaps the subject of the French
poem--the crown prince of powerful England as compared to
Suchenwirt's heroes, the greatest of whom were the King of
Hungary and the Dukes of Austria, Carinthia, and the Burgrave
of Nuremberg.

At the same time that the life of the Black Prince of
England provided impetus for a poem with a single hero as its
subject, similar to the *Ehrenreden,* famous battles, glorious
and inglorious, also provided popular subject matter for
poetry. Accounts of battles as well as detailed battle scenes
appear in Suchenwirt's works. The victories over the Austrians
at Sempach (July 9, 1386) and at Näfels (April 9, 1388) echo
throughout many Swiss poems. In the "Spruch von der Sempacher
Schlacht"[128] written immediately after the battle the poet
presents the failure of the Empire:

> Damit so ist der herschaft wol   7
> vil anders denn es billich sol,
> daß niemant redt umb sin sůn.

The arrogance of the Austrian Duke Leopold is contrasted to
that of the Swiss confederates. The opposition to the
nobility is clearly emphasized:

> Do hůb sich ein großer stoß,   55
> keiner da sines adels genoß:
> kam er den eidgnossen in die hend,
> er můst da nemen sin lestes end.

The main motif of another contemporary poem about the
battle[129] also compares the power of the confederates to that
of the nobility; the boasting of the nobles is juxtaposed to
the confederates' ability to handle their weapons. Here
Austria is not named specifically as the opponent, merely
alluded to under the rubric of the "lewe" (Habsburg lion).
The enemy is referred to as the "niderlendschen herren,"
i.e. the nobles from the Upper Rhine region. There is less
specific enmity between the Swiss and the Austrians, rather
more the opposition between the free Waldstätten and the
nobility, most notable of the House of Austria. This song
serves as a component for Hans Halbsuter's more famous
"Sempachlied."[130] Here also the hostility between the
peasants and nobility is obvious:

> Herzog Lupolt von Oesterrich   Str. 43
> was gar ein freidig man
> keins gůten rats belůd er sich,
> wold mit den puren schlan,
> he gar fürstlich wolt ers wagen:
> do er an die buren kam,
> hands in zetod erschlagen.

The great Sempach song, the so-called Halbsuter version,
does not appear until 1531. It contains sixty-six or sixty-
seven seven-line strophes depending upon the manuscript.
Wackernagel, Lorenz, and von Liliencron suggest that the poem
is actually a composite from several very different poems.[131]
Von Liliencron analyzes the various parts as follows: 1) The
song about the confessional pilgrimage of the lords from the
Netherlands to a priest in Switzerland who is symbolized by
a steer. 2) The account of Duke Leopold of Austria arriving
at Willisau and burning the city upon his departure. 3) The

duke's arrival at the gates of Sempach and his taunt
requesting breakfast for the mowers (i.e. stragglers) in the
fields. The poet introduces the Swiss fighters. A spy is
sent out to determine whether the Austrians want to fight.
The battle begins. 4) The account of Winkelried's heroic deed
which decides the battle for the Swiss side.[132] 5) The story
about a duke of Cleve who was treacherously drowned in the
Sempach Lake while fleeing. 6) How the Duchess of Austria
received the report of her husband's death and sent a wagon
to fetch his body. 7) Several preliminary, connecting,
explanatory, and concluding strophes by means of which the
author attempted to make one poem out of several.

The battle of Sempach was preserved in folk art through
historical songs designed for the pleasure and edification of
the Swiss confederates who took part. But the same event was
also preserved for posterity by Peter Suchenwirt who was
writing for the court at Vienna, more specifically for the
brother of the slain Duke Leopold. According to Austrian
documents Leopold believed he would encounter only a small
force at Sempach; but a powerful army had gathered including
soldiers from the four Waldstätten of Lucerne, Schwyz, Uri,
and Unterwalden. The Duke could not have forseen this
development. The exact number of troops on either side
varies from document to document. Suchenwirt claims that the
Austrians were outnumbered:

> Der furst wolt rawmen nicht daz velt   XX,185
> Den veinden da zu tratze,
> Chlain waz sein her, groz waz die welt
> Auf seinem widersatze.

Halbsuter makes the same claim for the Swiss side:

> „das völki ist also clein: Str. 19,2
> söltind unser puren schlahen,
> unser lob das wurde clein,
> he man sprech: die puren hands getan!"

Later Halbsuter mentions that 450 Austrians were killed:[133]

> Sin fürsten und auch herren   Str. 44
> die litend große not
> si woltend sich dapfer weren,
> die puren lands geschlagen ztod;
> he das ist nun unverschwigen,
> vierthalb hundert bekrönter helme
> sind uf der waldstat bliben.

Experienced men advised Duke Leopold not to under-
estimate the Swiss peasants. However, the Duke and his
knightly supporters took this advice to be cowardly. The
foot soldiers proved to be dangerous opponents since they
could easily wound or kill the horses, thus rendering the
heavily armored knights helpless.

Suchenwirt's account omits any reference to a retreat;
it emphasizes the bravery and loyalty of the Austrians:

> So wart der edl fürste gut   XX,215
> Mit wernden henden funden,
> Piz daz er sein ende nam
> Pey seinen getrewen herren....
> Grafen, ritter, edl knecht   221
> Mit eren da verdurben,
> Di mit gantzen trewen slecht
> Pey dem fursten sturben.

Halbsuter, on the other hand, stresses the ignominious defeat
and flight of the Austrians:

> Also vertreib der stiere   Str. 42
> den löuwen uß dem korn
> sin tröwen und prangnieren
> was ganz und gar verlorn,
> he es stat im übel an,
> ja daß der löuw dem stiere
> sin weid mit gewalt müßt lan.

Suchenwirt's account of the battle is disappointing to
the historian hoping to hear the Austrian side; even though
Suchenwirt was writing shortly after the battle he does not
include as many details as the Swiss versions written much
later. The reason for this discrepancy lies in the purpose of
Suchenwirt's poem. The poem "Von fünf fürsten, von dem von
Maylan, von marchgraf Sigmund, von Karlus, von hertzog
Wilhalm von Osterreich, und von hertzog Lewppold von Osterreich"
was conceived as a warning against disappointments and
capricious changes of fortune illustrated by the fates of five
unlucky princes who met with disaster about the year 1386.
Thus the emphasis of the poem is upon Duke Leopold's arrogance
and subsequent demise, not on the battle of Sempach per se.

Poems by two heralds (?) from the thirteenth century
illustrate the combination of several genres which influenced
Suchenwirt: historical songs, heraldic poetry, and allegorical
blazon.

The deposition of King Adolf of Nassau and the election
of King Albert of Austria took place at Mainz on June 23, 1298.
Both kings had been prepared to fight since the beginning of
the preceding year and set up military headquarters near
Göllheim not far from Worms. On the evening of July 1 King
Albert claimed that he was merely on his way back to Austria
in an attempt to avoid a battle when he was attacked by King
Adolf's men under Count Palatine Rudolf (Adolf's son-in-law)
and Duke Otto of Lower Bavaria; Rudolf and Otto claimed that
they too were merely passing by Göllheim when they were
attacked by Duke Henry of Carinthia and Duke Ulrich von Walsee.

Once the battle began it was carried through with great
determination and bravery on both sides. King Adolf was
unhorsed and left unconscious for a while, but he bravely
continued fighting until he died a heroic death. His son
and many of his followers were taken prisoner.

This battle is immortalized by two contemporary poets,
Hirzelin and Meister Zilies von Seine. Unfortunately both of
their accounts are fragmentary. Hirzelin,[134] who supported
the Austrian side, indicates that he is a traveling singer:

> Hirzelin, friunt, daz si geseit   278
> dir und aller varnden diet.

His home was probably in the area of Lake Constance since he
lists many northern Swiss knights and is only familiar with
major nobility outside of Switzerland such as the princes of
Austria, Carinthia, and Bohemia. The fact that he portrays
the dukes Henry of Carinthia and Ulrich von Walsee in such
complete detail, not merely noticing their generosity to the
poet, points to a more intimate relationship with them.

> Sin edliu hant chan swãre   180
> bŭzen aller gernder diet,
> di er mit willen ie beriet.

Hirzelin writes completely within the realm of courtly
observations. He alludes to Wolfram von Eschenbach and
Walther von der Vogelweide to give credence to his own account.
The two descriptions of arms indicate that French heraldic
expression had already taken over the entire language of
heraldry. This French veneer remained popular in Austria

until the time of Emperor Frederick III and remained the single
most distinguishable characteristic of heraldic description.[135]
Hirzelin described the Carinthian arms (or, three lions sable)
and Duke Henry himself as follows:

> Ze Paris auf pytipunt   144
> wart tecche und wapenrocch bereit
> dem fürsten druch sin werdicheit.
> Schilt und banir sin was gelich
> geteilet, halp von Osterrich,
> daz ander gar von golde
> nach werder wibe solde,
> dar auz drei lewen gaben glast
> von chotzer siden swarz gebast,
> widersehende ob einander;...
> Sust chom der furst dort her gerůrt.   156
> Sin helm der gab vil liehten schin:
> zwen swarze flügel Cherubin
> der engel het darauf gedent
> mit guldin leubern rich verwent
> geblasunniert fůet den helm.

This coat of arms is half Austrian, half Carinthian. The
coat of arms of Ulrich II von Walsee is introduced by a
request from a lady:

> Die einiu sprach: „wis uns bereit   272
> und sag uns, lieber Hirzelin,
> wie sin wapen muge sin?"

Naturally Hirzelin was delighted to reply:

> Ich sprach: vrowe, ein saphir rich   281
> von der Poy der schilt ist glich,
> dar durch ein strich geit richen glast,
> von wazerperlin drin gebast;
> des selben ist teche und wapenroch,
> dar under er manich rich gezoch
> hat getan ze velde....
> daz auf helm nie wurd gedent   297
> zwen braune flugel so rich verwent,
> dar durch ein bar tiuwer rich,
> di sint dem schilt wol gelich.

Suchenwirt similarly blazons the coat of arms of Ulrich III
von Walsee, a white fess on a black field:

> Der schilt was chostper und reich,   XIII,207
> Saffirn brawn gar meisterleich
> Gereichet und geheret;
> Des glentzen ist vercheret
> Von des pittern todes slag;
> Dar inn ein vasch getzieret lag
> In parraweis von perlin vyn.

Both Suchenwirt and Hirzelin identify the white fess with the
word "pearl;" incorrectly they also label the black field

"sapphire brown." Suchenwirt employs the same expression when
he describes the black Carinthian lions as "von praün saffieren
scheinen sach man auz den golde reich drea leon" (VI,202) (see
also p. 167).

The other side of the battle of Göllheim, the side of King
Adolf of Nassau, is described by Meister Zilies von Seine, also
a traveling singer.[136] Meister Zilies, from the Rhine region,
wrote laudatory and heraldic poems which were conceived
primarily because he expected to be recompensed by those whom
he lauded. Adolf Bach maintains that the greatest part of his
production, including death laments dealing with individuals in
high positions, has been lost. Meister Zilies' most important
work includes the 302 fragmentary lines about the battle at
Göllheim probably written in the fall of 1298.[137] King Adolf's
participation in the battle and his death make up the core of
the poem. The poet was not personally present at the battle
but obtained his facts from eye-witnesses. He calls King
Albert's men the *viande* (1,3) while referring to King Adolf's
army as *van unser siden* (1,194).

The fragments begin in the middle of the battle with
vigorous struggles which eventually led to the death of King
Adolf. An Austrian knight (the name is missing) presses
forward; he meets a Nassau knight who is identified by his
coat of arms, an anchor, and who fights to the death:

> Ich meynen, de den anker droich.   1,10
> Sin ors ho vnde stolz
> Quam noch sneller dan eyn bolz
> Also mit sporen dar gemeint...

Then King Adolf joins his men in the tumult and fights his
way forward, searching for King Albert whom he wounds in the
eye or by whom he is wounded in the eye:

> Hey sûchte den van Oisterrich.   1,58
> Van dem hey zû hant kirde sich.
> Mir sade eyn ritter, de id sach,
> Det hei in vnder ougen stach.

King Adolf turns away from Albert because some knights from
Zweibrücken, Leiningen, Veldenz, and Rauh-Wildgrafen intrude.
After his fall Adolf fights without his helmet because it
weighs too much for his injured head, "Sin hoyft was des

helmes blois" (1,69).

The description of Adolf's death is missing, but not
the poet's lament:

Ich muys den ri^enen koninc clagen,   1,98
Want an eme wart erslagen
Eyn cristen koninck, ein greue wert,
Eyn ritter kone, de sin swert
In wiues deynste dicke erzoych.
Sin eydil herze was so hoych,
Dat may geyne vndait drin inquam.

The battle continued to rage; numerous Nassau heroes are
praised, especially Count Eberhart von Katzenellenbogen. The
capture of Adolf's son Ruprecht is missing.

Another fragment of 184 lines by Meister Zilies entitled
"Die Böhmenschlacht"[138] describes the battle at Dürnkrut on
August 26, 1278; basically it is a glorification of Rudolf of
Habsburg and his deeds in this battle. The author reveals no
real knowledge of the incidents of the battle but portrays
general battle scenes richly embellished with description and
interpretation of arms.

Although King Rudolf of Habsburg received, according to
a treaty of 1276, the territories of Austria, Styria, and
Carinthia after a three year long struggle with King Ottocar
of Bohemia, still another decisive battle took place between
the two kings at Dürnkrut. Both Rudolf and Ottocar took an
active and brave part in this battle. King Ottocar finally
met his death. The poem begins with Rudolf's army, banners
flying, ready for the attack. There is a long description
of King Rudolf:

An in geleget wart ein plade   2,14
Wal gestichit unde geslan.
Zu hant sach man dort her dran
Ein künincliches wapincleit,
Dar ane des richis are steit,
Ingesigel unde zeichen...

Ottocar at the head of the Bohemian army also prepared for
battle. The beginning of the battle is missing. The battle
is frantic. Rudolf prays before entering himself. Rudolf
breaks through the Bohemian lines; Ottocar is furious and
presses forward. Both kings lose their horses but receive
replacements. Rudolf is aided by a knight with a lion in his

coat of arms:

> Awoy, eyn ors dort here drůch   2,83
> Den man, den lewen vn den aren.
> Dis zeichen kůnt is man vn barn.
> Dar up was ouch reycht gelimpf.

The Bohemian king falls. The lines missing here probably
describe the victorious return of the Austrian army into camp
at the end of the battle. Among the returnees is Count
Eberhart von Katzenellenbogen covered with wounds who is
received with honor by King Rudolf.[139]

   The duel between the kings is portrayed in allegorical
grandeur; the heraldic animals battle in place of their masters:

> We, wi stolzliche dar   2,128
> Die flügil erswang der adel ar,
> Gen des lewen clawen hi!...
> Under dem arn sich ein lewe barc,   2,143
> Der ouch gen disme lewen vacht.

The imperial eagle defeats the Bohemian lion, a white
leaping lion on a red field:

> Van hermlī eyns lewen war   2,58
> Nach ich, up kelen dar gestracht.

The poem concludes with the blazon of King Rudolf's coats of
arms; the imperial arms of a black eagle on a gold field and
his Habsburg family arms of a red lion on a golden field:

> Up golt van zabel eyn adelar   2,173
> Was geslayn vn gelait.
> Van me riche hi^e dese waypē drait....
> Van arde hi^e andeir waypen hait: 2,176
> Eyn lewe in hoher werde stait,
> Van roider keyle up golt geslain,
> Dey hi^e vil dicke hait gedain
> Herzenschrickes lere.

Because this is a heraldic poem it is understandable that the
poet does not depict history completely accurately. The
description of the battle is nothing but a framework using
traditional materials to glorify King Rudolf and the most
important event of his reign.

   It is clear that the knight's deeds were closely
identified with his arms and a blazon of these arms was a
form of flattery or praise. Although the goal of political-
historical songs was primarily to record a particular event
or battle, to eulogize a heroic figure, or even to effect a
change in policy a description of coats of arms invariably appears.

"TOURNAMENT AND SIEGE POEMS"

The genre of poetry which I call "tournament and siege poems" belongs to the larger genres of heraldic poetry and political-historical poetry. These poems provide prototypes for Suchenwirt's *Ehrenreden* for several reasons: they report history quite objectively in verse form; they are frequently written by heralds; they include heraldry as an integral part of the account; and, generally, the blazons of arms are technically correct.

"Tournament and siege poems" also illustrate the shift in focus from imaginary heroes and events to real ones. In the middle of the thirteenth century Konrad von Würzburg blazons the coats of arms of real knights who take part in an imaginary tournament at Nantes; Jacques Bretel portrays a real tournament which took place at Chauvency in 1285; and similarly an anonymous poet or herald describes a real siege which took place at Caerlaverock Castle in 1300. In each of these three examples heraldry appears almost for its own sake. The recording of arms is more than a mere list, however, for the authors obviously take delight in the pictures they portray. But, more importantly, the mere blazon seems to provide honor to the bearer of the arms. Thus the descriptions of arms represent an accurate account of a historical or imaginary event, give the event credence, and also honor the individuals depicted.

Konrad von Würzburg portrays a tournament in honor of beautiful ladies held on the plain of Nantes (following the tradition of brilliant tournaments allegedly held there in the past by King Arthur), at which King Richard of England, the epitomy of generosity and nobility, wished to gain honor and fame. The poem entitled *Turnier von Nantes* begins with the purpose of such a gathering explained in courtly language and in terms of courtly goals:[140]

> Dô wart an im bewæret wol   67
> daz man den milten kûme sol
> ûz edelm muote bringen.
> swer in mit râte twingen
> wil ûz sîner frîen art,

weizgot der leidet im die vart
die frîez herze triutet.
swie vil man im gebiutet
daz er unmilticlichen lebe,
sô wirt gevellet doch sîn gebe
rîlîche ûf alter unde ûf jugent.
in lêret angeborniu tugent
daz er ûf êre warte.
daz edel muot unarte,
deist gar ein ungehœret dinc.

Four thousand knights are divided into two opposing
sides, the *Tiuschen* versus the *Walhen*. The Germans appear
under the leadership of King Richard of England, the main hero
of the poem, and the *Walhen* under *der Kerlingœre voget* (King of France)
and the King of Spain. The most noble participants are
described in groups of seven. The first day is spent in
individual combat, the victory of King Richard is clearly
emphasized. On the second day of mass combat Richard again
emerges as the victor of the winning side. The tournament
concludes with the capture of the King of Spain.

Some scholars have identified King Richard of the poem
with Richard the Lionhearted. However, it is unlikely that
Konrad would have praised Richard the Lionhearted who was the
opponent of the German crusaders, was held prisoner by the
German Emperor, and died in 1199. Jakob Baechtold, on the
other hand, believes that the *Turnier von Nantes* was modeled
after a tournament held at the coronation of Richard of
Cornwall as King of the Romans in May 1257 at Aachen.[141] It
is not at all impossible that Konrad was present at this
coronation and inspired by it. The presumption is that
Konrad was alluding to the double election of Richard of
Cornwall and Alphonso X of Castile and Leon, and that he
gave the victory to the first chosen and thus legitimately
crowned king.

On Richard's side Konrad places the kings of Scotland
and Denmark, the dukes of Brabant, Brunswick, and Saxony, the
Landgrave of Thuringia, the margraves of Brandenburg and
Meissen, and the Count of Cleve. Among the opponents appear
the King of Navarre, the Count of Champagne, the princes of
Burgundy and Lorraine, "ein herre von Britanje" (Duke of

Brittany), the counts of Artois, Bar, Blois, and Nevers. This
alignment does not seem to reflect political considerations,
nor the tournament itself, but rather poetic freedom on the
part of the author. The individual knights, however, are
based on historical personages as is seen by the blazon of
their coats of arms. Paul Ganz uses the shields to determine
the date of the poem which he places between 1265 and 1269.[142]

The coat of arms of the leader of the Kerlingære, gold
fleurs-de-lis on a blue field, is described as follows:

> er fourte an sîme schilte   534
> durch hôher werdekeite schîn
> fünfzehen liljen guldîn,
> die glizzen wünnichlichen dâ.
> von Orient safîre blâ
> den plân mit glaste zierten,
> darûz die liljen smierten
> schôn unde lobelichen gar.

This is a variation on the old coat of arms of France, with
five *fleurs-de-lis* on the top row, then four, three, two, and
one in the succeding rows, to form a triangle.

Charles Boutell claims that he found evidence for the
oldest quartered coat of arms, that of Castile and Leon, on
the gravestone of Eleanor, Queen of Edward I, in Westminster
Abbey from 1291:[143] the golden Castilian castle on a red field
and the black lion of Leon on a white field. Konrad's blazon
of these same arms is earlier no matter what dating system
is accepted for his works, since he died in 1287. He
describes the coat of arms of the King of Spain:[144]

> ûf sîme schilte erlûhten   548
> vier stücke, als im daz reht gebôt:
> zwei wâren wîz, zwei wâren rôt,
> und liezen sich dâ melden.
> in den zwein rôten velden
> geleit alsam ein lieht rubîn
> zwô bürge wâren guldîn,
> dô sach man ûz den wîzen
> dâ zwêne löuwen glîzen,
> die lûhten swarz ‹reht› als ein brant.

The Spanish arms also appear quartered in the *Clipearium
Theutonicorum* by Conrad von Mure (1242-1249, see p. 28), but
with the incorrect colors--black lions on a gold field and
two red cities (castles) on a silver field:[145]

Rex Hispanie duos gilvo tibi nigro leones. 3
In niveoque duas urbes rubeas ibi pones.

The Spanish arms are the only quartered arms found in the
Zurich Roll, here again with the incorrect colors. However,
about the same time the *Zurich Roll* was being compiled, it
became fashionable to quarter coats of arms, and many famous
arms date from the fourteenth century.

Konrad displays considerable finesse in describing
complicated heraldic charges which as yet had no specific
names; for example, the double lily border (trêcheur) in the
shield of the King of Scotland (or, a lion rampant within a
double tressure flory counterflory gules):

ein rant geblüemet drumbe gienc   366
⟨sô⟩ rôt als ie kein rôse erkant.
⟨ouch⟩ was enmitten ûf den rant
geleit ein guldîn strickelîn.
die bluomen sach man ûz und în,
die von dem rande lûhten
und alse liljen dûhten
gestellet an ir bilden.

Konrad is often called the first heraldic poet. His
works, excluding the *Turnier von Nantes,* illustrate the conventional
use of heraldry to symbolically describe fictitious heroes.
In the *Turnier von Nantes* he departs from tradition to portray
a realistic situation with real heroes. However, he should
not be considered the first heraldic poet according to either
of the definitions discussed above: he was not the first poet
to include heraldry in his work; since he did not compose
Ehrenreden, he could not have been the first to do so. On the
other hand, according to Gustav Seyler, Konrad was a herald:

Der berühmte Dichter *Conrad v. Würzburg*...der sich in seinen
jüngeren Jahren in einer den späteren Herolden entsprechenden
Stellung befand und darum nicht bloss eine ungewöhnliche
Wappenkenntniss sondern auch eine niemals übertroffene
Meisterschaft im Beschreiben der Wappen besass, führt in
seinem *Turnei von Nantheiz* auch das Wappen der Grafen von
Cleve an.[146]

Paul Ganz agrees with this appraisal: "Seine eingehende
heraldisch-juristische Bildung, die historische Kenntnis der
Wappen deutscher und welscher Fürsten und Grafen legen Zeugnis
ab, daß er sich eingehend mit historisch-genealogischen und
auch heraldischen Studien befasst haben muß."[147]   Arnold

Galle, on the other hand, disagrees completely with this
evaluation and goes to some lengths to disprove it:

> Die gröste geschicklichkeit in der ausführung erscheint ohne
> alle innere anteilnahme, die verknüpfung mit dem stoff ist
> rein äusserlicher art, die fäden, welche eine feste verbindung
> mit dem grundstock der dichtungen und damit eine organische
> einfügung hätten ermöglichen können, fehlen fast ganz: gründe
> genug für ein absprechendes urteil.[148]

He claims that Konrad's descriptions, excluding the historical
arms, are "kalt und tot, mit dem letzten wort der beschreibung
verschwindet auch das interesse."[149] Where Seyler praises
Konrad's correct usage of tincture, Galle claims this is
purely accidental use of primary colors. Where Seyler extols
Konrad's professional blazons, Galle points out the many
mistakes, regarding not only historical coats of arms, but
also the rules of heraldry and heraldic terminology. Galle
also claims that Konrad's use of materials and precious stones
is capricious.

In the poem the Count of Cleve wears a red escutcheon
on a white field:

> mit eime schilte wîzgevar,   516
> der was mit hermîn überspreit.
> der ander schilt was drîn geleit
> der ûzer glanzen kelen rôt.

This is exactly reversed from reality (i.e. gules, an inescutcheon argent).
The English arms also appear reversed as three red leopards
on a gold field:

> mit golde lieht von Arâbîn   310
> was im sîn velt bedecket,
> und waren drîn gestrecket
> entwerhes drî lêbarten...
> und wâren ûz rubînen   318
> nâch hôher wirde lône.

Konrad also blazons the coat of arms of the dukes of
Brittany, gold and blue (checky or and azure), incorrectly
as white and red:

> blanc und rôt schâchzabeleht   594
> wart sîn glanzer schilt gesehen.

Galle asserts that in the *Turnier von Nantes* Konrad simply
described the coats of arms of those knights who interested
him, who struck his fancy; those knights for whom he worked,
such as the great southern German families, were not

particularly fascinating. He omitted the arms of Bohemia, not
because he was not fimiliar with them, but because he was
indifferent.

Galle's criticisms appear unduly harsh. Konrad was
obviously attracted by heraldry even though he does not seem
to be as completely versed in it as a professional herald would
have been. His mistakes, however, are not more numerous than
those found in contemporary heraldic books or rolls. Furthermore accurate heraldic blazon was not his primary goal. His
fascination seems to lie in the overall visual picture which
the blazon of arms invokes. Thus he describes not only the
shield and helmet, but frequently the tabard and horses'
bardings as well. The difference of approach becomes clear
in comparison with Suchenwirt, the professional herald.
Suchenwirt does not make mistakes in his blazon. On the other
hand, Suchenwirt does not describe the individual knight in
battle with the arms worn on a particular occasion, but rather
the historical family arms of the individual. For him the
hero of the *Ehrenrede* is more important than his coat of arms,
i.e. the subject of the poem is the individual, not the coat
of arms. While Suchenwirt portrays the individual, Konrad
paints a colorful picture of a tournament. At the same time
Suchenwirt, the professional herald, maintains a strict order,
blazoning first the shield, then the helmet, creating a unity
lacking in Konrad's works. This order was undoubtedly not
originated by Suchenwirt since Konrad mentions the activity
of the "cnappen...die von den schilten rîche und von den
helmen sprâchen" (11. 1105-1107), and the anonymous author of
the lament honoring Count William of Holland (see pp. 42-43)
limits himself to a description of the shield and helmet.
Suchenwirt was very probably following the rules established
for heralds which were, in the fourteenth century, becoming
quite rigid.[150]

Konrad's delight in pageantry is echoed in the poem
by Jacques Bretel[151] (see pp. 21-22) describing a tournament
which was organized by Louis de Looz, Count of Chiny, and
took place at Chauvency in October 1285. The poem provides

very accurate information regarding the organization and execution of a tournament. Here this task is assigned to the herald Bruiant. The guests and participants arrived on Monday morning. The first two days were spent in individual combat. Bretel lists the names of the knights in each joust and comments either on the joust or on its outcome. In the interludes between battles Bretel discusses chivalry, the valor of individual knights, etc. The evenings are spent in song and dance. On Tuesday the king of heralds, Maignien, is sent out to invite more knights to participate in the mass tournament on Thursday. The program for this is organized on Wednesday. The actual *mêlée* is described in great detail. The day ends with a poetic sermon on love. On Friday the knights and ladies attend mass, dance, dine, discuss the various events of the week, and finally depart.

Bretel especially emphasizes the role of the herald. He questions the herald Bruiant about the identity of each combatant:

> Qui fu chascunz et de quel terre. 306
> Lors me respondit Bruiandiaus:
> "Je cognois grant partie d'iaus.
> "C'est la li cuens de Lucembourc,
> "Chevaliers preus et plain d'onor:
> "Aprés, son frere Walerant,
> "Chevaliers preus et compaignant,
> "Gent et cortois et large asséz."

During the jousts the heralds attend the ladies, comment on the abilities of the participants, and cheer the combatants while they fight.

The host and hostess of the tournament, the Count and Countess of Chiny, are Louis V of Looz (1268-1299) and his wife Jeanne de Bar († after 1295). Their arms, a gold cross between two gold bars on a red field (gules, two bends sinister between a cross couped or) are blazoned in the poem as follows:

> De toutes armez paréz fu, 3159
> Ainsi vermoilles comme feu,
> A deus bar d'or et a croissetes
> Petites, asséz joilÿetez.

One of the guests, Conrad Warnier de Hastat, is well-known because of his position as governor in Upper Alsace. He was

invited to the tournament and requested to bring his son
Conradin who had won fame fighting against King Ottocar of
Bohemia. Bretel describes Conradin's arms, a red St. Andrew's
cross on a gold field (or, a saltire gules) as follows:

> Mes iex tournai a si bone eure   896
> Que je vi tout a descovert
> Un chevalier d'armes couvert
> D'or fin a un çaintour vermoil,
> Et si porte par desparoil
> Une moleste d'or en chief.
> Hyraut escrïent de rechief:
> "Hastat a Conradin l'anfant!"

The herald identifies the knight by his arms and comments on
his career, his bravery and valor.

Similarly in a fragment of fifty-seven lines Meister
Zilies[152] employs the setting of a tournament rather than that
of a battle to show off his heraldic proficiency. This poem
is a glorification of the knight Adolf von Windhövel from
the Rhineland and of his deeds in a tournament. The fragment appears to be the conclusion of a rather long poem
probably written about 1300; documents pertaining to Adolf
von Windhövel exist from 1296 to 1303.

During the course of the tournament a lady describes the
coat of arms to the poet (herald?) who then identifies the
knight (probably in the complete poem several knights are
so identified):

> ,Ich wil dich siner wapin manin   4,5
> Vf trouwe, of du in bekennes,
> Dat dǔ vns den ritt^s nennes,'
> Sprach die frouwe minneliche.

She then describes the shield:

> ,He vurt ein scilt vā siluer riche,   4,9
> Dar in ein krǔz von keln roit....'

The poet replies that the knight is Adolf von Windhövel:

> ,Frouwe, ich nennē vch dē man,   4,39
> Den ir dort gewapent seit.
> Im is eren yil gescheit.
> It is min h^s Alf vō Winthouile...'

The poem concludes with praise and admiration for Adolf.

The tournament poems by Konrad von Würzburg, Jacques
Bretel, and Meister Zilies illustrate the poets' love for
heraldry placed in the refined, courtly setting of a

tournament. The poem celebrating the siege of Caerlaverock
Castle[153] in July 1300 demonstrates the same love of blazon
but in a more technical, less refined, setting. The author
may have been a herald; the poem is frequently referred to
as a roll of arms even though it is much more comprehensive
than a mere list of participants (see p. 28).[154] The language is the French of the English court. The form consists
of rhymed couplets, the verse most commonly employed at the
time. It contains the accurate blazon of over one hundred
knights from the reign of Edward I, including the King and
Prince of Wales. If it is indeed the first roll of arms,
it would indicate that the science of heraldry was already
perfected at a time when it is often considered to have been
in its infancy. Besides blazoning the arms of the participants
of the siege, the author frequently describes their personalities; he also provides valuable information regarding the
method of arraying an army and conducting a siege.

The castle of Caerlaverock on the northern shore of the
Solway Firth lay on the invasion route to Scotland of King
Edward I. As soon as the English army arrived at
Caerlaverock, around July 10, it was quartered by the marshal;
the soldiers proceeded to erect houses for accommodations.
Soon afterwards the military engines and provisions were
brought by the navy, and the footmen immediately marched
against the castle. A short, but sharp, skirmish took place
in which several men were killed and wounded. The loss
sustained by the infantry caused the men at arms to hasten to
their assistance:

> Meint en i court, meint en i saut,   672
> E meint si haste si de aler,
> Ke a nulli ne en daigne parler.

The author points out some of the knights who particularly
distinguished themselves in the assault.

> Cist ne vont pas cum gens meüres   718
> Ne cum genz de sen alumees,
> Mes cum arses e enfumés
> De orguel e de malencolie
> Car droit ont lour voie acuellie
> Juk a la rive du fossé.

The followers of Sir Thomas of Richmont advanced to the draw-
bridge and demanded entrance; they were answered with stones:

> ...on li respont   726
> De grosses pieres e cornues.

Reinforcements were provided by the followers of the Prince
of Wales; the walls were battered with considerable effect
by Sir Adam de la Forde; Sir Richard de Kirkbride assailed
the gate of the castle in so vigorous a manner

> Car onques fevres de martel   806
> Si sur son fer martela,
> Cum il e li sien firent la.

The author also praises the bravery of the besieged. They
showered huge stones and arrows upon their enemy, making
retreat difficult. They repelled assault upon assault and
defended the fortress for one whole day and night until the
next morning about nine o'clock. It was impossible to resist
the effect of three ponderous battering engines which killed
a soldier on the inside; when the roof fell in, stones entered
from all sides. Finally the besieged begged for peace, but
the soldier who displayed the banner of peace was shot through
his hand into his face by an arrow. They surrendered the
castle to the King of England and threw themselves upon his
mercy:

> Car le chastel au roi rendront   929
> E en sa grace hors vendront.

The marshal and constable of the English army immediately
commanded that all hostilities cease and took possession of
the castle. The English were extremely astonished to find
that the whole number of the enemy garrison amounted to only
sixty men. The King granted them mercy and bestowed upon
each a new robe:

> Ki vie e menbre lour dona   940
> E a chescun robe nouvele.

The King ordered his banner and that of St. Edmund, St.
George, and St. Edward to be raised. Lord Clifford was
appointed guardian.

The poem begins with a list of the participants and
a blazon of their arms; a typical example is that of Roger
de la Ware, a white lion and white crosslets on a red field

gules, semé of crosslets argent, a lion argent):

> Rogers de la Ware ovec ues,   181
> Uns chevaliers sagis e preus,
> Ki les armes ot vermellettis
> O blonc lyoun e croissellettes.

Later the author integrates the narrative with the description
of the coats of arms. Richard of Kirkbride, who assailed and
battered the castle, wore a green indented cross on a white
shield (argent, a cross engrailed vert):

> Meinte pesant piere e quaissable   800
> Cil de Kirkebride i porta
> Mes le escu blanc devant bouta
> O la crois verde engreellie
> Si ke mult fu bien asallie
> De li la porte du chastel...

The author notes that Brian Fitz Alan and Hugh Pointz
bore identical banners of gold and red horizontal stripes
(barry or and gules) and that a dispute arose between them:

> Le beau Brian le Filz Aleyn   353
> De courtoisie e de honnour pleyn
> I vi o baniere barree
> De or e de goules bien paree
> Dont de chalenge estoit li poinz
> Par entre li e Huet Poinz
> Ki portoit tel ne plus ne meins
> Dont merveille avoit meinte e meins.

But he leaves the reader wondering about what kind of an
authority or court would have settled the dispute. This is
one of the earliest records of such a disagreement; clearly
this problem was of some concern to the knights of the Middle
Ages.

The authors of these "tournament and siege poems"
appear to have been more interested in the heraldry than in
the details of the tournament or the siege. These poems are
representative of poetic blazon of the time; the poets were
not only concerned with properly describing the correct arms,
but also with the problem of placing this blazon into a
poetic context, a difficulty not encountered by the herald
compiling a heraldic book or roll such as the *Zurich Roll*.
The poetic blazon is clearly a prototype of the blazon which
appears later in the *Ehrenrede*. In none of the other prototypes discussed above does the blazon appear in such

completely contained form, in a form which could be trans-
ferred word for word to the *Ehrenrede*. Consider, for example,
Konrad's blazon of the arms of the Prince of Saxony:

> Der fürste rîch von Sahsen   390
> ze velde ouch in der rotte quam,
> das wâpencleider wünnesam
> von glanzer sîden glizzen.
> er hæte sich geflizzen
> ûf eine ritterlîche tjost.
> gebriten was von rîcher kost
> in sîn gewant zam unde wilt.
> der herzog einen tiuren schilt
> von zweier varwe stücken
> ·für sich begunde drücken
> nâch ritterlichem rehte.
> sîn halbez teil strîfhte
> von zobel und von golde was;
> daz ander teil, als ich ez las,
> erschein durliuhtic wîz hermîn,
> und was von rôten kelen drîn
> geleit ein halber adelar.

Konrad first describes the Prince's clothing as viewed by
the audience at the tournament; then he blazons the shield
(party per pale: barry of sable and gold; argent, a half
eagle gules); he completes the picture with a description
of the helmet:

> der fürste wolgezieret gar   405
> ûf sîme glanzen helme cluoc
> ûz eines phâwen zagel truoc
> zwô wünniclîche stangen,
> bestecket und behangen
> mit golde lieht und edele
> biz an die zwêne wedele
> der phâwenspiegel viderîn,
> die glanzen wünniclichen schîn
> ûf der plânîe bâren.
> die stangen beide wâren
> ûf den helm dur liehten prîs
> geschrenket schône in criuzewîs.

None of the blazons from the tournament at Chauvency or
the siege of Caerlaverock Castle is as comprehensive as
Konrad's; nevertheless, the poets are careful to put in a
good word for the knight in question; for example, the only
criticism of Walter de Beauchamp at Caerlaverock was that
he was too rash and daring:

> Puis i ot Watiers de Beauchamp   319
> Sis merlos de or el rouge champ

[Chivallier, selon ma cuidance,]
Uns des mellours fust entre touz
Se il ne fust trop fiers e estouz.
Mes vous ne orrez parler jamés
De senescal ki ne ait un mes.

His arms (gules, a fess between six martlets or) are blazoned
correctly. Suchenwirt, too, maintains that a shield is a
lovely sight to behold, especially when borne by such a noble
as Burkhard von Ellerbach, the Younger (quarterly, vert and or):

Den schilt man hat noch rainer lust   IX,223
Gesehen dik vor seiner prust:
Smaragden grün pei golde reich
Quartirt, der dike ritterleich
Erwirert ist vor vrawen chlar.
Ir nemt des helmes ewen war,
Der auf des heldes haubet stat,
Wo man sich werleich vinden lat;
Do fürt der edel auzerchorn
Noch dem schilde reich tzwai horn,
Als im di manhait ie gepot,
Dar under er sich dik in not
Durch ere hat gefrumet.

Thus "tournament and siege poetry" is clearly a prototype
for Suchenwirt's *Ehrenreden* which also include an expanded
poetic blazon.

GELRE

The prototype most similar to Suchenwirt's *Ehrenreden* is found in the works of the herald Gelre. According to Victor Bouton[155] Gelre was born about 1310/1315 and died about 1372. His real name was Heynen, but he took the professional name Gelre in honor of his masters, the dukes of Gelders. Froissart mentions that a herald by the name of Gelre, who spoke French, was present at Buironfosse in 1339.[156] Paul Adam-Even[157] believes that Gelre was Claes Heinenzsoon (known as Beijeren), king of arms of Gelders, herald of the counts of Holland from 1375 to 1414. In 1406 the new Duke William IV of Bavaria, Count of Holland and Zeeland, granted money to a Claes Heinriczsoon for services rendered to his father, Duke Albert (1358-1404). In 1407 the precise title of his office is given as "Beyeren le héraut, roi de ruyers, notre serviteur." In 1411 he is described as Claes Heyensoon, die men het Beyeren, onsen eerhald, Conninc van den Wapenen der Ruyeren." If Adam-Even's thesis, that there is only one man involved and not a father and son, is correct, then Gelre must have been born later than Bouton's dates. He could have been in the service of the dukes of Gelders before entering the service of the Wittelsbach family, the counts of Holland in 1375. Seyler, on the other hand, considers Beijeren merely to have been Gelre's predecessor in the official position of herald and not related by blood.[158]

Beijeren is known as the author of a heraldic book of sixty-two leaves with 1,098 coats of arms. On the last leaf is the inscription: "Explicit iste liber per manus Beyeren quondam gelre armorum regis de ruris." This heraldic book includes the arms of the participants of a tournament at Compiègne in 1278, at a siege at Gornichem in 1404 (with 120 shields), at a tournament at Mons in 1313 (191 shields), a campaign to Friesland and Kuinre in 1396 (404 shields). Beijeren is also the author of a chronicle of the counts of Holland written about 1409, which, among its ninety-nine emblazoned coats of arms includes not only those of the

counts of Holland, but also those of the Emperor and the
bishops of Utrecht; in addition it contains fourteen heraldic
poems about well-known lords from Holland.

As a herald Gelre traveled extensively to such far away
places as Lithuania, Hungary, Scotland, and Aragon. He
carried messages to the burgraves of the Rhineland and
Westphalia, to the leaders of the Teutonic Order in their out-
posts of civilization. He was present at the battles of
Crécy and Poitiers.[159] His first master, Duke Renaud, was an
ally of King Edward III of England. Gelre was one of the
heralds who carried King Edward's challenge to Philip de
Valois when the French and English armies were face to face
on the field of Buironfosse.

Gelre is best known for his heraldic book, *Wapenboeck*,
which is prefaced by heraldic poems in Middle Dutch. This
armorial illustrates the fact that such collections are by no
means confined to the heraldry of the country of origin, but
that heralds were obviously also expected to know the arms of
potential opponents. Since the Duchy of Gelders was part of
the Roman Empire, Gelre's *Wapenboeck* begins with a shield
ornamented with the arms of the Emperor. The coats of arms
of the seven electors are followed by those of a great number
of dukes and counts, each with the numerous knights of his
courts. The shields for all the kingdoms of Europe with
their political subdivisions fill the end of the manuscript.
It includes over 1,800 painted coats of arms. The details,
especially the helmet decorations, the technique, the style,
and the reliability of the arms are valuable to scholars
interested in the fourteenth century. However, it is not a
pretentious book but a functional collection of arms for the
herald himself, executed on thick parchment. The frontispiece
illustration of Emperor Charles IV and the seven electors is
well sketched but does not contain costly pigments. Although
the heraldry of the *Wapenboeck* has received considerable
attention (comparisons have been made with the *Zurich Roll*
and other heraldic books),[160] no one has seriously looked at
Gelre's poetic work from the point of content, form, or style.

Gelre's heraldic poems are especially important in the history of literature because they are so similar to Suchenwirt's *Ehrenreden* and other High German heraldic poems which preceded the *Ehrenreden* in their structure, form, manner of presentation, and manner of description of coats of arms, that they suggest a uniform German genre of heraldic poetry originating in pre-literary times: only the artistically more significant examples of this genre have probably found a place in literature via the route of oral presentation.[161] This continuity of the genre of heraldic poetry may be due to conversations among heralds at various tournaments, on campaigns, during trips in service of their masters. It is possible that Suchenwirt and Gelre met each other at some time during their careers. They also may have come in contact with the Chandos Herald and with Froissart, the historian.

The Gelre manuscript begins with a poem about the challenges or threats of eighteen knights, who are both described and emblazoned, against the Boar of Ardennes, Duke Jean III of Brabant, in January 1334. The challengers include the counts of Flanders, Namur, Reinecq, Marck, the dukes of Limburg and Bar, the King of Bohemia, and the Bishop of Cologne, etc. At the end of the poem is an illustration of a captured boar dressed in the tabard of the dukes of Brabant.

Second is a poem about the battle of Staveren of 1345. This is a series of poetic blazons of fourteen participants on the side of Count William I of Hainaut-Holland who died in the battle; these include the Count of Hoeren, the lords of Antoegne, Lynge, Merweende, Haemsteden, Asperen, Avelyns, Gheraert Mitten Baerde, Wouter van Mani, Willem van Naeldwyc, Dirc van Waelcourt, Symoen van Teylinge, Jan Lusserulis, and Claes Oem. In the manuscript the coat of arms as well as the name of each knight accompanies the blazon. The poems about each knight range in length from four to eight lines.

Gelre names the participants in the battle according to their coats of arms. There is no attempt to introduce the subject of the battle, to give the details of the struggle, or to come to a conclusion. Gelre appears to be more interested in blazons than in the battle itself. The descriptions of

arms are quite sophisticated in their technical accuracy; for
example, Gelre indicates labeling in the arms of Heer Symoen
van Teylinge:

> Die viifte wapende hem van goude,
> Een leeu van keel, alst wesen zoude,
> Van zilver een baresteel,
> Dit waren siin wapen al geheel. (p. 10)

A red lion on a gold field, a label of silver.

This seems to me to be typical of "tournament and siege
poems" where knights pass by the poet or herald who blazons
their coats of arms and identifies them. On the other hand,
Hellmut Rosenfeld[162] considers each of these little poems to
be an *Ehrenrede* in itself. Since there appears to be a lacuna
in the manuscript,[163] he claims that the poem was originally
much longer and that it fit the typical genre of heraldic
poetry as a composite of shorter *Ehrenreden*. An example of
such an *Ehrenrede* is the section devoted to Heer Dirc van
Waelcourt:

> Nu zal ic u den vierden nomen,
> Den hooschen, trouwen enten vromen.
> Hi droech van goude, dair in geset
> Een aern van keel, ic wilt ghiit wet.
> Hi had gesocht menich aventure,
> Een barestele van lasure.
> Gevoet, gebect was die aern
> Van lasuer, ic noomt u gaern. (p. 9)

Gelre blazons the arms: a red eagle with blue beak and claws
on a gold field, a blue label. He also praises the knight
but does not name him (except in the margin next to the
emblazoned shield). This does not conform to the *Ehrenrede*
formula defined in the introduction and discussed in chapter V.

The third poem is a chronicle of the dukes of Brabant
beginning with Priam, King of Hungary. It recites their
history and genealogy and is similar to the fourth poem, a
chronicle of the counts of Holland. These two poems were
composed in 1332 and 1325 respectively.

The chronicle of the counts of Holland concludes with
Margarethe, the same Empress of Bavaria about whom Suchenwirt
writes (see p. 33). Two anonymous death laments honor
Margarethe's closest relatives: her father William III of
Holland († 1337) and her brother William IV of Holland († 1345,

see pp. 42-43). Suchenwirt and Gelre could have been familiar
with one or both of these poems. Margarethe became ruler of
Holland upon the death of her brother and for many years was
involved in civil war against her own son. Gelre stood
clearly on Margarethe's side; he closes his chronicle with the
following tribute to her without even mentioning her son:

> Margriet, siin zuster, nemet goom,
> Hadde Lodewiic den keyser van Room,
> Ende hertooch van Beyeren was becant;
> Zi wart gravinne ontfaen int lant
> Ende zi regneerde voir waer
> Bicant in Hollant wel x iaer.   (p. 32)

Karl Helm suggests that Suchenwirt was not only familiar with
the anonymous poems but also with Gelre's chronicle.[164]

Finally the manuscript includes twelve *Ehrenreden* similar
to those of Suchenwirt. Most of the nobles honored are from
the Netherlands and the Rhineland, but the Count of Holstein
and Count Rudolph IV of Nidau are also included. In almost
all the *Ehrenreden* a woman, an allegorical figure, appears and
talks to the poet or herald. In the poem dedicated to Johan
van Spanem the lady tells Gelre she is going to give him the
task of helping her decorate a new room with coats of arms.
Of course she only wants extraordinary, brave, and honorable
knights on her walls:

> Eyn edel vrou sprac tot my:
> Hoir, Gelre, nu wil ic dy
> Bekummeren mit eynre zaken;
> Ich doe eyn nye kamer maken,
> Die ich mit wapen wil doen malen,
> Du salt my bescreven halen
> Ridder, die des wairdich siin
> Dat ich in die kamer miin
> Malen mach zonder miswende.   (p. 67)

Gelre is happy to make suggestions, but she interrupts to
describe one special knight who has fought against the
Prussians and against the heathens overseas, who has made
pilgrimages and bloodied his armor in battle and on the
tournament field, etc. Gelre requests a description of his
arms:

> Ich sprach: Vrou, nu maert my kont
> Zo wie der heelt ghewapent si,
> Dair ichen mach erkennen bi.   (p. 69)

The lady first blazons the coat of arms (checky or and azure
with a label gules):

> Velt gescaectafelt mit lasure;
> Dair op zo leecht eyn barenstele
> Van viif hanghen, root van kele.
> Elck hanc is durch graven,
> Viif lettren siin dair up verhaven.   (p. 69)

Hidden within the arms the five points of the label reveal the
first name of the hero which the lady happily cries out:

> ...Johan
> Spanem, Spanem roep men dan.

She then describes the helmet:

> Ende draecht den helm, dien ich visiere,
> Van sinen wapene eyn conversiere,
> Dair eyn guldiin croon op steyt;
> Van pawenvedren dair uyt gheit
> Eyn stanghe riiclic ghestacht.   (p. 70)

The helmet is also gold and blue, with a golden crown on top
from which a peacock feather flies. She concludes her out-
pourings with a more general description of the hero and with
another reference to Gelre. Johan van Spanem will have the
first place on her walls.

This poem differs from others discussed above because
it is not a death lament. The allegorical figure, the general,
but not specific, description of the hero's deeds, and the
blazon of the coat of arms are present, but the hero is
referred to in the present tense. This is a laudatory poem,
an *Ehrenrede*, written by a herald who carefully and correctly
blazons the coat of arms. Five other poems by Gelre follow
a similar formula: allegory, general enumeration of deeds,
no death lament and no prayer of intercession, but with a
blazon of the coat of arms. At the end of each of his poems
Gelre emblazons the arms--the shield and the helmet.

Gelre's other *Ehrenreden* adhere to a somewhat different
formula. The deeds of the hero are enumerated in great detail.
In the case of deceased heroes there is a lament and intercessory prayer. The poem honoring Heinriic van Nueft, for
example, begins with the poet's plea to God for aid in this
noble effort:

> Nu helf, heer alder werelt God,
> Dir tse love zonder spod:

> Wold ich zo gaerne dichten;
> Nu hilf mir berichten. (p. 33)

He laments the death of the noble and courtly knight:

> Dair om zo moes ich claghen
> Eyn ritter, die na ritterscaft
> Geworven haet na heiles craft,
> In ritterlicher wise. (p. 33)

He then describes his specific deeds: at Hategans, Volenho, Gaernaten, Allesier (where he was the best), Stenvoirt, Honcoert in France, Doornic (where the English King also fought), Waerle (where he was well known), Scutdorp, Aldenzeel, Kovelen, Montaboer, Relichousen, etc. He fought in Lombardy, at Milan, undertook a campaign to Prussia against the heathens, accompanied Count Enghelbrecht van der Marcke to the Holy Sepulcher and Mount Sinai to the grave of St. Catherine:

> Door no zo voer he over meer
> Mit zinen geboren rechten heer,
> Greve Enghelbrecht van der Marcke,
> Hyn tso dem heilighen zarcke,
> Door Cristus in begraven lach,...
> He quam tso monte Synay,
> Die heilige waerde wandels vry,
> Die maecht sint Katrine
> Lies eem genade vurscine. (pp. 37-38)

Gelre praises the hero's spiritual and knightly virtues. He blazons the shield and helmet with the proficiency of a professional (argent, a fess gules, in chief a lion gules):

> Fiin paerliin lighen menichfalt
> In daem scilt pollieret:
> Dair midden durch vertsieret
> Eyn faes, der lecht in berwiis,
> Alsam der edel robiin priis
> Verwe voir alle steyn haet;
> Eyn dyamant obder robiin staet
> In eyns lewen forme;
> Tso stride ind och ten storme. (p. 40)

The helmet consisted of silver mantling, a red crown topped by silver feathers:

> Often helme moes ich ghien:
> Die covertuer van hermel fiin;
> Dair ofh eyn croon van robiin,
> Vus liechter verbe brindet.
> Door tusschen wael besinnet
> Tween vluechlen vus der gronen gaen;
> Mergriis sal vuer verbe haen. (p. 40)

The poem concludes with an intercessory prayer to the Virgin

Mary and with the revelation of the name of the hero:

> Helf Maria, moeter, reyne meit,
> Die keyne sunder nicht voirseit,
> Das unse bete nicht werde blint;
> Bid vuer vuem diin liebe kint;
> Zo doe wir alle willichliic:
> Her hiet van Nueft her Heinriic.   (p. 40)

The works of Gelre are representative of both heraldic
poetry as broadly defined and of the narrowly defined *Ehrenrede*.
Despite the limited information regarding his biography his
identity as a herald is well established--a herald who
emblazoned a heraldic book and who wrote heraldic poetry.
Clearly Gelre's *Ehrenreden* represent a departure--perhaps
development--from the other heraldic poetry discussed in this
chapter. The formula of his poems and their relationship to
the only really similar poet of the time, Peter Suchenwirt,
will be discussed in chapter V.

SYNOPSIS: HERALDIC POETRY

Hellmut Rosenfeld in an article entitled "Nordische Schilddichtung und mittelalterliche Wappendichtung"[165] poses a number of thought-provoking hypotheses about the nature of heraldic poetry which will be examined in detail in the following pages. The geographical distance between Gelre in the Netherlands and Peter Suchenwirt in Austria allows them to be considered representative of the genre. Their death laments and *Ehrenreden* suggest a similar scheme. They often begin with a humility formula or appeal to God which is common in medieval poetry:

> Gelre   Nu hilf, herr alder werelt God,
> Dir tse love zonder spod:
> Wold ich zo gaerne dichten;
> Nu heilf mir berichten.   (p. 33)

> Suchenwirt   Got her, nu chum mir zestewer
> Durich deines todes smertzen,
> Daz sich deins fron'n geistes fewer
> Entzünd in meinem hertzen.   (V,9)

Then they express praise and in the case of death laments sorrow for the deceased and an account of his battles and deeds; there follows a technical description of the coat of arms (shield and helmet, seldom the tabard) with the name of the hero; and they conclude, in the case of a lament, with a prayer for intercession for the soul of the deceased. Generally there is no smooth transition from the lament to the blazon, but instead the description of arms usually acts as an independent entity, often itself introduced by another humility formula, also a typical topos:

> Gelre   Kund ic na hogher wairdicheit,
> Siin helm, siin scilt, siin wapencleit,
> Mit rechter consten blasinieren.   (p. 65)

> Suchenwirt   Chund ich nu wol verchünden
> Den underschaid der wappen sein.   (IX,220)

This is often followed by another appeal to God or "Art" or concludes with another intercessory prayer.

The isolation of the description of the coat of arms within the entire poem and the specific parts of the poem let one surmise that two types of poems are combined. The blazon

probably had only a very brief praise or lament introduction
which was either expanded or replaced by a laudatory song or
death lament. The lyrical death lament is made up of three
elements: lament, praise, intercession; Suchenwirt's poem
honoring Duke Albert (V) illustrates this type where the
blazon is missing. Scandinavian laudatory songs and
Suchenwirt's poem about Duke Albert's Prussian campaign (IV)
illustrate the contents of a laudatory song: praise of the
hero, coupled with an individual campaign or more likely a
biography, usually concluded with the author's praise of the
generosity of the hero. With the scalds this forms a
definite genre, an ornamental decorated style of description;
with German poets the genre is not so fixed, but the topos of
spilliute or minstrels praising the generosity of their patrons
is very common.

The death lament and laudatory song have thus literally
coalesced, if Rosenfeld's analysis is correct, with the
original or archetypal poems describing coats of arms which
contained only brief introductory flourishes. This longer ·
form is reduced in Gelre's poem about the battle of Staveren
which does not describe a single individual but rather the
entire body of knights who took part in the battle; Rosenfeld
maintains that the breadth of the task caused the reduction
of the various parts. Actually Gelre concentrates on the
shield of each participant in two to four rhymed couplets,
seldom with a word of praise for the bearer of the arms.
Here Rosenfeld hypothesizes a fixed form of heraldic poem
which includes perhaps a humility formula, praise of the
hero's deeds, etc. (he does not say exactly what) and he
suggests that Gelre departs from this model because the
battle which he is describing involved too many individual
participants. In the same vein Rosenfeld considers the Latin
poem of Conrad von Mure, the *Clipearium Theutonicorum*, to be
purely scholarly whereas the blazon rhymes of the professional
Gelre point to other connections, but he fails to explain
himself further. There does not appear to be any substantial
difference between Conrad's blazons and Gelre's blazons in

the poem describing the battle of Staveren; both Conrad and
Gelre identify knights as concisely as possible in the
established poetic fashion. On the other hand, in his
Ehrenreden Gelre's purpose is more than mere identification:
the more involved and complicated blazon honors the knight
within the context of his heroic deeds.

The historical song about the battle at Göllheim by
the herald Hirzelin (see pp. 59-62) could possibly be a
fragment of a larger description of the battle, two independent heraldic poems as parts of a lost cycle. This would
represent an intermediary stage between the individual *Ehrenrede*
and Gelre's series of blazons from the battle of Staveren.
The first part of Hirzelin's poem would include the description
of the battle, the heroic deed of Duke Henry of Carinthia,
concluding with his arms and his name; the second poem would
similarly include the battle description, the heroic deed
of Ulrich II von Walsee, also concluding with his arms and
his name. Both parts fit Rosenfeld's definition of a heraldic
poem even though the introductory laudatory song in both cases
is more like a historical song.

The same battle of Göllheim is portrayed from the
Nassau side in a historical song by Meister Zilies von Seine
(see pp. 62-63). Rosenfeld maintains that, from the fragments
extant, Meister Zilies also divided the battle into heraldic
poems about individual knights. Thus in the fragment pertaining to the heroic deed of Gerlach of Kleen Rosenfeld finds the
typical herald's formula:

Meister Zilies   Hedde ich sinne vn̄ kůnst
                 Vnde sůysser minnen dene gůnst,
                 So wolde ich in vyseyern.   (1,198)

Suchenwirt   Wer ich der chünsten nu berait,
             Daz ich visiert die wapen sein!   (VIII,236)

However, in Meister Zilies' poem the actual blazon is
missing.

In Meister Zilies' song about the battle at Dürnkrut
("Die Böhmenschlacht," see pp. 63-64) the battle of kings
symbolized by a battle of their armorial animals suggests to
Rosenfeld that the author had literary ambitions. This

symbolic representation is typical of a herald, according to
Rosenfeld, but emanates from the sphere of masterful *Spruchdichtung* as Konrad von Würzburg demonstrates in his song "Dem
adelarn von Rôme" (32,316). The rest of the poem, however,
reflects the typical sphere of heraldic poetry, especially the
conclusion: after Rudolf's victorious return the poem ends
abruptly with a technically proficient heraldic-poetic formula
which includes the arms and name of the hero:

Meister Zilies Vp golt van zabel eyn adelar
      Was geslayn vn̄ gelait.
      Van me riche hi dese waypē drait.
      Van arde hi^e andeir waypen hait;
      Eyn lewe in hoher werde stait,
      Van roider keyle up golt geslain,
      Dey hi^e vil dicke hait gedain
      Herzenschrickes lere.
      Hye ist eyn rich burgere,
      Koninc Rodulf, dey d^g kronē ple^{y}git.
      Wisset, dat hi^e hait gesiegit
      Eyn lewe, eyn ritter vnde eyn ar. (2,173)

   Hirzelin justifies the inclusion of heraldic description
through women who ask about the arms of various knights; he
thus turns a battle into a tournament-like event with an
audience of women. Meister Zilies used the same justification
for the description of the arms of Adolf von Windhövel on the
occasion of a real tournament (see p. 72). Here the poet
meets three women (possibly the allegorical figures of *Frau
Ehre, Frau Minne,* and *Frau Tugent*) who lament the virtuous knight
and describe his arms in order that the poet (herald?) might
identify him, or they ask him for the coat of arms and name
of a hero who is beyond reproach. The same technique is
employed also in the laments for Count Werner of Honberg,
Count William of Holland, in Suchenwirt's lament for Ulrich
von Pfannberg, and Gelre's lament for Adam van Mabbertingen.
Gelre employs this form in his *Ehrenreden* honoring living
heroes, as does Hans Rosenplüt in his poem about Louis of
Bavaria (1460). Similarly, Gelre's rhymes on the battle of
Staveren and the "tournament and siege poems" have their
antecedents in the tournament poem of the herald Johann
Holandt who describes a tournament at Schaffhausen held in
1392.

The variety of situations found in heraldic poetry
suggests that it is much older than the fragments available
today. The polemic against heraldic poetry written by
Seifried Helbling (1282-1299)[166] points to its popularity
since an isolated phenomenon would not have produced such a
forceful reaction. Seifried Helbling appears to know what
form a heraldic poem should take, and he continually alludes
to the coats of arms of epic fictitious characters as well as
to contemporary figures. However, it is not the professional
heralds but rather the epic poets of the time who first reveal
glimpses of the genre. The prime example is the *Turnier von
Nantes* by Konrad von Würzburg. According to Rosenfeld, this is
not a unified poem, but a combination and hyperbole of various
sub-genres of heraldic poetry. The beginning and ending
emphasize the generosity of King Richard to wandering minstrels--
a topos typically found in poetry written by such *spilliute*.
The second part of the *Turnier von Nantes* portrays first
individual combats and then the mass tournament. The direction
of the poem is away from the battle and towards the deeds of
the hero; the parts are independent of each other, formulated
like the historical songs of Hirzelin and Meister Zilies about
the battles at Göllheim and Dürnkrut. Konrad attempts to
interweave into his work as many coats of arms as possible
regardless of whether the knights are mentioned again or
whether they distinguish themselves. The descriptions of the
knights' arms are reminiscent of a parade passing by, similar
to Gelre's heraldic rhymes about the Staveren battle, to the
siege of Caerlaverock Castle, and to the tournament at
Chauvency. According to Rosenfeld Konrad has simply taken
heterogeneous parts and put them together into a "half epic"
work; thus it is natural that the epic style would influence
the description of coats of arms, making the *Turnier von Nantes*
not the paradigm of heraldic poetry but rather its reflection
in the language of the epic poet.

If Edward Schröder's thesis is correct, namely that
Konrad wanted to honor the generosity of King Rudolf of
Habsburg,[167] then this work glorifies the same man as

Meister Zilies' "Böhmenschlacht:" a comparison of both poems
demonstrates the difference between *Buchgedicht* and *Wappendichtung*, and it also shows that both go back to a rich pre-
literary or non-literary tradition of heraldic poetry in the
sphere of the *spilliute* and *farende liute*.

Knowledge of the individual hero and of his coat of arms
was a prerequisite for the herald whose duties also included
carrying messages, delivering invitations to battles and
tournaments, the *Helmschau*, organizing tournaments, etc. The
blazons in the *Clipearium Theutonicorum* compiled by Conrad von
Mure, despite the fact that he wrote in Latin verse and was
not a professional herald, are generally of professional
quality. Conrad does, however, occasionally blazon incorrectly,
as in the case of the arms of the Duke of Brabant (sable,
a lion or) which appear as the arms of the dukes of Limburg
(gules, a lion argent crowned or):

> Dux Brabante, tuus clipeua rubet, hunc ita pingam   16
> Albam, quod caput hic auri diademante cingam.

The Brabant arms are blazoned correctly and no less profes-.
sionally by Konrad von Würzburg in his *Turnier von Nantes:*

> Der fürste wert von Brâbant   504
> quam dar als im gezæme was.
> man sach in kêren ûf daz gras
> mit eime tiuren schilte gar,
> der schein von zobel swarzgevar,
> und was nâch hôher werdekeit
> ein guldîn löuwe drûf geleit
> der gab ‹der› heide liehten schîn.

The difference in these blazons lies in the nature of the two
works--one is a heraldic book, the other a poem about a
tournament. Conrad von Mure strives for clarity and
conciseness; Konrad von Würzburg is concerned with the
picture he is painting of a tournament field filled with
colored shields. Konrad von Würzburg departs from the
earlier practice employed in his other works of depicting
symbolic arms for fictitious knights; here he blazons the
actual shields of true knights at an imaginary tournament.

The herald Gelre emblazons rather than blazons the
arms of the dukes of Brabant in his *Wapenboeck*. However, he
blazons a similar coat of arms, that of Reynout van

Valkenboirch (gules, a lion argent):

> Als stu diin kamer siist ontwinden,
> Dair zal tu eyn leeu in vinden,
> Geslitstair van kele scone,
> Die van hem zelven draecht eyn crone.
> Op zilver es die leeu gesat;
> Ich hoir voir wairheit spreken dat,
> Dat he den leeu heeft ghedraghen
> Diick dairt vrunt ind viant zaghen,
> Ind men siin manheit nie en sach slapen.   (p. 83)

Similarly at the siege of Caerlaverock Castle Henry, Earl of
Lincoln leads the vanguard bearing a purple lion on a
saffron banner (or, a lion gules):

> Henris li bons quens de Nicole,   37
> Ki prouesce enbrasce e acole
> E en son cuer le a soveraine
> Menans le eschele premeraine,
> Baner out de un cendal safrin
> O un li'oun rampant purprin.

Suchenwirt, too, appears concerned with the visual image
when he describes the arms of Leutold von Stadeck--on a red
field, a pearl (silver) lion with a gold tongue, teeth, and
claws grasping menacingly at the enemy:

> Der schilt den veinden was bechant   XV,196
> In strum und auch in streites not:
> Der was von edlen rubein rot,
> Dar inn ein lew von perlein reich
> In planch weis, den man vraidichleich
> Sach inn dem schilde chlimmen
> Und gen den veinden limmen,
> Recht als er lebt in tzornes pein;
> Den sach man vor der pruste sein
> Den veinden streben dikch zu var:
> Tzung, tzend, und chlaw von golde chlar.
> Des lewen chraft ist nu gelegen!

These same Stadeck family arms are emblazoned by Gelre
who also emblazons the arms of Austria, Styria, Carinthia,
Bohemia, Cilli, Chappel, Walsee, Ellerbach, and Hohenzollern.
The overlap of subject material employed by the heralds and
poets of the time is truly remarkable.

It is possible that heralds had mnemonic devices which
supported their knowledge of arms. But it is not very
probable that such mnemonic devices would be included in
death laments and in *Ehrenreden*. Rosenfeld claims that the
professional factual description of arms did not bring any

special honor to the individual since arms were inherited
(for example, Hirzelin's description of the arms of Ulrich II
of Walsee agrees essentially with Suchenwirt's of those of
Ulrich III). I believe, on the other hand, that whereas the
blazon of a coat of arms may not personally describe the
individual, it does honor him by symbolically giving him
status, continuity, his own "place under the sun." Rosenfeld
makes a distinction between the professional heralds, whom
he places in the same category as *spilliute*, and the epic poets
such as Konrad von Würzburg. He refrains, however, from
classifying Gelre and Suchenwirt who were both poets and
heralds *(spilliute ?)* and whom he highly praises.

It appears that Rosenfeld, from investigating the works
of Gelre and Suchenwirt, reasons that there must have been
earlier models containing elements common to their work which
influenced them. I agree that Gelre and Suchenwirt appro-
priated the various parts of earlier poems--death lament (with
its lament, praise, and intercession), historical songs of
battles, heroic deeds, etc., descriptions of tournaments and
sieges replete with heraldic material--and thus originated the
heraldic poem of the fourteenth century. They did not, however,
follow a well established practice, although there may have
been pre-literary or non-literary heraldic material available.
The specific format of presentation of this material seems to
originate here.

PART TWO: PETER SUCHENWIRT

SUCHENWIRT'S LIFE

The documentation pertaining to Peter Suchenwirt, the
best known German herald of the fourteenth century, is very
meager. Neither his birth date nor his death date are known.
All official evidence relating to Suchenwirt's life is
connected with his house in Vienna on the *Chürbaumerstrazz* (now
the Seitzergasse) near the old Babenberg ducal court.[168]
Suchenwirt's name appears in twelve documents from June 16,
1377 to December 16, 1407 (the last pertaining to his widow)
found in the Vienna archives.[169] On December 24, 1382 Peter
Suchenwirt and his wife Ursula sold one of their houses in the
Chürbaumerstrazz to the painter Leinhart and his wife Margarete.
Subsequently on March 28, 1383 Suchenwirt rented from the
painter Leinhart the courtyard between their two houses as
well as the rooms overlooking the courtyard. The street
received its name from the Spanish goat (or cordovan) leather
which was worked by the many cobblers who lived there. Here
also, on this street not far from the court, lived painters,
and parchment makers, as well as the herald and heraldic poet
Peter Suchenwirt. On February 4, 1386 however, Duke Albert
III gave by proclamation many of the houses on the street to
the Carmelite monastery: "...die cappellen und daz gesêzze
in dem Münczhof und den Münczhof darzu gelegen unser
vorvardern gesezzen und wonhaft gewesen sind." Besides the
house of "Muschals suns des juden," which Duke Rudolf IV had
already given the Carmelites, Albert bestowed upon the
Carmelites the following houses: "Hainrich dez Pairleins haus,
Peters des Suchenwirtes haus, Leinharcz maler haus, Ulrich des
schuster von Schêrding haus, Dietrichs des schuster haus,
maister Dyetreichs des pognêr haus, der Helblerin auf dem Hof
haus und Jäckleins von Amsteten haus, die all umb daz kloster
gelegen sind und ettleich auf den Hof stössent."[170] The fact
that the monastery and the churchyard are mentioned indicates
that the complex was already under construction. There is

no mention in the documents indicating that Albert gave
Suchenwirt the house in 1377 as some speculate,[171] nor
whether he compensated him for the loss of the house in 1386.

Suchenwirt's language, perspective, and sympathies
suggest that he was an Austrian. It is possible that he was
in the service of King Louis of Hungary and Burgrave Albert of
Nuremberg before settling at the Habsburg court in Vienna.
Based on a document from Munich, May 31, 1354, Ludwig Schönach
speculates that Suchenwirt may have visited Bavaria on his
wanderings:

> Markgraf Ludwig von Brandenberg verpfändet dem Runttinger
> für schuldige 244 Regensburger pfennige das gericht in der
> Neustadt samt allem zubehör. beim dritten der aufgeführten
> acht schuldposten heisst es: acht pfunt umb zwen hengst, der
> ainer worden ist Friderich unserm pfeiffer, und der ander
> dem Suchenwirt.[172]

The best source of information about Suchenwirt's life is
found in his poetry. Unfortunately, however, he does not tell
about himself in an organized chronological fashion. It has
been suggested that each of his *Ehrenreden* was dedicated to a
different master under whom he had served; this would have
been impossible since, Henry of Carinthia, for example, died
in 1355 when Suchenwirt must have been very young. Other
Ehrenreden appear to have been written in close succession--
too close for Suchenwirt to have changed masters each time.
However, there is considerable evidence that the heroes of the
Ehrenreden were associated with each other, that most of them
were members of a grail society in Vienna known as the *Societas
Templois* (see pp. 187-190).

Finally, the name Suchenwirt appears in eulogy form in
a poem by Hugo von Montfort (1357-1423), a younger contemporary
who was with Suchenwirt on the famous Prussian crusade in
1377. Hugo's poem indicates that Suchenwirt was well known and
admired during his lifetime:

> Solt ichs als blasinieren,   V,129
> Die wappen also zieren,
> Des wer mir ze vil.
> Der silmen zal, der stunden zil
> Der mag ich nit gewalten,
> In minem sinn behalten.

Darzuo gehört der Suochenwirt,
Der dik mit red als nahe schirt,
Man mocht es grifen mit der hant;
Er ist in mangem land erkand.[173]

All other information about Suchenwirt must be extracted
from his works. In his poems Suchenwirt refers to himself,
his masters, his contemporaries, to events, politics, social
and moral problems. His last poem was written before November
1395, i.e. after the death of Duke Albert III and before the
Austrian territories were divided among Albert's son and
nephews. His first poems were written in the 1340's and
1350's: for example, the poem dedicated to Duke Henry of
Carinthia was written sometime after 1347, the last event
mentioned in the poem, and the *Ehrenrede* dedicated to Herdegen
von Pettau was written after Herdegen's death in 1352. Thus
it is possible to establish the approximate years of Suchenwirt's life from 1320/30 to at least 1395.

Otfried Weber divided Suchenwirt's life into three
periods:[174] 1) the period of his activity as a blazoner of
arms and heraldic poet in Austria, then at the court of King
Louis of Hungary, and later in the service of the burgraves
of Nuremberg, ca. 1350-1361, when he wrote mainly *Ehrenreden;*
2) the period after the death of his lord, Albert of Nuremberg,
and the time of his wanderings through Germany, ca. 1361-1371/2,
when he wrote didactic and religious poems; 3) the period of
his poetic activity in Vienna and at the court of Albert of
Austria, ca. 1372-1395, when he wrote political occasional poems.

These divisions are based on a faulty chronology of the
poems and much imagination; Weber uses stylistic and linguistic
criteria to establish Suchenwirt's poetic development from his
earliest days to his more mature years. Then he uses this
evidence to corroborate the chronology of the poems and the
periods of Suchenwirt's life. Unfortunately there is no real
evidence that Suchenwirt served at the courts of Louis of
Hungary or Albert of Nuremberg. However, most the events
about which Suchenwirt writes did occur within his lifetime.
Although Suchenwirt uses the first person *ich* in almost all
his poems, he himself does not usually intrude into the poems.

His "I" is an impersonal one--often merely a matter of
convention. The poems contain tantalizing clues to dates and
events. The death dates, for example, of most of the heroes
of the *Ehrenreden* are known; but it is impossible in most
cases to determine when Suchenwirt actually wrote the poems
honoring them.

Suchenwirt was of bourgeois origin; he claims to be *ein
gernder man,* i.e. to belong to the class of *farende liute:*

> ...„Ich nym durich er güt   XXIX,22
> Und pin tze recht ein gernder man."

As such he was dependent upon the generosity of his various
patrons; he explains in the same poem:

> Durich notdurft meinez leibs nar   XXIX,3
> Nam ich der pideben herren war,
> Als gerndem orden wol antzimpt,
> Der güt durich got, durich ere nympt.

Occasionally he complains about the lot of a *gernder man:*

> Der fürsten gab chumt altzu sain,   VI,101
> Ir helf, ir trost ist in tzu chlain.
>
> Di Milt was e gewaltig   XXI,41
> Der fursten manigvaltig,
> Di ist an peiden arm lam.
> Des pin ich chargen herren gram,
> Di rechter milde sein gehaz.

He even jokes about his willingness to accept all invitations:

> „Ir vrawen, pit nicht vaste,   XXV,110
> Wann ich pin leicht ze laden."

The poem "Die red haizzt der new rat" begins with the following
words:

> Ich rait eins tags nach meiner nar,   XXII,1
> Als ich noch suech durch daz iar
> Di pidiben herren manigvalt.

However, in another poem he looks back upon his life with
gratitude for this same generosity which he had often
questioned:

> Waz ich ye von den milten nam   XLIV,94
> Und noch von in geholffen wirt,
> Dez chan ich Peter Suechenwirt.
> Laider nicht gedankchen
> Mit worten, mit gedankchen.

In "Von dem Phenning" he portrays himself as a sophisticated,
well traveled man, widely known among the nobility:

> Ich rait allain in fremdew lant,   XXIX,1
> Daz ich den edeln würd bechant.

Evidence for Suchenwirt's childhood, his schooling, and his training in the herald's art comes strictly from his poems. Unlike Wolfram von Eschenbach, Suchenwirt claims to be able to read and write:

> Di sprüch von der minne   XXV,61
> Aus maisterleichem sinne,
> Der ich ein tail zu deutsche laz.

Although there is no direct proof of his literacy, it appears logical that a herald, whose duty it was to compile heraldic books and rolls, would be able to read and write, especially a bourgeois herald in the fourteenth century. In the poem "Die red haist der brief" Suchenwirt describes a letter he would like to write:

> Chund ich in meinem hertzen tief   XXI, 1
> Schreiben ein gerechten prief,   2
> Daz die materig würd sigehaft   3
> Auz meiner chranchen sinne chraft,   4
> Der ich zu tichten hat gedacht,...   5
> Allrest so wirt mein prief geschribn.   24

Obviously the above is a poetic statement; he phrases his desire either in the subjunctive or passive as a matter of convention. It is possible, but not probable, that he employed a scribe to write for him. He also claims to know (perhaps to have read?) the old heroic stories about Parzival, Wigalois, and Lanzelot:

> Was man in alten püchen sait   X,74
> Von Parcival, von Gamuret,
> Von Wyguloys, von Lantzulet,
> Von manigen helden güte tat.

He was also familiar with the Helbling satires, the *Wachtelmare*, Freidank, Neidhart, Ulrich von Lichtenstein, Frauenlob, Hadamar von Laber, Heinrich von Mügeln, as well as the *Nibelungenlied* and other heroic epics. Above all Suchenwirt demonstrates love and admiration for Konrad von Würzburg. He attempts to emulate Konrad's *Goldene Schmiede* in his own poem praising the Virgin Mary entitled "Di siben frewd Marie:"

> Nu hat mein sin nicht chreffte,   XLI,7
> Als vor mit maisterscheffte
> Von Wirtzpürch maister Chünrat

> Dich wirdikleich gepreiset hat,
> Maria müter unde mait.

On the other hand, he did not have a scholarly education; his French was not very good and he did not know Latin:

> Auch maniger mir unchundig waz   XXV,64
> Von vrantzois, von lateine.

> Ich chan laider nicht latein...   XLI,1523
> Daz klag ich Peter Süchenwirt.

In the poem "Die red haizzt der froind sin" he writes:

> In Daniel ich daz las.   XLIII,42

It is impossible to determine whether in his later years he had taught himself Latin, whether he had read a Middle High German translation, or whether he was writing figuratively. Nevertheless the usual religious ingredients are not lacking in Suchenwirt's works. He appears familiar with the Bible as well as with the Church fathers: St. Mark, St. Luke, St. Augustine, St. Jerome, Dionysius, Isidor, Philo Judaeus, the *Historia Ecclesiastica*, to name a few, are quoted especially in such ostentatious pieces as "Di siben frewd Marie."

Suchenwirt provides very few really definitive clues about himself or about his opinion of his own role in life. This is not unusual in the Middle Ages when roles were well established, widely recognized, and taken for granted by all (Suchenwirt writes of *gerndem orden, ritters orden, früchtikleichem orden, pæbstleichen orden,* etc.). He claims to be a herald, even a good one. However, he also engaged in the activities of historian and political commentator. An analysis of these roles should lead to a better understanding of Peter Suchenwirt, the finest example of a heraldic poet.

MANUSCRIPTS AND RESEARCH

There are fifty-two poems by Peter Suchenwirt extant in at least thirty-three different manuscripts.[175] The table, APPENDIX I, shows which poems appear in which manuscripts.

The main manuscript A, Vienna, Nationalbibliothek MS 13045, 503 pages, 13.5 X 19, paper, dates from the beginning of the fifteenth century. The first 483 pages contain poems by Suchenwirt, then follow fifteen blank pages, and the manucript concludes with a Tobias prayer. Each of the forty-six Suchenwirt poems begins with a large red initial; the poems are written on both recto and verso in one column of fifteen to thirty lines copied by a number of different scribes.[176] The existence of MS A was first made known to Alois Primisser by Hofrat von Hammer in 1820. It had been found among the books of the late Prince Prosper von Sinzendorf; the owner was then Count Georg von Thurn who placed it in the care of Primisser. The manuscript is frequently referred to as the Sinzendorf-Thurn manuscript. The poems were not entered into the manuscript according to subject matter, a defect which Primisser remedies in his edition by first placing the *Ehrenreden*, then the historical and political occasional poems, moral allegories and spiritual didactic poems, and comic poems. MS A is considered most important because it contains the largest number of poems.

The second most important manuscript, B, Schlierbach, Cistercienserabtei I, 27, 804 pages, 20 X 28.5, paper, once belonged to Job Hartmann Enenkel von Albrechtsberg who died in 1627 in Vienna. It probably originates from the beginning of the seventeenth century: "Ex illo antiquo curabat describi an 1625 Jobus Hartmannus Liber Baro Enenkelius" (p. 4). Furthermore, the scribe claims: "Dises Heldenbuech...Ist abgenommen vnd geschriben mit meins vnderschribnes handen, aus dem alt vor 200. Jahren geschribnen buech...vnd miers mitgetheilt Im 1625. Jar" (p. 434). Twenty-one Suchenwirt poems are copied in double columns. Unfortunately Primisser did not know about the existence of this manuscript when he

compiled his edition. In 1878 Godfried Edmund Friess edited
the five poems (1-5) from MS B which do not appear in MS A
(except for the first seven lines of 5 at the beginning of MS A).
Despite the fact that MS B was copied from a now lost model
some 250 years after the composition of the poems, the
manuscript is very important for Suchenwirt text criticism
since it not only adds to the total corpus but also eliminates
gaps contained in MS A: III, VII, X, XVII, and 5 appear in
complete form in MS B while they contain lacunae in MS A.

Manuscript C, Vienna, Nationalbibliothek MS 10100a,
242 folios, 20.5 X 32.5, paper which also originates from
the seventeenth century (ca. 1645), is an anthology containing
the works of several poets including Konrad von Würzburg,
Heinrich Teichner, Jacob Peterswald, Heinrich von Freiberg,
as well as verse and prose texts from the sixteenth and
seventeenth centuries. Ten of Suchenwirt's poems are included
in this manuscript which belonged to Christoph Adam von
Fernberg who lived in the first half of the seventeenth century.

The other manuscripts contain only a few poems each. Of
these Franz Kratochwil described twenty-one in 1889.[177] Otfried
Weber lists thirty-three manuscripts and describes their
relationships among each other.[178] These minor manuscripts
are described below in alphabetical order:

a   A sheet of paper with between 46 and 50 lines of verse.
In 1878 this sheet was cut up and pasted into the empty pages
of MS A; it was probably originally copied from MS A.

b^1 Berlin, Staatsbibliothek Preußischer Kulturbesitz
MS Germ. 361, 164 folios in quarto, 14.5 X 21.5, paper
second half of the fifteenth century.

b^2 Berlin, Staatsbibliothek Preußischer Kulturbesitz
MS Germ. 488, 395 folios, 20.5 X 30.5, paper, copied by a
single scribe, "mertin ebenreuter" (f. 257^r), in 1530 (f.
313^r), dedicated to "dem hochwirden fürsten vnd hern herren
Melchor zobel bischoff zu wirzbur" (f. 260^r).

d^1 Dresden, Landesbibliothek MS M 203 (105), 83 folios
in quarto, paper, fifteenth century.

d^2 London, British Museum MS Add. 24946, 293 folios,
17 X 30, paper, fifteenth century. The manuscript belonged

to the Weigel family in Leipzig.

f   Freiburg, University Library MS 362, 93 folios, 21.5 X 29, 1445.

g^1 Gotha, Landesbibliothek Ch. B. 271, 201 folios, 14.5 X19.5, paper. The manuscript originated in 1443 (f. 190^r), belonged to Augustin von Hammerstetten, and was dedicated to the Elector of Saxony in 1497 (ff. 1-8).

g^2 Gotha, Landesbibliothek Ch. A. 985, 9 folios, 19.5 X 28.5, paper, copied before 1439 (f. 9vb).

h^1 Heidelberg, University Library MS Cpg. 355, 166 folios, 14.5 X 20, paper, second half of fifteenth century (the date 1458 appears on the front cover).

h^2 Heidelberg, University Library MS Cpg. 393, 97 folios, 15.5 X 21.5, paper, second half of fifteenth century.

h^3 Heidelberg, University Library MS Cpg. 4, 236 folios, 21.5 X 31, paper (with three parchment folios at the beginning), copied after 1479 (ff. 210^v and 230^v) by Conrad Schreyber of Ötingen (f. 197^v).

k   Kremsmünster, Monastery Library MS 69, 173 folios .in quarto, paper, from the first half of the fifteenth century (before 1440).

l   Donaueschingen, Fürstenberg Library MS 104, known as the "Liedersaal Codex," 269 folios, from the end of the four-teenth century. This manuscript was edited by Joseph von Laßberg between 1821 and 1825.[179]

m^1 Munich, Staatsbibliothek MS Cgm. 393, 319 folios, 15.5 X 21.5, paper, completed after 1470 (f. 282^v).

m^2 Munich, Staatsbibliothek MS Cgm. 1113, 160 folios, 21 X 29, paper, the second half of the fifteenth century.

m^3 Munich, Staatsbibliothek MS Cgm. 4871, 146 pages, 20.5 X 26.5, paper, copied by two scribes at the beginning of the sixteenth century.

m^4 Munich, Staatsbibliothek MS Cgm. 270, 388 folios, 21 X 29.5, paper, copied by two scribes in 1464 (f. 388^v).

m^5 Munich, Staatsbibliothek MS Cgm. 379, 255 folios, 15 X 21, paper. The date 1454 appears on f. 166^r and the date 1474 on f. 225^v.

m^6 Munich, Staatsbibliothek MS Cgm. 690, 309 folios, 15.5 X 21.5, paper, completed in 1496 (f. 307^V).

m^7 Munich, Staatsbibliothek MS Cgn. 5919, 433 folios, 21.5 X 31.5, paper. The manuscript was copied about 1510 (ff. 320^r, 410^4, 412^r, 414^r) by Ulrich Mostnach (f. 69^r) in Bavaria.

m^8 Munich, Staatsbibliothek MS Cgm. 444, 221 folios, 14 X 19.5, paper, from Wessobrunn, compiled after 1422 (f. 7^r) by eleven scribes including Johannes de Eyra (f. 66^r) and Jacobus de nouo foro (f. 208^V).

n Weimar, Landesbibliothek MS Q 566, 166 folios, 15.5 X 21, paper, copied in 1479/80 (f. 57^r). The codex originated in Nuremberg where it was in the possession of the poet Hans Folz.

p Prague, National Museum MS X A 12, 368 folios, paper. The manuscript belonged to Jörg Roggenburg from Augsburg (f. 353) and was copied by the scribe Clara Hätzlerin who completed the task in 1471: "anno domini Augspurg 1471 Clara Hätzlerin" (f. 353). The manuscript was edited by Carl Haltaus in 1840.[180]

r A songbook from the second half of the fifteenth century bought by Ludwig Bechstein in 1835, now lost.

s Seitenstetten, Benedictine Monastery MS 286, unnumbered folios in quarto, paper, from the beginning of the fifteenth century.

st Stuttgart, Landesbibliothek Cod. poet. et philol. Q 69, 298 folios, 15 X 21.5, paper, from the middle of the fifteenth century.

t Prague, National Library and University Library RVI Fc 26, 261 folios, 20.5 X 29, paper, from the fifteenth century, copied by a scribe known as Leonardus after 1467 (ff. 200^V, 237^r, 260^V).

w^1 Vienna, Nationalbibliothek MS 2848, 300 folios, 21.5 X 29.5, paper, copied after 1469 (f. 1^r).

w^2 Vienna, Nationalbibliothek MS 2969, 308 folios, 14 X 20.5, paper, fifteenth century.

W Wolfenbüttel, Herzog-August-Bibliothek Cod. Guelf. 51.2 Aug., in quarto.

w[o] Wolfenbüttel, Herzog-August-Bibliothek Cod. Aug 81. 16 (No. 2806), 71 folios, 21 X 29, paper, beginning of the fifteenth century, shortly after 1412 (f. 67rb).

The first text edition of Suchenwirt's poems was published by Alois Primisser in 1827[181] and was based primarily on MS A. Besides manuscripts A and C, Primisser was also familiar with h[1], h[2], h[3], and s. The poem "Vom Würfelspiel," not contained in any of these manuscripts, was published in the *Liederbuch der Clara Hätzlerin* in 1840.[182] Thus the forty-six poems from MS A, the five additional poems from MS B published by Friess,[183] plus the poem "Vom Würfelspiel" complete the total of fifty-two published poems.

A brief survey of the meager research to date on Peter Suchenwirt will indicate the type of material on which this investigation is based and will suggest the possibilities for future directions of inquiry.

Suchenwirt's name first appears in scholarly literature at the end of the eighteenth century in a literary history by Erduin Julius Koch[184] and in a list of poems from Heidelberg manuscripts in the Vatican Library compiled by Friedrich Adelung.[185] In 1809 Bernhard Joseph Docen included a few lines about Suchenwirt in the *Museum für Altdeutsche Literatur und Kunst*.[186] A year later he discovered Suchenwirt's poem lamenting the death of his friend Heinrich Teichner (XIX).[187] In 1812 Friedrich Heinrich von der Hagen published information about the manuscript tradition of poems XX, XLII, and XLVI.[188] In the same year Docen reported a new Suchenwirt manuscript and published parts of poems XX and XLI.[189] Julius Max Schottky edited the Teichner poem in 1818 in the *Jahrbücher der Literatur*.[190] In 1821 Alois Primisser described the newly discovered major Suchenwirt manuscript (MS A) and published excerpts from some of the poems.[191] He then began an edition of all the known Suchenwirt poems. In 1822 Schottky discussed the importance of the poem "Von hertzog Albrechts ritterschaft" (IV) as a source of information about crusades to Prussia.[192] In the

same year Joseph von Laßberg printed the "Widertail" (XXVIII)
with no author given in the third volume of his *Lieder-Saal*.[193]
Primisser's complete edition finally appeared in 1827. His
notes and glossary added considerably to the knowledge of
fourteenth century courtly life, treating such concepts as
knighthood, tournaments, hunting, court festivals, the art of
warfare, armor, and weapons. The early date of this edition
is responsible for the many examples of Suchenwirt's
vocabulary and syntax which appear in the *Mittelhochdeutsche
Wörterbuch* by Benecke, Müller, and Zarncke and other Middle
High German handbooks. Primisser documents in detail the
historical activities of Suchenwirt's heroes. Because he did
not supply an adequate bibliography, it is extremely difficult
today to trace his sources. Primisser's text is basically a
diplomatic edition. However, he does make some modifications
to facilitate its use: he standardizes the punctuation and
capitalizes the beginning of each line as well as proper names
and places; he resolves all abbreviations; the "tz" and "cz"
of the manuscript are rendered as "tz," while "z" replaces
"ß;" he distinguishes between "ů" representing the umlauted
"ü" and "ủ" representing the diphthongs "ue" and "uo," all
of which were variously rendered by the different scribes;
where an "e" appears above "a," "o," or "y" in the manuscript,
which he attributes to scribal carelessness, Primisser omits
it in the text. Generally Primisser maintains that incon-
sistencies add flavor to the text and illustrate the typical
practices of the fourteenth century and later centuries in
which the manuscripts were copied. The 1827 edition was
reprinted unchanged in 1961,[194] and there has been no new
edition.

Also in 1827 Eberhard Gottlieb Graff noted another
manuscript with the poem "Widertail."[195] However, this
manuscript was forgotten until one hundred years later when
Heinrich Niewöhner rediscovered it.[196]

The Primisser edition aroused interest in the language
and person of Suchenwirt. August Koberstein published a
detailed analysis of Suchenwirt's language in four school

programs between 1828 and 1852.[197] While his work may have
been of interest at the time of its publication, it is now of
limited value because the methodology is outdated. The only
attempt at an historical analysis of Suchenwirt's poems was
made by Karl Heinrich von Busse in 1843.[198] Von Busse was
concerned with crusades into Livonia which were not verified
in other historical sources. He also traced the geography
described in the poem about Duke Albert's Prussian campaign.
From this time on Suchenwirt's name appears in publications
of historical source material--but with no added information.[199]

After Koberstein the first Germanist to show an interest
in Suchenwirt was Franz Kratochwil. Beginning with a superficial biographical study in 1871,[200] he wrote a very complete
and detailed essay on the state of the Suchenwirt manuscript
tradition eighteen years later;[201] the difficulties posed by
this essay for the modern reader are the result of the
linguistic techniques used by Kratochwil, which were in
keeping with the state of the art at that time, but are now
superseded. Kratochwil described twenty-one manuscripts and
attempted to establish relationships among them. The history
of MS A was elaborated upon by Julius Pölzl[202] who traced its
location after it was stolen from the library of Count Georg
von Thurn shortly after 1827. The thief offered the manuscript to the Vienna Hofbibliothek in 1846 for one hundred
ducats. Despite the complaints of Count Georg von Thurn, the
library maintained possession of the manuscript although it
was considered lost by the academic world until Professor
Friess rediscovered it in 1877.

Suchenwirt's language provided the material for a
dissertation on temporal conjunctions in the works of Suchenwirt and Hugo von Montfort by Ewald Frey in 1893.[203] Wilhelm
Uhl provided the *Allgemeine Deutsche Biographie* with an article
and bibliography on Suchenwirt.[204] In 1897 Joseph Seemüller
published one of the best articles to date entitled "Chronologie der Gedichte Suchenwirts" giving not only a chronology
but also a close analysis of their content.[205] A definitive
chronology, however, has yet to be formulated. Seemüller also

published the first article discussing Suchenwirt as a
literary figure in Vienna in the fourteenth century.[206]   In
1910 Albert Morey Sturtevant[207] compared two versions of the
poem "Der Widertail" (XXVIII) from MS A edited by Primisser
and MS 1 published in Laßberg's *Lieder-Saal*.   He examined
the vowels, consonants, and the pronoun *daz* and the conjunction
das to illustrate the difference between the Bavarian (MS A)
and Alemannic (MS 1) copies of the original poem. One of
Seemüller's students, Felizitas Freiberger, wrote a dissertation on Suchenwirt's use of *geblümte Rede* in 1913.[208] She
concluded that Suchenwirt used *geblümte Rede* as a stylistic
tool consistently throughout his work and that this device
says nothing about him as a poet or about the development of
his poetry.

In 1912 Ludwig Schönach added to Suchenwirt's biography
with the publication of a document from 1354 mentioning
Suchenwirt's name in Bavaria (see p. 96).[209]   Albert Leitzmann
made a number of corrections to Primisser's edition in an
article in 1919.[210] In 1931 Niewöhner made known eight new
manuscripts in which Suchenwirt poems appear.[211] In his
Geschichte der deutschen Literatur bis zum Ausgang des Mittelalters
Gustav Ehrismann[212] updated the biography and bibliography compiled
by Uhl.

The last major study about the poet, planned as preliminary work for a new text edition, was the dissertation of
Otfried Weber published in 1937.[213] Weber discussed six major
themes (Suchenwirt's life and influence, the manuscript
tradition, the history of the origin of the poems, the style,
prototypes, and influence of Suchenwirt's works on later
generations). Unfortunately many of his theses are highly
speculative. For example, excluding an exact birth and death
date, Weber has formulated an almost complete biography of
Suchenwirt which includes an analysis of his linguistic,
stylistic, and poetic development in the manner of biographical nineteenth century literary scholarship.

Hellmut Rosenfeld considered the entire genre of
heraldic poetry, its Scandanavian antecedents and Suchenwirt's

predecessors, in an article in 1936.[214] The question of
Suchenwirt's possible relationship with Gelre and his knowledge of anonymous laudatory poems was raised by Karl Helm in
1938.[215] Hans Friedrich Rosenfeld contributed an article to
the *Verfasserlexikon* in 1953 based primarily on Weber's study
and including his errors.[216]

At a conference, the "Kolloquium über Probleme der
altgermanistischen Edition" in 1966, Hans Blosen presented a
sample of the methodology he is applying to a new edition of
Suchenwirt's works, the publication date of which is as yet
uncertain, but surely lies several years ahead.[217] The poem
"Der Widertail" appears in the largest number of manuscripts
and is thus representative of the many problems involved.
Blosen maintains that Primisser's edition is generally quite
reliable. However, the many new manuscripts which have been
discovered since 1827, especially MS B which has never been
published in its entirety, make a new edition in the not too
distant future a necessity.

In his literary history published in 1970 Hans
Rupprich[218] again summarized the information about Suchenwirt
found in Uhl, Ehrismann, and Rosenfeld, but he also provided
a framework for Suchenwirt within the literary genre of
Herolds- und Wappendichtung in the fourteenth century. This well
written synopsis is the only readily accessible recent treatment of Suchenwirt. Like all summaries it provides minimal data.

Attempts have been made to analyze Suchenwirt's language,
to formulate his biography, and even to trace several
military-religious campaigns, but no one has examined Suchenwirt's individual poems for their insight into Suchenwirt's
Weltanschauung. From the above it is evident that a number of
major research projects should be undertaken to present a
comprehensive picture of Suchenwirt and his contribution to
German literature. This investigation primarily considers
the genres of *Ehrenreden* and political and historical
occasional poems which represent Suchenwirt's contribution
to the broad genre of heraldic poetry.

Various attempts have been made by scholars such as
Primisser, Seemüller, Weber, and Blosen to date Suchenwirt's
poems. Primisser assumes that the poems are in chronological
order in MS A. However, in his text edition he grouped them
according to the subject matter, the *Ehrenreden* also according
to the rank of the hero. Seemüller approached the poems
through internal evidence--events mentioned in the poems
themselves--and dates thirty-one of the fifty-two poems
approximately. The result of his calculations suggests that
most of the poems were indeed in chronological order in MS A.
The chart on page 111 represents Seemüller's results.[219] The
decisive element in ascertaining the chronology of the *Ehrenreden*
is the time between the death of the hero and the composition
or recitation of the poem; unfortunately this cannot be
determined since there is no documentary evidence pertaining
to their performance. A possible reason for the composition
of *Ehrenreden* will be discussed below.

In a further attempt at dating Blosen[220] has examined
the various ways in which Suchenwirt referred to himself: in
the earlier poems he called himself "Suchenwirt." In the
middle of his poetic activity (based on Seemüller's chronology)
he named himself "Der Suchenwirt," perhaps under the influence
of his friend Heinrich Teichner who called himself "Der
Teichner." In the later poems he used the full name "Peter
Suchenwirt." Once he writes modestly: "Ich Peter tummer
Suchenwirt" (XLI,24). These observations lead only to very
general conclusions or speculations that as a herald he used
the professional name "Suchenwirt" and later as a recognized
man of some position (house owner) he employed the more
established double name "Peter Suchenwirt."[221]

Suchenwirt's poems range in length from fifty-seven
lines to 1,540 lines. His works include a number of different
genres which could be identified as follows: four death
laments (II, III, V, XIX), eighteen *Ehrenreden* (I, VI, VII, VIII,

CHRONOLOGY OF POEMS

VI	"Von Kernden hertzog Hainreich" in or after[222] 1347
XII	"Von her Herdegen von Petaw" in or after 1352
1	"Uon Hawnfeld her Mariez" after 1353, perhaps before, in or after 1357 .
4	"Von hern Albrechten von Rawchenstein" in or after 1354
2	"Von hern Hansen uon Chappell" after 1354, before, in or after 1358
XI	"Von graff Ulreich von Phfanberg" in or after 1355
3	"Von herzog Albrechten uon Oesterreich" between May 1356 and July 20, 1358
II	"Von der Kayserin von Payrn" in or after June 1356
I	"Von Chünik Ludwig von Ungerlant" in or after July 1356
IX	"Von hern Puppli von Elrwach (dem jungen)" second half of 1357
X	"Von her Puppily von Elrwach (dem iungen)" after December 1357
III	"Von hertzog Albrecht von Östereich" after July 20, 1358
XIII	"Von hern Ulrich von Walse" in or after 1359
XIV	"Von hern Fridreichen dem Chreuzzpekch" in or after 1360
VII	"Von purgraf Albrechten von Nurnberch" in or after April 1361
XVII	"Von hern Fridreichen von Lochen" after the beginning of 1365
XXIX	"Von dem Phenning" between 1365 and 1373
XXVII	"Der rat von dem ungelt" between 1365 and 1379
XV	"Von Leutolten von Stadekk" in or after 1367
XVI	"Von graff Ulreichen von Tzili" after July 26, 1367
VIII	"Von her Pircharten Ellerbach dem alten" in or after 1369
XXII	"Die red haizzt der new rat" 1372/1373
XXXIV	"Von der fürsten tailung" between 1375 and 1379
IV	"Von hertzog Albrechts ritterschaft" in or soon after 1377
XVIII	"Von hern Hansen dem Trawner" after June 7, 1378
XXXV	"Von tzwain päbsten" end of 1378
XX	"Von fünf fürsten..." second half of 1386
XXXVII	"Von der fürsten chrieg und von des reiches steten" 1387/1388
XXXVI	"Die red haizzt der umbchert Wagen" end of 1388
XXXVIII	"Daz sind Aristotiles rêt 1394
V	"Von hertzog Albrecht säligen in Östereich" between August 29, 1395 and November 1395
XXXIII	"Daz ist der getrew rat" before November 1395, but after V

IX, X, XI, XII, XIII, XIV, XV, XVI, XVII, XVIII, 1, 2, 3, 4),
eleven historical and political occasional poems (IV, XX, XXI,
XXII, XXVII, XXIX, XXXIII, XXXIV, XXXV, XXXVI, XXXVII),
fifteen moral allegories and spiritual didactic poems (XXIII,
XXIV, XXV, XXVI, XXVIII, XXX, XXXI, XXXII, XXXVIII, XXXIX, XL,
XLI, XLII, XLVI, "Vom Würfelspiel"), and four comic poems
(XLIII, XLIV, XLV, 5). These labels are only very general, for
naturally there is considerable overlap of subject matter
within the individual poems. For example, the poem "Von
dem Phenning" (XXIX) contains elements characteristic of a
moral allegory and of historical and political poems. The
all-powerful persuasion of money is personified as an old
man whom the poet meets. Personification is a typical device
of the moral allegories where the virtues such as truth, shame,
generosity, love, constancy, and others appear as allegorical
ladies. Furthermore, in "Von dem Phenning," the old man
talks to the poet from the fount of his experience; he
discusses not only moral and didactic subjects, but more
centrally, the politics of the Empire. Throughout all of Germany and even farther the *Phenning* leads the poet and distinguishes
miserly princes from the generous ones. This poem could be
viewed as a type of travel directory for Suchenwirt's colleagues, his fellow wanderers who were always seeking generous
patrons.

The historical and political occasional poems are
generally based on a single historical event or political
issue--the split of the Church of 1378 (XXXV), the futility
of a tax on wine (XXVII), the defeat at Sempach (XX), the
battle between Padua and Milan (XXXVI), the Prussian crusade
of Duke Albert III (IV). The poem about Albert's Prussian
crusade is similar to one by Friedrich von Sunnenburg which
reports about the campaign of the King of Bohemia to Hungary;[223]
furthermore, its form is adapted from rhymed chronicles and
shorter historical poems concerning a single event, such as
the battle of Sempach and the battle of Göllheim (see pp. 56-
63). The symbols of the warring powers in "Di red haizzt der
umbchert Wagen" (XXXVI) are taken from their coats of arms

in keeping with existing customs as in "Die Böhmenschlacht" by Meister Zilies (see pp. 63-64). I disagree with Seemüller who maintains that Suchenwirt contemplates the events which he discusses from a greater distance than did the authors of historical songs.[224] On the contrary, Suchenwirt appears to be very concerned with the matters about which he writes-- even about events chronologically and geographically removed from him. Thus, he depicts the surrender of the "dog" of Verona, Antonio Cane della Scala, to the "cart" of Padua, Francesco Carrara, and the "serpent" of Milan, Galeazzo Visconti, from a knowledgeable partisan perspective. The historical songs about the battle of Sempach, on the other hand, though also entirely partisan, were composed many years after the fact with questionable historical accuracy. The composition of the poem "Von fünf fürsten" (XX) appears to be unique: quite diverse subject matter is unified from the entirely superficial perspective of contemporaneousness. In the introduction Suchenwirt implores kings, princes, and nobles to pay attention (a frequent motif in the historical· song) to the astounding happenings in the world; his reportorial style is truly a precursor of the modern newspaper.

Suchenwirt warns the sons of Albert II (or perhaps Albert III) against dividing up their land in the poem "Von der fürsten tailung" (XXXIV). Neither generation observed this good advice: the sons of Albert II, Albert III and Leopold II, divided their lands, as did their sons, Albert IV and his cousin William. Suchenwirt tells a parable about a piece of wood which can only be broken after it is once split. In a similar poem "Daz ist der getrew rat" (XXXIII) he again implores the young dukes not to divide their lands, emphasizing his advice with examples from the Bible, with a parable of the mutiny of the elements, and finally he describes the misfortune of the princes of Brunswick who maintained the imperial crown and sceptor for one hundred years until they lost them through war and disturbances caused by the division of land among the children.

In a poem entitled "Die red haist der brief" (XXI) the poet imparts to the young lords of the court advice about life

from a well-traveled, mature, worldly man. He even makes
diplomatic suggestions. However, he subtlely disguises this
in an allegorical setting. He would like to write a letter
but the personifications of *Ehre, Zucht, Scham, Wahrheit, Treue,
Stetigkeit, Gerechtigkeit,* and *Milde* have become sick and lame;
good knights stand outside the gates of the courtyard while
Lose and *Schmeichler* find entrance; friends desert friends; and
the knights practice simony and usury instead of protecting
widows and orphans. Here Suchenwirt combines political
commentary and diplomatic advice with allegory and didactic
lessons.

Suchenwirt never fails to criticize evil; even in the
historical and political poems he shares in the moralizing
tendencies of the bourgeois poets of the fourteenth century.
This tendency (disregarding the comic poems) is evident in all
his work, as different as the subject matter may be. But his
didacticism is regularly based either upon a contemporary
event or, if his poem is from its inception didactically
oriented, upon current conditions. The combination of both
directions, the didactic and the historical, permeates his
entire literary production.

Suchenwirt's moral allegories and spiritual didactic
poems follow the tradition of Frauenlob, Regenbogen, Heinrich
von Mügeln, Heinrich von Neustadt, Suchensinn, Meister Altswert,
and others. The distinction between moral and spiritual
didactic poems is not sharp. "Daz ist di verlegenhait" (XXXI)
is purely secular or worldly in its treatment of inherited
riches and marriage for money as the cause for uncourtly
lazy epicurean life. In "Was Vbels ainem yeglichem usz Spil
chom" Suchenwirt traces the detrimental results of playing
dice, through various classes in society. He departs from
the didactic message to sketch little genre pictures, which
not only portray everyday life in a convincing manner, but
also indicate his own contact with various classes of society.
The well-known allegorical ladies of the time appear frequently;
in the *Ehrenrede* dedicated to Ulrich von Pfannberg (XI) they
mourn at the hero's graveside. But all is not well with these

ladies: *Zucht* and *Scham* are sick, *Wahrheit* has a sore tongue, *Treue* has broken her foot, *Stetigkeit* has a heart ache, *Gerechtigkeit* fell down the stairs, and *Milde* is lame in both arms. *Frau Minne* wakes from a ten year sleep and finds that everything has changed. She pokes fun at the narrow, tight clothing of the modern knights. To recall and reintroduce the old courtly customs she decides to hold a tournament in the Freudenau; *Frau Ehre* recommends Suchenwirt as the herald. Here Suchenwirt combines allegory with the *Ehrenrede*.

In another poem *Frau Stetigkeit* and *Frau Minne* discuss the characteristics of two lords of the court, a good knight who demonstrates constancy and a bad knight who pays homage to the sins and evils of his time (XXVIII). *Frau Minne* wears a bright gown and *Frau Stetigkeit* is dressed in blue, one of the few references in Suchenwirt's work to popular color allegory.

The didactic poems deal also with the ten commandments, the seven deadly sins, the Last Judgement, and the seven joys of the Virgin Mary. "Di red von dem jungsten gericht" (XLII) portrays the apocalypse in typical medieval terms and pictures. The description of the transitory nature of everything earthly, the separation of families, and the appearance of the Lord Judge are especially poignant. "Di siben frewd Marie" (XLI) is a laudatory poem of 1,540 lines praising the mother of God based on *Die goldene Schmiede*, a work which Suchenwirt cannot praise enough. Concomitant with the flowery language and Konrad's mystical symbols is scholastic wisdom: the nine choirs of angels recite Dionysius and Isidor.

In the love allegory Suchenwirt was obviously following a wide-spread practice; he is original only in the reflections which form the core of a typical framework. Similarly the combative motif, color allegory, and the hunt motif were widely popular. The personification of the *Phenning* appears to be his own device even though it may not have been original in principle. The same theme contained in "Was Vbels ainem yeglichem usz Spil chom" is treated elsewhere as are the teachings of Aristotle to Alexander the Great.

Moral and religious subject matters such as the ten

commandments, the deadly sins, avarice, the Last Judgement are found in numerous works in the thirteenth and fourteenth century. Suchenwirt himself admits that his poem about the seven joys of Mary was inspired by Konrad von Würzburg; in a similar fashion Regenbogen discussed the seven sorrows of Mary.[225]

Another genre includes comic poems *(Scherzgedichte)*, lying tales *(Lügenmärchen)*, and other word games. In the poem "Die red haizzt der froind sin" (XLIII) Suchenwirt was more concerned with the rhymes than with the contents which do not make sense. The last word of the first line can be read backwards and then it corresponds to the last word of the third line; the second and fourth lines are similar:

> Ich suecht gedicht in sinnes chor   (roch)   XLIII,1
> Und sprach: got mir gelükch geb.   (beg)
> Mich daucht, ich trüg der frewden roch,
> Do ich chom auf der chunste beg.

Another poem, "Die red ist Equivocum" (LXIV), 118 lines long, does make sense despite its fifty-nine identical rhymes. Here in rapid succession is an appeal to the Holy Ghost, a confession of sins, an admonition of the folly of man, a request to God for mercy and to the Virgin Mary for intercession:

> Heyliger geist, sterkch mein gemüt,   XLIV,1
> Mich hat mein torhait vil gemüt,
> Dovon ich trag der sunden last,
> Ich pitt dich, daz du mich nicht last.
> Herr, du pist der ewig hort,
> Ich wort vil gern, daz mich hort.

Suchenwirt also engages in the old genre of *Lügendichtung* or *Lügenmärchen*. In the 114 lines of "Ein red von hübscher lug" (XLV) he brings together all kinds of unrelated and impossible things:

> Mir sagt ein offen wolgesmyrt,   XLV,108
> Ich hiez davon nicht Suchenwirt,
> Daz ich nindert vinden chan
> Ein henn, die maistert tzwelf han,
> Daz si ier legten ayer.
> Ein ströbeiner Peyer,
> Dem was die werlt so wol bechant,
> Des pin ich chünig in Schottenlant.

Finally Suchenwirt parodies his own *Ehrenreden*. The poet asks: "O where can I find the wisdom to comprehend the

weak reputation of the hero?" His heart searches for fame and
honor as a cat searches for a mouse; it determines how the
mouse lives, when it eats and drinks, and positions itself outside the mousehole. The hero's reputation dissolves among
nobility as salt dissolves in warm water. Whenever he tries to
serve ladies, he finds he is so full of milk and rolls that he
cannot move. His heart melts on the fire of love as a cold
stone melts on a block of ice. He oversleeps many tournaments,
jousts, and good deeds. His first campaign was to Acre where
he killed a year old calf. He was so distressed that he had
surpassed himself in the battle that the shock made him take
to bed for five and a half years. He undertook three more
campaigns, the fourth to Prussia. Arriving in time for Vespers,
he noticed that his back and limbs were stuck together; he gave
up adventures entirely when his coat was burnt in a fire. His
shield has a border of liverwurst with a nosebag of straw in
the middle. On his helmet sauerkraut in mustard sines in
the sun:

> die roten mündel muezzen   5,120
> mich pitten umb den namen sein
> und daz ich chünd der wappen schein:
> uon leberwursten ist der rant
> ein futtersakch in rant pant,
> in einem schilt ein habestro.
> ir zarten frawen nu seit fro,
> daz ich in hab czu uelde pracht.
> sein helm glast aus hoher acht,
> seint ich es müzz chunden doch.
> ein grozzer hafen sawrkoch
> glest auf dem helm wunichleich,
> daz er die cziehen sein bestreich
> da haymen an der sunnen.

The poem concludes with the name of the hero, Sumolff Lapp von
Ernwicht.

Suchenwirt displays a great deal of interest in the
abstraction of "art," especially in the introductions to the
Ehrenreden, but also in his other poems. Most frequently he
laments that he does not possess "art:"

> Nu pin ich der chunst ein gast,   VI,171
> Daz mich unchünsten uberlast
> Hat laider nu besezzen.

> Ich pin der chünste laider ploz   VII,44
> Und an getichtes maisterschaft.

Under the label "art" he includes wisdom, strength, ingenuity,
inventiveness in the method of presentation, decorative speech,
ability to rhyme, count and measure syllables:

```
Wo nu getichtes rechter hort,     III,1
Wo witz und wol gebegne wort,
Wo wol bedachte sinne
Mit weisheit auz und inne
Geplümt, der chunsten rant durchgraben,
Spech, fundik, maisterlich, erhaben?

Wo ist nu rechter chünste hort,     XVIII,15
Di spähen fünd, reim, unde wort
Mit silben tzal der lenge?
```

In its perfection he calls it "meisterliche Kunst" or "Meisterschaft." He is unremitting in the repetition and variation of
praise for "art," in the lament, even in self-recrimination,
that he is not master of "art." Often he attaches a plea to
the Holy Ghost for enlightenment and aid. He maintains that
the flowering *(blüemen,* also *florieren)* of speech belongs to true
art: he claims that the poem *(Rede)* "Di schön Abentewr" (XXV)
was composed for the sake of *geblümte Kunst*; "Daz sind Aristotiles
rêt" (XXXVIII), on the other hand, he did not decorate with
flowery words and thus he, Peter Suchenwirt, demonstrates his
inferior or limited art.

He considered it especially appropriate to "flower"
(blüemen) at the beginning and conclusions of the *Ehrenreden,* and
often he introduced the blazon with a few thoughts about art.

```
Pluemt ich nu end und anevank,     XIV,5
So würd di red ein tail tze lank.
```

This "blümen der Rede" refers both to grammatical as well as to
intellectual forms, but also, as in "Di schön Abentewr," to the
form of the whole.

Where he laments his own inability *(Unkunst)* he generally
overrefines the language to a pomposity which is unacceptable
to the modern reader; it is as though he were trying to prove
his ability to "flower" and were merely affecting modesty. In
a more sober mood, however, he explains his inability to
"flower" by his lack of knowledge of Latin which makes the
Holy Scripture unattainable:

```
Di heilig schrift ist mir unchunt,     XLI,1522
Ich chan laider nicht latein,
```

Davon ist meiner chünste schrein
Mit maisterscheffte nicht getzirt.
Daz klag ich Peter Süchenwirt.

Except for the beginnings and conclusions the narrative
style in the *Ehrenreden* is not particularly moving since Suchenwirt avoids "flowery" language and concentrates on a fairly dry
enumeration of facts. However, the 1377 Prussian campaign in
which he personally took part becomes vividly alive in his
description. Thus he seems to vacillate between a stylization
of epic material which requires courtly phraseology and a
personally colored presentation.

Suchenwirt's language is informal without being
monotonous. Popular epic influence is evident when he gives
his knights such epitaphs as: "der hoch genenndich," "der
muotes frech," "der wandels freie," "der eren fruot," "der
hôchgeteuert," "der stolze degen auserwelt," "der hôchgemjot,"
etc. His heroes pursue their goals "durch hôhen preis," durch
abenteure," "durch ritterschaft,"'durch preisbejag." This
points to courtly epics as do the technical expressions of *crey,*
tjost, schumpfeutere (one of his favorite words, implying a
glorious battle or encounter, which he even makes into a verb),
scharmützel, sturm, etc. Often he introduces the lyrical motif of
"red mouths," i.e. young ladies who are present to lament the
dead hero. His frequent bold images are remarkable; they go
back to the Old Testament or mystical symbolism. The bold
knight seeks out the holy ground like a well-trained blood
hound; the reputation of the bad knight, on the other hand,
dissolves like glue under a stream of water. This type of
language and these metaphors must have been very popular at
that time, for Suchenwirt appears to have achieved some fame
among his contemporaries according to Hugo von Montfort.[226]
Suchenwirt's poems written in honor of his employers,
Albert II and Albert III of Austria, are representative of
his work: two are death laments in the tradition discussed
above and one belongs to the genre of historical and political
poetry, i.e. a poem about one historical event. None of these
poems belongs to the genre of *Ehrenrede,* as strictly defined,
which will be discussed later. All of them contain heraldic

elements and are clearly descendants of the traditions discussed
above, namely death lament, historical and political songs, and
"tournament and siege poetry." A line by line examination of
these three poems will illustrate Suchenwirt's poetic style,
the type of subject matter which interested him, and his
manner of presentation.

The poem entitled "Von hertzog Albrecht von Östereich"
(III) dedicated to Albert II (1298-1358) is a death lament
including a description of the deceased's coats of arms but
with no specific mention of his deeds, very similar to the
lament honoring Count William of Holland (see pp. 42-43).
Albert was known as the "lame" and the "wise" and was referred
to by Suchenwirt as the elder *(der alte)* to distinguish him
from his son Albert III. Suchenwirt paints a lovely picture
of Albert's noble soul and only refers to his deeds in general
terms.

The poet asks: where is the treasure of poetic art, of
cleverness, words, meaningful wisdom, where is the exalted
shield of art? Yes, to be sure, I cannot tread the path of art
since wise masters have already cut down the forest of art.
Poor me, I must work like one who has lost his mind while clever
ideas are being cut up continuously. Oh, I would be happy with
only the smallest portion of this noble art! (III,1-60).

The poet laments the loss of the highest treasure of
loyalty, the noble prince, who never consciously did anger,
who aided widows and orphans in their need, was a mighty
shield of peace, an atoner and mediator for princes. Albert
lived in peace and unity among his many neighbors. He was
well-known for arbitrating neighborly disputes, such as between
the Walsee family and the Bohemian and Moravian leaders.
Thomas Ebendorfer von Haselbach characterizes:

> Sed et alias inter suos crebrius exuberantes spumas litium,
> et potentiae rigore, et patientiae persuasione aequo moderamine
> consopivit: quia omnes semitae ejus fuere pacificae.[227]

Similarly, he reconciled the citizens of Passau with their
bishop (this dispute is described in the poem dedicated to
Hans von Traun, XVIII,398-447). Albert acted as arbitrator
between King Louis of Bavaria and the Archbishop of Salzburg

and used all of his powers to bring together the Emperor with
the Pope and the Church. He strove with all his might, but he
did not succeed. Emperor Charles IV named Albert judge to
resolve the misunderstandings between him and the children of
the deceased emperor. Albert's obvious wisdom in such under-
takings and in this particular decision were praised by
contemporary writers other than Suchenwirt.

Suchenwirt writes: wisely and powerfully he ruled his
household treasury of justice; one never heard of perjurous
statements or letters by him since his heart was like his
mouth; he was so wise that he reigned true and did not condone
evil. For these reasons his praise and fame were never
refuted (III,61-83).

Other sources also confirm that kings and emperors
came to Albert for advice: Emperor Louis, Emperor Charles,
King John of Bohemia, and King Louis of Hungary among others.
There is an anecdote about the blind King John of Bohemia who
came to confer with Albert about action to be taken against
Louis of Brandenburg. After completing their secret talks,
the blind John could not find the door and the lame Albert
could not leave his chair to open the door.[228]

Again the poet implores: oh, if I could only paint
what greatness lay in this prince! His heart never mellowed,
because it was so manly, even when it delivered harm to him.
He even collected noble hearts around him while in foreign
lands. Where else was there so active and energetic a prince
with such a sick body? He did not avoid heat or cold, rain
or snow: he suffered all the elements for honor and fame.
With his sick body he traveled through woods, rocks, fields,
and marshes (III,84-97). Regarding his sickness and his
activities Thomas Ebendorfer writes:

> Albertus dux vero membrorum compagne contractus factus est,
> ad opera militaria exercenda propria in persona inhabilis...
> in sella gestatoria ubique in Dominiis suis circumfertur...[229]

Thomas Ebendorfer praises Albert's sagaciousness, his discrim-
inating use of his power as judge, and the fact that he held
open court of justice at least once a week.

Suchenwirt continues: although his body lies dead, his

praise lives on, as a keel does not sink but floats on the water.
Your blooming branch, oh justice, has unfortunately withered...
(III,98-114).

  The description of arms is unclear in the Primisser
text since about ninety lines are missing from MS A. However,
these lines do appear in the Schlierbach manuscript published
by Friess. They represent the beginning of the blazon of the
arms of Styria, Carinthia, and Austria. Suchenwirt portrays
the typical medieval funeral scene. Twelve knights on horseback
surround the tomb. The shields and banners and swords are
held upside down by three knights:

   ich sach uon ersten einen schilt 6,76
   nach der panir, der was uerczilt
   der spiczigen perg die ort ze tal.

For Styria a silver fire-spitting panther with gold claws on
a green field (vert, a panther argent, armed or, spitting
flames of gules):

   sein grüner glast was worden ual 6,79
   chain smaragd in den schildt was
   recht als der reif das grün gras
   mit seiner chelt gefelbet,
   also hat sich geselbet   .
   des schildes glast nach chlagunder gir,
   darin geperlt das panthir
   daz was ee chlymmende fraydig,
   daz was czu schauen laidig,
   der swanz war nach dem ruk gepogen
   der perlein glast was ser betrogen
   mit plaichen silber tünchelfar,
   ,der chlavn gold uerplichen gar'...
   Auz seinem munt des feures stam III,120
   Gab nicht mer rot, als im ee zam.

One knight was carrying the Austrian arms, a red shield with
a white fess (gules, a fess argent), and the helmet with a
peacock feather:

   Des rot unertik scheinet. III,138
   Di par, di ee geseinet
   Mit morgen-tau geperlt lak.

The helmet with its fancy decoration dangled forlornly from
the horse:

   Von phaben fedren einen quast III,151
   Der was zurütten und zerfürt,
   Des orses hüf der quast perürt;
   Der spiegel glitz was worden sal,

Chron unde quast hing hin ze tal,
Vorprochen und vercheret gar.

Finally Suchenwirt blazons the Carinthian arms: the shield is
divided in half horizontally, on one side a gold field with
three brown (black) lions (or, three lions passant sable); on
the other side a red field with a white fess (gules, a fess
argent):

> Von golt und von rubeinen,   III,163
> In plank weis gleich geteilet,
> Mit schanden ungemailet,
> Des goldes art gamillen var,
> Die hat der tod verderbet gar
> Mit seiner chelde pitter,
> Mit swindem ungewitter.
> In dem golt getzieret was
> Drey leben praün von ademas.
> In parre weis gelenket,
> Di het der tod verrenket,
> Rück par si lagen alle drey,
> Gelastes und gestaines frey;
> Der rubein rot vercheret gar,
> Dar in man sach geseinet chlar
> Ein par von edler plüte weiz
> Die het des pittern todes fleiz
> Vorderbet und verreret.

The above descriptions are liberally sprinkeled with Suchenwirt's
own words of lament. He personifies the shields which themselves
are sad and bitter at the death of Albert.

   The poem ends with a plea for intercession by the Virgin
Mary and for the mercy of God. Here also the subject of the
poem, the deceased Duke Albert, is named for the first time.
It was typical in a death lament as well as in an *Ehrenrede*
to mention the name of the honored one at the conclusion of
the poem. Suchenwirt's poems in MS A include the titles which
tell the reader the name of the subject. In any case, much like
American political convention nominations, there was no doubt
in the audience's mind regarding the identity of the person
being honored.

   Although Albert's specific deeds are not enumerated as in
the *Ehrenreden,* Albert II does figure in the accounts of other
heroes (XIII, XV, XVIII).

   Suchenwirt describes the campaign of Duke Albert III
to Prussia in 1377 in a poem entitled "Von hertzog Albrechts

ritterschaft" (IV). Suchenwirt accompanied Albert as official court poet and recorder and specifically names himself several times in the poem (IV, 410, 425, 475, 554, 570). This account is especially valuable since none of the chronicles describes this particular campaign in any detail. There is no reason to doubt its historicity, however, since several contemporaries do mention the expedition. Leopold Stainreuter writes in his German chronicle:

> Nach Kristi gepürd tausent drew hundert siben und sibenczig jare tet auch der selb hochgeborne fürst herczog Albrecht ein mechtige merkleiche Preussenfart und ward da ze ritter, und in der zeit ward herczog Albrecht sein sün geporen.[230]

Thomas Ebendorfer writes also about the year 1377:

> ...Princeps se ad Prussiam contra Infideles et Schismaticos dimicaturus contulit, ibique accinctus militari gladio cum multis ex suis, revertitur ad propria domina mulat cum gloria.[231]

Kaspar Schütz describes this campaign in somewhat more detail in his Prussian chronicle:

> Bald nach diesem kam [1377] um Preußen Hertzog Albrecht von Österreich, mit zwey vnd achtzig Rittern vnd ihren Geferten, die auch lust hetten sich mit den Unchristen zu sehen, und zu versuchen, denen zu Gefallen und guter Gesellschaft halben, der Hochmeister selbst mit seinem Volck vnd ihnen in starcker anzahl auff Littawen zog. Da sie aber keinen Widerstand funden, verheerten, verwüsten und durchstreifften sie die beyden Gebiete Kaltenenen vnd Weducke, vnd zogen also vngefochten wieder nach Preußen.[232]

Gutherie and Gray's general world history contains only the following terse account:

> Bald darauf kam der Herzog Albrecht von Oesterreich mit 62 Rittern und 2000 Soldaten nach Preußen, mit welchen der Hochmeister, ohne einen Feind gesehen zu haben, Pastov, Caltenen und Weduke verwüstete.[233]

The inglorious and dastardly wasting, burning, and killing is omitted by other Austrian chroniclers although, of course, emphasized by native ones. Suchenwirt writes:

> Der schaden tet mit seiner wer   V,77
> Den haiden weib und chinden.
> Die Littaw heten do chain her:
> Der fürst wolt nicht derbinden,
> Pis daz man da drew lant verhert.

Several literary histories have ascribed this poem to Konrad von Würzburg, a mistake caused by an incorrect listing in the Schwandtner manuscript catalogue.[234] At the end of the poem Peter Suchenwirt clearly names himself as author:

>Mit trewen rat ich Süchenwirt   IV,570
>Den edeln tzucht und er:
>Nu volget meiner ler!--

Duke Albert III was born in 1347 and died in 1395; he
became duke in 1365 upon the death of his older brother Rudolf
IV. His younger brother, Leopold, died at the battle of Sempach
in 1386. Suchenwirt discusses the strained relationship between
Albert and Leopold in the poem "Von fünf fursten" (XX) where he
accuses Leopold of high living, a warlike, fiery and jealous
nature, and claims that he took away many of his peaceful
brother's possessions. Albert, on the other hand, was possessed
of a mild and peaceful nature, and did not like to fight. He
undertook the campaign to Prussia solely for the purpose of
winning his knighthood. Later he went to the aid of the city
of Triest against Venice (XVIII,476), engaged in a war with
Bohemia, and was compelled to exercise the sword of justice
against the robber counts of Schaumberg and Rore in his own land.
His last military campaign against King Wenceslaus of Bohemia
(mentioned several times by Suchenwirt, XXXVII,89; XXXVIII,333,
336) cost him his life. Albert became sick in camp, had himself
brought to his hunting castle at Laxenburg, and died there on
August 29, 1395. His first wife, Elisabeth of Bohemia died
without children. His second wife, Beatrice, Baroness of
Nuremberg, whom he married in 1375, bore him a son Albert in
1377 (IV,523-530) while he was on the Prussian campaign (see
also V,121).

The poem "Von hertzog Albrechts ritterschaft" (IV) begins
with a declaration of the purpose of the expedition:

>In trug sein hertz und auch sein wil,   IV,8
>Daz er tzu ritter werden wolt.

Julius Max Schottky elaborates on the importance of such
campaigns which served in the fourteenth century as substitutes
for crusades to the Holy Land:

>Nächstdem, daß man von diesen Reisen dieselben Folgen erwartete,
>die man sich von einem Kreutzzuge nach Pälastina versprach,
>gehörte es gewisser Maßen jetzt zum guten Ton gegen die Preußen
>gezogen zu seyn. Damen geboten den Rittern diese Gottesreise,
>um ihren Muth, wie ihre Ergebenheit zu prüfen; man wollte von
>dem Großmeister zum Ritter geschlagen seyn, und wohl auch manches
>in dringender Gefahr gethane Gelübde auf diese Art lösen, zumahl

da sie eine leichtere war, als der Zug übers Meer. Es vereinigte
sich demnach Religionseifer mit Ruhmsucht, Eitelkeit oder Trieb
nach Abenteuern, um den bedrängten Preussen den Todesstoß bey-
zubringen. Wer nur immer von höherem oder niederem Adel ausziehen
konnte, zog gegen die Unglücklichen, und vermehrte Winrichs
siegreiche Scharen.[235]

The exact date of the Prussian campaign poses some
interesting questions. The accounts cited above indicate that
it took place in the late winter. According to another
document Count Hermann von Cilli drew up his last will and
testament on the eve of St. Catherine's Day (November 25) in
1377 before setting out on this expedition.[236] To me the most
convincing evidence is the established date of the birth of
Albert IV on September 21, 1377, an event which took place
before the army returned to Vienna.

The exact size of the expedition is also debatable.
Suchenwirt says:

> Mit im [Albert] rayt manig edel chnecht   IV,12
> Und manig ritter wol geporn,
> Da sach man reyten auzerchorn
> Fumftzig werder dinst man.

He then names the five counts who accompanied Albert:

> Von Maydburk waz der ain,   IV,23
> Graff Hansen den ich main,
> Von alter edel und von gepurt;
> Da rayt graff Haug von Munfurt,
> Dem trew noch eren nie geprach;
> Von Czil drey grafen man da sach
> Mit grozzen eren manigvalt,
> Graff Herman sey von erst betzalt,
> Sein sun und auch sein vetter.

Hans von Maidburg, who in 1407 was the provincial marshal in
Austria; Hugo II von Montfort (†1423), who later gained fame
as a poet; Count Hermann von Cilli, one of the richest and
most powerful landowners of his time; Hermann's son Hermann II
and his nephew William. The elder Hermann's dignity and
authority are indicated by the fact that it was he who had
the honor of dubbing Albert a knight (IV,268).

The Austrians rode from Vienna to Laa on the Thaya river,
the place of assembly, where they were joined by more knights
and more soldiers; then they continued on to Breslau and
Thorn. At Thorn they first came into the territory of the
Teutonic Order. A magnificent feast was prepared in Albert's

honor; the ladies and maidens of the city dressed in beautiful
gowns with pearls and entertained him royally:

```
Da sach man widerglaste     IV,72
Von mundelein und von wangen;
Mit perlein, porten, spangen
Di vrawen sich da tzirten
Und gen der lust vlorirten;
Chron, schapel, unde chrentze
Sach man und vil der tentze
Mit tzuchten und mit eren.
```

They continued on to Marienburg where Albert was graciously
received by the Grand Master, Winrich von Kniprode,[237] the
greatest and most successful of all the Teutonic masters. Here
Winrich held two banquets in honor of the Austrians. Then at
Königsberg one banquet followed the other. Albert displayed
the great splendor of the Austrian court by holding a large
feast and by presenting gifts of gold and silver. The
expense of the banquets is emphasized by Suchenwirt through
the types of wine offered:

```
Di tisch sach man beraten     IV,114
Mit Welchisch und mit Oster wein,
Chlarn Rainfal schancht man ein
In gut gevezz in rechter chost.
```

Welscher wine refers to some type of southern wine, *Oster* wine
to eastern wine, probably Greek; and the *Rainfal* (Latin
Rifolium) came from the Proseckerberg at the source of the
Timao river in Istria. Later a *Wippacher,* a Carniolian wine,
is mentioned, as well as the *Lutenberger* wine from Lutenberg on
the Mur river in what is now Yugoslavia.[238] The question
remains as to whether these expensive wines were brought along
or whether they were available in Prussia.

After ten days, on the last day before setting out against
the heathens, the Grand Master held the impressive ceremony of
the *Hochmahl am Ehrentisch.*[239] According to the custom, which
Suchenwirt suggests was old and established, only the ten or
twelve most worthy knights were invited to the table of honor.
The bravest, most famous, the ones who had distinguished themselves on the battlefield, were awarded this honor and were
announced by the heralds. On this occasion Konrad von Krey,
the captain of the Austrian forces, was given the first

Ehrensitz, the highest honor. The utensils, dishes, and goblets were of gold and silver. Later other members of the army were summoned to other tables to enjoy the food, music, songs, and festivities which lasted five or six hours. In Germany and Austria it was considered a great honor to have been present at an *Ehrentisch* of the Teutonic Order in Prussia.[240]

The army rode through Samogitia to Insterburg, past a castle built on the Angerapp river by Commander Ludolf König (†1345) and restored by Grand Master Winrich. After passing by Insterburg the military train came to the Suppen river which it crossed via four bridges (this river could be the more easterly Russian-Polish Szeszuppe which then flowed near Ragnit into the Russe to the Kurisch Haff). From there they continued along the Memel river. Suchenwirt describes the details of this military operation including the problems of fording rivers:

> An di Suppen, da man sach   IV,180
> Vir prukken uber slahen;
> Daż wazzer ist, als wir sahen,
> Nachen gantzer glefen tief;
> Auf yeder pruk man wenig slief
> Von getret und von gedranch.--

They crossed the Memel with the aid of 610 boats:

> An di Mimil tzu der tzeit,   IV,187
> Daz wazzer ist pogen schuzzes weit.
> Da chom man tzu den schiffen,
> Di marner da tzu griffen
> Und warn willichleich berayt,
> Mit mue und auch mit aribayt
> Von mitten tag tzu fesper tzeit
> Swemt man uber daz wazzer weit
> Pey den schiffen, daz ist war,
> Mer wen dreizzik tawsent gar!
> Der schiff der warn mit der tzal
> Tzehen und sechs hundert über all.
> Dez hers ertrunchen da nicht mer
> Drew pferd, ain chnecht, an widercher,...

Since this was one of the largest expeditions, one thousand men were required to prepare the roads for the army. Despite this Suchenwirt insists that the roads in Prussia were even worse than those in Hungary:

> (In Ungern ist man ungewan   IV,208
> So poz geverd auf slechter haid!)

Not only were the roads terrible, many of the men became sick, and it was difficult to find suitable camping places at night. But each morning the army set out happily to fight against the heathens:

> Des margens frue man froleich gacht   IV,236
> Mit vrewden in der haiden lant:
> Da wart gesprengt und gerant!

According to the customs of the Teutonic Order the Commander Ragnit rode at the front of the army; the banners of St. George, the Grand Master, Styria, Austria, and many others followed--a colorful picture!

They crossed the Samogitia border into Lithuanian territory. At the first village they surprised a wedding celebration:

> In ein lant, daz haist Sameyt,   IV,257
> Da vand man einew hochtzeit;
> Di gest chomen ungepeten!
> Ein tantz mit haiden wart getreten,
> Daz ir wol sechtizig bliben tot;
> Dar nach daz dorf mit vewr rot,
> Daz es hoch in di luften pran.

This description could be understood as purely poetic with · many grains of irony, but the account coincides with others by Suchenwirt. The Christians overran the land, burned and laid waste to everything in sight.

After this first success, the most distinguished and respected knight on the campaign, Count Hermann von Cilli, knighted Albert III. This was the purpose of the entire campaign since knighting in heathen territory was considered much more honorable than at home. As he dubbed Albert, Hermann exclamed: "Pezzer ritter wenne chnecht!" Following this admonition, Albert himself knighted seventy-four more men in honor of the Blessed Virgin.

The evening was continually disturbed by angry heathens. The next day the army was divided into small groups which dispersed throughout the countryside to ferret out the heathens. Marshal Gothort von Line directed this operation brilliantly. The heathen men were killed on the spot, the women and children taken prisoner:

```
Gevangen wurden weib und chind,    IV,331
Es was ein gemleich hof gesint!
```

But Suchenwirt portrays a sad picture of barefoot children
bound to their mothers' bodies:

```
Man sach da vil manigem weib    IV,333
Tzway chind gepunden an irn leib
Ains hinden und ains voren;
Auf einem pferd an sporen
Chom si parfuz her geriten!--
Di haiden grozzen chumer liten,
Man vieng ir vil, und al tzu hant
Di hend man in tzu samen pant;
So fürt man si gepunden
Gleich den iagunden hunden.
```

The prisoners were huddled together within a fence to allow
the weary warriors a sound night's sleep. On the third day
the army arrived in the territory of Rossiene where they
began a new offensive.

```
Da sach man wuchsten, prennen,    IV,363
Slahen, schiezzen, und rennen
Haid ein, pusch ein unvertzagt,
Recht als, der füchs und hasen iagt.
So fluhen si die widervart!
```

Conrad von Sweinwart killed the heathen captain, a heroic
deed which overjoyed the Christians and angered the heathens
who fought with renewed energy using guerrilla tactics for
which they were quite famous.

When all the heathens had disappeared into the woods
and bogs, Count Hermann held a feast in honor of the new
knights, eighty-two in all. It was the first time that
Rainfal, Wippacher, and noble *Lutenberger* wines were drunk
here. More men were knighted so that the total of new
knights grew to 108. After they had crossed, cleared, and
burned the territory of Eragola (a total of eight days in the
wilderness), they returned through heavy wind, rain, and hail
to the Memel. Duke Albert returned by ship to Königsberg. He
was accompanied by the brothers Ulrich, Wulfing, and
Friederich von Stubenberg and many others to the Kurisch Haff
where they were caught and buffeted about in a violent storm.
The difficulties of those who returned by land, including
Suchenwirt, were equally perilous. They traveled through
the wilderness of Grauden which Suchenwirt described as the

worst territory he had ever experienced:

> So poz gevert ich nye gerayt,   IV,475
> Daz sprich ich wol auf mein ayt!

Primisser identifies the areas mentioned by Suchenwirt as follows:

> Russien = White Russia
> Aragel = the territory of Carelia or Cargapolia
> die Wildniß Grauden = the area near Graudenz on the Vistula river

He is clearly puzzled by the distances involved in his hypothesis: "Die größte Schwierigkeit biethet der Name Aragel dar, welches kaum für Carelien oder Cargapolien gesetzt seyn kann, da diese Landschaften zu weit vom Wege abliegen."[241] Karl Heinrich von Busse agrees that these distances make the entire campaign "unwahrscheinlich und abenteurerlich"[242] and thus identifies the names as follows:

> Russien = area near Rossiene--an old city in Samogitia, seven
>   miles from the 1845 Prussian border
> Aragel = four miles eastwards from Russien, area of Eragola
> die Wildniß Grauden = the strip of land on the left bank of the
>   Memel between the river and the Prussian border to Grodno

Because of the terrain (as Suchenwirt clearly asserts) these distances would be difficult but not impossible to cover. Thus from Insterberg the army crossed the Memel above the castle of Ragnit and from there pushed ahead in Samogitia. Three days after this invasion it reached the area of Rossiene, and then it turned to Eragola where, according to the then prevailing customs, all settlements within reach belonging to the heathen Lithuanians were devastated. They spent eight days doing this (IV,419) and then spent three days returning to the Memel. On the other side of the Memel, they came to an area known as the wilderness of Grauden (namely Grodno) which the army crossed in a westerly direction, probably toward Schirwind. Thereupon the crusaders, who were exhausted by unfavorable weather and bad roads, and together with them Suchenwirt, continued to Königsberg. This was all within the realm of possibility. The correct identification of place names, the knowledge of which was not available at that time except through one's own observation or through exact reports from travelers, is evidence for the fact that Suchenwirt did not fabricate his report out of thin air.[243]

Finally the entire army was reassembled at Königsberg.
Albert honored the ten bravest knights from various areas with
gold and silver goblets full of coins: Jeschko Schwab from
Bohemia, Ulrich from Redlitz, a knight from Kolowrat, Heinrich
List, Albrecht Meissner, Rupprecht Chraft from Cologne, Ekhart
from Scotland, William, Ritschart, and Loys from France. He
designated Konrad von Krey as commander of the returning
forces. Finally Albert received thanks from Master Winrich
for undertaking this campaign:

> Der maister und der orden   IV,507
> Durch hoches preyses horden
> Danchten dem von Osterreich,
> Daz er so rechte zuchtichleich
> Geraist het mit irm her.

And Albert put on another fancy banquet with the best of
wines. At Riesenburg he received the news of the birth of
his son Albert IV, on September 21, 1377. He stopped in
Schweidnitz to visit his cousin, the widowed Duchess Agnes.
After four days the army continued to Austria via Poland and
Moravia.

Suchenwirt concludes the poem with a summary of the
purpose of such a campaign, namely for the glory of knighthood,
and everything it stands for:

> Wer gut ritter wesen well,   IV,561
> Der nem vrawn Eren tzu gesell
> Und auch sand Jorgen, daz ist recht.
> „Pezzer ritter wenne chnecht!"
> Daz wort er in dem hertzen trag,
> Di weil er lebt ainen tag,
> Mit willen, werchen, gutter tat.
> So sprichet er den schanden mat,
> Und wirt sein nam mit lob getziert.

Suchenwirt's account of Albert's Prussian campaign
presents several points which should be restated. Albert,
despite his mild and peaceful temperament, set out upon this
expedition because it was the thing to do--in one campaign he
could win enough heavenly and earthly honor (*êre*-fame) to
last for the rest of his life. Throughout the expedition
Suchenwirt emphasizes the sumptious banquets--the food and
wine, the gold and silver utensils. As a herald he should

have been very used to such displays of wealth and grandeur.
According to his descriptions these feasts compared favorably
to those back home in Austria even though they were held miles
away in the territory of the Teutonic Order. Suchenwirt is
also quite explicit in his descriptions of the plundering of
the heathen lands. He never admits any personal animosity
towards the enemy. It would be interesting to know whether
Albert concurred in the disapproval of such actions which
Suchenwirt seems to assert. This poem could be viewed as
an anti-war statement by Albert put into Suchenwirt's mouth.
Similarly Suchenwirt emphasizes the physically unpleasant side
of the soldier's life--the mud, the cold, the rain, and the
hail. He never really presents the campaign as a glorious
expedition even though it did have its glorious moments of
feasting.

Suchenwirt's account illustrates the dichotomy of
research on Prussian military crusades which are usually
called *Reisen* or *Fahrten* (here *Preußenfahrt*), i.e. "journeys" or
"campaigns." Such campaigns are characterized as either
dangerous ventures into the heathen unknown lands or as
"eine fröhliche Jagd" in the sense of courtly sport. Even
though the techniques of these campaigns did not vary much
from 1200 to 1400 and there is contemporary information such
as that found in Suchenwirt's poem, such campaigns have been
carefully studied only in the last few years. The most common
type of expedition is called by Friedrich Benninghoven "die
reine Verherrungsreise." He says: "Bei ihr ist das militärische
Ziel ein indirektes: Schädigung der wirtschaftlichen und kriegerischen Kraft des Angegriffenen durch Verwüstung und Plün-
derung in weitestgehender Art."[244] Thus, the object is not
only to collect as much booty as possible, but also to weaken
the agricultural and economic potential of the enemy, thereby
strengthening one's own. The religious elements provide a
spiritual justification for the operation.

The area of Prussia, Lithuania, and Latvia was sparsely
populated: in the thirteenth century there were two or three
people per square kilometer, scarcely more in the fourteenth

century.[245] The most propitious times of the year for such
expeditions were in the winter when the moors and bogs were
frozen and sleds could be used, and in the summer when these
same moors and bogs were dried out. Fall and spring were
characterized by rain, mud, and swollen rivers. This suggests
that Albert's campaign indeed probably took place in late
summer. The time of year was also important for the feeding
of the troops. During harvest time an invading army would
need few supplies since it could live off the land. The size
of the army and the extent of the expedition would also depend
upon the possibilities of obtaining local supplies. A small
army could cover more territory and did not require as many
supplies, but it was less effective militarily. Albert's army
appears to have been very large, Suchenwirt claims 30,000 strong.
Generally the armies were divided into divisions. A special
commando cleared the way through the wilderness with axes and
knives. Spies and signalmen *(Wartleute)* also played an important role. The army had to cross a difficult border wilderness
area to reach the heathen population. A camp or *sowalk* was
established from which the men would ride out in small groups
of ten to twenty in a radius of ten kilometers to plunder. In
a description of a similar expedition in 1372 Hermann von
Wartberge lists nine different *sowalk*.[246] Comparing this
account with another description of an operation in 1378
it is difficult to determine whether these were a series of
night camps or whether they represented a chain of march
advancements.[247] Communication was by means of horns and
messengers. The booty was collected in the central camp for
transportation back home. A typical expedition lasted from
two to four weeks with generally about two weeks in enemy
territory.

Benninghoven concludes his study of medieval military
campaigns in the East Baltic region with the following
observation:

> Es handelt sich hier in keiner Weise um „Wehrsport" irgendeiner
> mühelosen und gefahrlosen Art, sondern um die Betätigung und
> Ausführung wohldurchdachter strategischer Überlegungen unter den
> Bedingungen der Zeit, die von beiden einander bekämpfenden
> Mächte (wie auch von deren Nachbarn) in gleicher Weise unter-

nommen wurden.[248]

He maintains that medieval campaigns into Prussia, Lithuania, and Latvia have much in common with modern warfare: the bombing of territories deep within the *Hinterland* in World War II, the various forms of partisan or guerrilla warfare of recent years with the "burnt earth" policies and goal of crippling the agricultural potential and psychologically wearing down the opposition of the people. Furthermore, the Middle Ages did not recognize the difference between the legal status of combatants and noncombatants because the sharp distinction between public and private rights was missing. The concept of "total war" seems to have reasserted itself in the twentieth century.

Suchenwirt's death lament in honor of Albert III, who died on August 29, 1395, was perhaps his last poem. The poem entitled "Von hertzog Albrecht säligen in Östereich" (V) begins with an appeal to the Holy Ghost. Suchenwirt laments that bitter Death has taken away a prince whose noble heart was constant, modest, and calm. He was a fair and just judge who loved the Holy Scripture and God's commandments so much that he sent to Paris to find teachers for his university in Vienna. Thomas Ebendorfer describes Albert's affinity for scholars in some detail. Albert was the second founder (after Rudolf IV) of the University of Vienna where he appointed as teachers of the Holy Scripture Masters Heinrich von Hesse, Heinrich von Oyta, Heinrich von Langenstein, Andreas Kalker and others; other masters of the arts, doctors of law and medicine were assigned an appropriate year's pay, each according to his speciality. Albert had classrooms and apartments built and awarded the scholars and their pupils new freedoms. He obtained from Pope Urban VI the right to include theology in the curriculum. Suchenwirt's comments regarding Albert's role in the university are espeically note-worthy since they are usually overshadowed by historians in favor of his brother Rudolf.

When Thomas Ebendorfer was a child, he caught a brief glimpse of Duke Albert and later made the following

observation: "Homo pacis, militiae cultor, et divini cultus
amator."[249]   His shield was like an umbrella over many countries;
he prevented many wars.

The description of Albert's Prussian campaign of 1377 is
condensed into only twenty-two lines in this poem. Suchenwirt
emphasizes the knightly virtues of the Duke, mentions the
unnecessary damage inflicted upon the Lithuanians, and concludes with the purpose of the expendition: "Got und der
Magt zw eren."

Albert's religious nature is emphasized by an account
of his fasting and all night vigil before the Sabbath in
honor of the Virgin:

> Auf chainem pett er nicht enlag   V,85
> Di samptztagnacht der weise:
> Andächtichleich er dienstes pflag
> Got und der magt zw preise!

Albert reigned for thirty years, was a knight for
twenty years. He always appeared joyful, polite, and courtly.
He died much too soon, especially for the sake of the young
princes whom he raised so faithfully and fatherly. Upon the
death of his brother Leopold at Sempach in 1386 Albert took
over the protection and education of his four nephews. At
the time of Albert's death, William the Friendly was twenty-
five; Leopold the Magnificent was twenty-four; Frederick of
Tyrol was twenty-two; Ernst the Strong was twenty-one; and his
own son Albert IV was eighteen. Suchenwirt's concern for
these young men, their relationships with each other as well
as with their neighbors, proved to be well founded since their
territories were soon beset by strife and turmoil.

Suchenwirt concludes the poem by naming Albert, the
subject of the lament, by recommending his soul to heaven,
and by naming himself:

> In Österreich hertzog Albrecht,   V,143
> Der waz warhaft von iugent....
> Got liepleich anzwschawen:
> Des pitt ich Peter Swchenwirt
> Got und unser frawen!--

It is curious that to honor his master, the Duke of
Austria, Suchenwirt chooses the older type of poem, namely
the death lament, rather than the *Ehrenrede*. He does not

mention specific deeds other than the Prussian campaign; nor
does he blazon Albert's (i.e. the Austrian) coats of arms
which were well known and obvious to all his audience. It is
possible that the death lament with its long established
tradition was still considered the most accepted and most
respectful way to honor the deceased.

The poems dedicated to Duke Albert II and Duke Albert
III of Austria are replete with elements discussed above as
prototypes of heraldic poetry--the death lament, the description of a historical event (Albert's campaign to Prussia),
as well as the blazon of coats of arms. These poems also
illustrate the different roles assumed by Suchenwirt which
will be discussed below.

An overview of the genres which Suchenwirt employs
indicates a certain degree of independence. His works can
best be understood, in form and content, in the context of
his position within the courtly tradition. His starting
point is the epic form of a rhymed couplet; he often transfers
its non-strophic freedom to a strophe-like four line stanza.
He makes use of diverse epic and didactic content. However,
he does not confine himself in style and subject matter to
the imitation of his courtly antecedents. He does not
attempt laudatory poems dedicated to a cow, or chicken, or
pig as does the König vom Odenwald. He writes *Lügenmärchen*
for which Reinmar von Zweter already provided models, but he
completely avoids the obscene; he deliberately refuses to
praise unworthy princes:

> Ainer voligt pueben weis,   XXXVIII,317
> Der ander voligt trunkenhait;
> Daz ich daz an fürsten preis,
> Des tün ich nicht, auf meinn ait.

His contemporary, Heinrich Teichner, had built his copious
production upon moralizing religious poems; Suchenwirt is
closer to the older courtly precedents, more diverse, and
less concerned with the bourgeois. The poem "Daz ist die
verlegenhait" (XXXI), for example, is written from a courtly
perspective, and "Daz ist di geitichait" (XXXII) brings into
play the older personification of the *Wuchersack* which origi-

nated from the *Spruchform*.

Although Teichner touched upon numerous historical events and political questions in his poems, it is difficult to determine his own particular view. Suchenwirt also wrote historical occasional poems but with a much more acute historical sensitivity than did Teichner for whom everything could be resolved by morality. Suchenwirt sought to achieve direct results through his poetry (e.g. a repeal of the wine tax, a unification of Austria, etc.), and in this respect he is closer in the subject matter of his poems to the older writers of political *Sprüche*; however, he does not employ the abbreviated one strophe form of the *Spruch*. Nor is Suchenwirt a satirist in the same sense as the poet of the Helbling satires. The didactic element is present, but not to the same extent as in the case of Teichner. Suchenwirt's occasional poems are thus not direct imitations of existing models, even though their connection to related art forms is evident.

Suchenwirt attempts to characterize his works by emphasizing in one instance his art: "mit eren plumen durchfloriert: den rat gibt euch der Suchenwirt" (XXVII,104-105); in another the moral content of his poetry: "ich rat, ich straf, ich lere die yungen herren" (XXI,184-185) and "ich haizz der Suechenwirt, der dikch mit red so nahen schirt, man möcht ez greiffen mit der hant" (XXII,45-47), by advocating virtue and honor, by instructing the lords wisely, and by criticizing them with insight and with moderation. To be sure, Suchenwirt always addresses noble circles. However, his moral perspectives are not exclusively those of conventional courtliness; they are more general, based on religious teachings, more closely affiliated with the people. Even "the poor folk" have their turn, when, for example, Suchenwirt speaks out against the arrogance and gluttony of the rich, or when he perceives with an understanding glance that the feuds among princes and cities lead to the ruination of the peasants as well as to serious consequences for the warring parties. He castigates with acute economic sensibility the greedy, who for half value acquire the mill and the land of a neighbor.[250]

The candor of his rebukes, the objectivity of his observations, as well as his ability as a herald elevated Suchenwirt in the eyes of Hugo von Montfort, who considered him an unattainable ideal:

Darzuo gehört der Suochenwirt,   II,135
Der dik mit red als nahe schirt,
Man möcht es grifen mit der hand;
Er ist in mangem land erkand.
Das sag ich üch mit einem wort:
Er ist der best den ich ie ghort
Von got und von den wappen.
Da tribt er keine grappen,
Er vâchtz mit geblüemten worten an,
Des ich doch leider nit enkan.[251]

V. EHRENREDEN

Suchenwirt's *Ehrenreden* are laudatory addresses, written in rhymed couplets, in honor of a nobleman, usually dead--only three poems are dedicated to living men--and including a description of his coat of arms. As mentioned above, Suchenwirt frequently identifies himself in his poetry. The *Ehrenreden*, however, are a notable exception: he does not name himself in a single one (in contrast to Gelre, who does not follow a consistent pattern in this respect). One might speculate that Suchenwirt withheld his identity in his *Ehrenreden* because of their intended purpose, but, unfortunately, there is no direct evidence that they were recited before either a public or a private audience.

The most distinctive features of the *Ehrenreden* are the precise enumeration of the heroes' deeds and the blazon of arms. Suchenwirt's heroes are generally minor figures in the annals of world history. The chronicles of the time describe the deeds of these heroes only in conjunction with those of their masters who were members of the ruling houses. The chronicles report that these men were present at a particular occasion or that they participated in a certain campaign. Their specific contributions are seldom mentioned. The official documents pertaining to them consist of appointments to government positions or of matters of property or money such as those relating to Suchenwirt's house in Vienna. Only Suchenwirt and Gelre dedicate entire *Ehrenreden* to relatively unknown figures. In this respect they are following the precedent of earlier death laments which honored such men as Count Werner of Honberg, Count William of Holland, and Freiherr Konrad von Schlüsselberg, which though similar to the *Ehrenreden*, do not adhere to the strict formula.

Suchenwirt's *Ehrenreden* adhere to a fairly strict formula with respect to their content (see chart on pp. 142-143).[252] They may be divided into three major parts, reminiscent of the death lament discussed earlier. Introductions (part I) generally contain one or more of the three following elements:

an expression of regret that death has terminated a deserving
life; a laudatory statement concerning the subject of the
Ehrenrede; and an apologetic remark by the poet regarding his
inability to do justice to the task he is about to undertake.
The importance of this formalized introduction is indicated by
Suchenwirt's remarks in the poem dedicated to Friedrich von
Kreußpeck (XIV) where he excuses himself for omitting the
usual "flowers" *(geblümte Rede)* which would make the poem too long:

> Pluemt ich nu end und anevank,   XIV,5
> So würd di red ein tail tze lank.

Only once, in the poem honoring Burkhard von Ellerbach, the
Younger (IX), does Suchenwirt employ the courtly description
of nature in the springtime as an introductory motif:

> Di erd ist süzzer früchte vol,   IX,1
> Dar aüz pirt, als sich pilleich sol,
> Würtz unde chraüt, plüm unde gras.
> Was den winder trübich was,
> Daz hat tzu vrewden sich bechert;
> Der May auz süzzem lufte rert
> Des früchtichleichen tawes tror.

In one instance, in the poem dedicated to Moriz von Haunfeld
(1), the introduction is missing in the manuscript.

The body of the *Ehrenrede* (part II) is dedicated to a
description of the hero and his deeds. The core (part II B)
consists on an enumeration of his deeds, preceded by part II
A, a laudatory praise of his general moral, courtly, knightly,
and spiritual characteristics, and is followed by part II C,
a short repetition or elaboration of the general praise; in
the death laments (once also in an *Ehrenrede* honoring a living
person) there follows an intercessary prayer (part II D),
generally directed to the Virgin Mary.

The conclusion (part III) always contains a blazon of
the coat of arms (part III A), which is frequently introduced
with another admission of the poet's incompetence. Whereas the
first statement of humility at the beginning of the poem is
rather convincing, this second self-deprecation is conventional--
the poet is following the rules even though he knows perfectly
well how capable he is as a herald. The name of the hero (part
III B) is revealed for the first time, and this is formally
connected with a short praise or short lament, also with a

Suchenwirt's *Ehrenreden*

No. of Poem	*Ehrenrede* dedicated to	I Intro- duction	II Praise Deeds Praise Prayer				III Arms Deeds Prayer Name			Total Lines
			A	B	C	D	A (IIB)	(IID)	B	
I	Louis of Hungary	31	67	59	10		34		7	208
III	Albert of Austria	35	81				68	11	6	201
VI	Henry of Carinthia	45	80	32	18	22	20		5	222
VII	Albert of Nuremberg	25	40	120	14	9	24		9	241
VIII	Burkhard v. Ellerbach	29	3	167	24	12	10		5	250
IX	Burkhard v. Ellerbach	32	23	158	6		16		7	242
X	Burkhard v. Ellerbach	23	16	153	31	16	18		9	266
XI	Ulrich v. Pfannberg	82	183	26			18		19	328
XII	Herdegen v. Pettau	39	50			14	30		5	138
XIII	Ulrich v. Walsee	25	32	120	13	11	24		7	232

Suchenwirt's *Ehrenreden* (cont.)

No. of Poem	*Ehrenrede* dedicated to	I	IIA	IIB	IIC	IID	IIIA	(IIB)	(IID)	IIIB	Total Lines
XIV	Friedrich v. Kreußbeck	6	13	290	20	2	14			7	352
XV	Leutold v. Stadeck	9	22	135	25		26			9	226
XVI	Ulrich v. Cilli	21	2	138	22		30		7	8	228
XVII	Friedrich v. Lochen	20	3	138	6	4	22			7	200
XVIII	Hans v. Traun	37	2	472	30		12		6	11	570
1	Moriz v. Haunfeld	...	...	..54		16	(A+B=27=)		(=A+B=27)		..97
2	Hans v. Chappel	29	30	52			28		10	5	154
3	Albert of Austria	39	75			20	22	7		4	167
4	Albrecht v. Rauchenstain	27	42	50	4	12	18			5	158
5	Sumolf Lapp v. Ernwicht	7	56	56			18			5	142

short prayer; occasionally the battle cry of the hero is also
given.

A brief inspection of the chart makes it evident that
some of the poems deviate from the standard formula; the
following explanatory remarks, numbered according to the
poems, apply to these deviations:

I.   "Von Chünik Ludwig von Ungerlant" was written in
honor of the living King of Hungary, thus there is no lament,
nor a prayer for intercession for his soul (part II D).

III.   "Von hertzog Albrecht von Östereich" is a death
lament. The intercessary prayer (part II D) appears in the
conclusion (part III) between the blazon of the coats of
arms and the revelation of the name of the hero. The specific
enumeration of Albert's deeds (part II B) is missing and thus
the usual two sections of praise (parts II A and II C) are
combined into one, part II A, which acts as the main body.

VIII.   "Von her Pircharten Ellerbach dem alten" has a
very short section (part II A) of praise introducing the main
body which serves as the conclusion to the introduction (part
I). The formulaic quality is obvious (as can also be observed
in XVI and XVII):

Der willichleichen seine tag   VIII,30
Got und der welt gedienet hat
Mit wort, gedanchen, güter tat.

IX.   "Von her Puppli von Elrwach (dem jungen)" was
written before the death of young Burkhard and is lacking the
lament and intercessary prayer (part II D).

X.   "Von hern Puppily von Elrwach (dem iungen)," on
the other hand, was written after Burkhard's death and does
include a part II D. There the praise section (part II C)
provides the motivation for the intercessary prayer.

XI.   "Von graff Ulreich von Phanberg" differs from the
others in its allegorical setting which appears as a frame.
The introduction (part I) and the hero's name (part III B) are
expanded. Suchenwirt says very little about Ulrich's actual
deeds (part II B); instead, the main body of the poem (part
II A) consists of a conversation among six ladies--*Tzucht, Mazz,
Scham, Warhait, Staet,* and *Tugent,* and six knights--*Gotleib, Erwart,*

Getrewrat, Mildemar, Adelger, and *Manhaft,* which is unusually long when compared to the other *Ehrenreden.*

XII. "Von her Herdegen von Petaw" also does not contain information about the hero's deeds (part II B) and thus the two praise sections (parts II A and II C) are compacted into one (part II A).

XVI. "Von graff Ulreichen von Tzili" again has a short formulaic section of praise (part II A). The usual prayer concluding the main body (II D) is moved to the conclusion where it comes between the blazon of arms and the naming of the hero.

XVII. "Von her Fridreichen von Lochen" also has an abbreviated praise at the beginning of the main body (part II A):

> Ye vinden lan pay guter tat   XVII,22
> Mit hertz, mit willen und mit müt.

XVIII. "Von hern Hansen dem Trawner" not only has an abbreviated part II A, but the prayer at the end of the main body (part II D) appears in the conclusion and adds new historical information.

1. "Von Hawnfeld der Mariez" has a twenty-seven line conclusion (part III) in which the coat of arms and the name of the hero are so completely interwoven as to be indistinguishable. The usual second praise (part II C) is also missing but perhaps this was included in the introduction (part I) and in a first praise (part II A) which are missing from the manuscript.

2. "Von hern Hansen von Chappell" also transposes the intercessary prayer (part II D) to the end of the poem between the blazon and the hero's name. The usual laudatory section (part II C) is missing entirely.

3. "Von herzog Albrecht von Oesterreich" has, after the blazon of arms (part III A), additional historical information which according to its content whould belong in the missing part II B.

Besides numbers 1-4, Seemüller also sees a close

affinity among numbers VIII, XVI, XVII, and XVIII, all of
which have a short part II A and which appear next to each
other in MS A.

Although closely related, the death laments honoring the
Empress of Bavaria (II), Albert III of Austria (V), and
Heinrich Teichner (XIX) do not meet the requisites of an
Ehrenrede: none of the three includes the coat of arms of the
deceased; in the second and third Suchenwirt names himself
as author; less obviously the crossed rhyme departs from the
typical composition of the *Ehrenrede* with its rhymed couplets.
The lament dedicated to Albert III contains the typical
introduction (part I) and the main body may be divided into a
part II B (V,33-92) and a part II D (V,133-140); however, the
historical deeds of the hero are not included for their own
sake, but rather as proof for his moral characteristics of
wisdom, generosity, and courage, and between part II B and
part II D Suchenwirt departs from the usual formula to
present a short survey of the living members of the House
of Habsburg. The poems honoring Albert's father (III and 3)
and Herdegan von Pettau (XII) are heraldic death laments with
no description of the heroes' specific deeds, and thus they
do not meet the strict definition of *Ehrenreden*. The poem
entitled "Von hern Sumolf Lappen uon Ernwicht" (5), on the
other hand, meets the formal requisites for an *Ehrenrede,* but
as a parody it is obviously dissimilar in content. Seemüller
maintains that it must be omitted from the list of *Ehrenreden*
even though he dissects it in his chart.

The chart illustrates how similar the *Ehrenreden* are in
form, with only minor variations. Not only the impersonal sections of
the poems (I, II A, II C, II D) are formulaic in nature, but
also the individual parts (II B, III A) are quite similar.
Without any mention of personality differences, each hero
follows a similar life-pattern, which, of course, is not
unusual for men of similar social backgrounds. Typically,
they made a pilgrimage to Prussia where they were knighted.
They fought in the many wars in Italy, Germany, and countries
neighboring Austria. The more adventuresome volunteered for

action in the Hundred Years War in France or fought against
the Scots in Britain. Several made pilgrimages to the Holy
Land. Suchenwirt's descriptions of these deeds, however, is
highly stylized, often couched in courtly language reminiscent
of earlier days.

Suchenwirt adds to the general knowledge of his heroes,
but he does so in an erratic and inconsistent fashion. This
is due to his sources of information which were not always
based on personal experience. Thus he reports what was then
considered common knowledge, information not deemed suitable
for an official chronicle. The type of information and the
manner of its presentation will be illustrated in the close
examination of the *Ehrenrede* dedicated to Hans von Traun.

Gelre's *Ehrenreden*[253] (see chart on p. 148) may be
analyzed according to the same criteria as Seemüller devised
for Suchenwirt's. The first six *Ehrenreden* are similar to each
other and somewhat different from those of Suchenwirt. The
introduction (I) and general praise (II A) are very difficult
to distinguish from one another and could best be viewed as
a single section. Two of the poems refer to a few specific
deeds but do not elaborate in any detail. The others merely
describe the hero in general terms. The blazon and name of
the hero (parts III A and III B) are quite distinct and
usually contain praise with the blazon and name. Since these
are not death laments, there is no section of lament, nor a
prayer of intercession. In the poem dedicated to Johan van
Spanem a section of praise (II C) appears after the blazon
and name (III A and III B) which are so closely interwoven as
to be one. The final distinguishing characteristic of these
six poems from the six following poems is their brevity. One
could easily envision another part (II B) which would describe
the deeds of the heroes in detail and increase the total
length of the poems to compare with the other six poems.

The other six poems are remarkably similar to those of
Suchenwirt. The introduction (I) is distinct from the
beginning general praise (II A); there is a well-developed
part enumerating the deeds of the hero (II B); the specific

Gelre's *Ehrenreden*

Ehrenrede dedicated to	I Intro-duction	II Praise A	Deeds B	Praise C	Prayer D	III Arms A	Deeds (IIB)	Name B	Prayer (IID)	Total Lines
Johan v. Spanem	23	52				(A+B=20=)	21	(=A+B=20)		116
William v. Hennegouwen	5	40				14		9		68
Rudolph v. Nydou	15	6	12			10		5		48
Garaert v. Holstein	12	13	18			8		7		58
Reynout v. Valkenboirch	13	47				12		12		84
Van Virnenburch	5	84				14		5		108
Heinriic v. Neuft	11	8	181	13	5	18		1	5	242
Rutgher Raets	18	46	122	24		16		5	9	240
Adaem v. Mabbertingen	38	68	74	24		24		10		238
Hertooch v. Gulic	11	87	349	21		30		14		512
Diederiich v. Elnaer	12	4	132			25		6		179
Danyel v. Merwede	11	11	163			21		12	4	222

deeds are followed by more general praise (II C); sometimes there is a prayer (II D); occasionally a prayer is included at the end of the poem in connection with the name of the hero; and there is a distinct section of blazon and name (III A and III B). In the *Ehrenrede* dedicated to Heinriic van Neuft the name of the hero appears for the first time in the last line; this is preceded by a five line prayer of intercession. In the other two poems which have a distinguishable prayer in the third section, the prayer follows the name of the hero. The poem honoring Adaem van Mabbertingen departs from the usual formula: the blazon (III A) precedes the deeds of the hero (II B); then follow the praise (II C) and the name of the hero (III B).

The deeds of the heroes follow a similar pattern, but at the same time, are different enough to portray distinct individuals. Each knight made at least one trip to Prussia under the banner of Our Lady. Diederiich van Elnaer, for example, rode into Lithuania:

> Dair no he sint in Prusen reyt
> In Littouwen menlich streyt
> Onder onser Vrouwen bannieren,
> Do viel zeer hart dat scoffieren
> Do bleef vil manich heiden doot.   (p. 51)

Instead of imperial and neighborhood problems of central Europe, Gelre writes about the many battles in the Low Lands--the battle at Vollenho in which many Frisians lost their lives, the battles at Stavelo, Bornhem, Utrecht, Zallant, Swolle, Yseloorde. Heinriic van Neuft fought bravely at Vollenho:

> Ende streit dair na tse Vollenho,
> Des manich Vriese was onvro,
> Waer he zich ye hin keerde.
> Siin menlic moet eem leerde:
> He was vol alre tsoghet.   (p. 34)

The enemy was similarly unfortunate to meet Hertooch van Gulic at Stavelo:

> Thuuswaert nam hi sinen goom:
> Een was bi hem, die siin oom
> Wart doot geslagen, ter selver stonde;
> Des hi gewreecken niet en konde,
> Inder abdyen van Stavelo,

> Des was hi droevich ende onvro,
> End bat desen zelven Jongen heer
> Om te helpen wreecken siin zeer.   (pp. 101-102)

Unlike Suchenwirt Gelre names himself in four of his twelve *Ehrenreden*. In the poem dedicated to Hertooch van Gulic, for example, the lady inquires: "Are you not Gelre? Then in the name of God tell us about our hero!"

> En bistu niet geheiten Gelre?
> Du pleechst te dichten ente scriven;
> Heef aen; ten zal nyet achter bliven,
> Begin in die name ons Heren;
> Dat hi di wisen moet ende leren,
> Ende hi di int herte zende
> Te dichten tbegin mitten ende.   (p. 100)

By writing in the first person both poets identify themselves closely with their poems. Where Gelre does mention his own name, it is in an allegorical dialogue with a lady. In a similar situation, in the poem dedicated to Ulrich von Pfannberg (XI), Suchenwirt does not reveal his own name.

The motivation behind the *Ehrenreden* remains a mystery. They honor both living and dead heroes. Furthermore, in many cases they were written years after the death of the hero which precludes their function as funeral orations. There is no documentary proof that the heroes or their relatives commissioned the poems or remunerated the poets. The similarity between Gelre and Suchenwirt is striking. The possibility of their knowing each other or following a common model is very intriguing. Even where their poems differ, it is obvious that both heralds were part of the same literary climate.

The longest and one of the most interesting of Suchenwirt's *Ehrenreden* is dedicated to Hans von Traun (XVIII). There are very few references to this Hans von Traun. He came from a very old family which appears in documents in the eleventh century. Hans was the son of Hartnit von Traun and Abensberg and Adelburg von Hartheim. For many years he was curator in Freystadt (in the *Mühlviertel*); he appears in documents from 1362 and 1363 as provincial governor "ob der Enns." In 1320 he was listed as benefactor of the priests at Horsing. Valentin Preuenheuber includes a short biography of Hans' life in his *Annales Styrenses* which is in turn quoted by other biographers.

Primisser claims that Preuenheuber obtained his information
about Hans von Traun from Suchenwirt's poem since he cites as
his source "ex manuscript. de rebus gestis D. Joan, Baronis a
Traun."[254] This is not very conclusive evidence: the information quoted by Preuenhueber coincides with Suchenwirt's,
but this should not have been difficult to obtain.   Johann
Freiherr von Hoheneck quotes Preuenhueber's biography almost
verbatim and then actually cites part of Suchenwirt's *Ehrenrede*.
Unfortunately he does not indicate which manuscript he used.[255]
Preuenhueber states that Hans died in 1363 and was buried in
the monastery at Wyllering. However, Suchenwirt refers to
events in Hans' life which occurred in the years 1369 and
1370; Seemüller cites a document in which Hans appears on
June 7, 1378.[256]

The poem begins (part I) in allegorical fashion. The
order of knights is orphaned for Death has taken away the
darling of *Frau Ehre*. Suchenwirt compares himself and his art
with that of an inexperienced hunter in the wilderness. He
cannot detect the tracks of art and hunts confusedly over
many detours among the rocks and on dangerous precipices. Nor
does his hound catch the scent of the stag. The hunting horn
of his senses is deceptive since its resonances sound only at
half volume, with a broken voice, and direct him away from the
trail of art. Nevertheless the poet is not discouraged: "Nu
dar, nu dar, Her sin, wol an!" With the help of God he is
willing to hunt for truth and honor, to describe the deeds of
the hero:

> Gnad nu got, der milde,   XVIII,36
> Dem ich tze iagen pin berait
> Nach seiner verte wirdichait,
> Des hertz ye iagt auf ern pan!--

Suchenwirt launches into an enumeration of Hans' long
and eventful life, omitting the general descriptions of his
character typical of many of the other *Ehrenreden* (part II A
consists of only two lines).

The chronology of the events (part II B) cited in the
poem seems to be generally correct despite the fact that no
dates are given. Hans von Traun began his illustrious career

during one of the many disputes between Austria and her
neighbors. He took part in an engagement at Laa in 1332
between Austria and Bohemia in which the Bohemian brothers
Heinrich and Hans von Lippa were taken prisoner:

> Ein vechten resch vor La geschach,   XVIII,43
> Da man tze paiden seitten sach
> Sechs hundert werleich unde mer:
> Er [Hans] vocht nach seines hertzen ger
> So mandleich durch der veinde schar.

He participated in a campaign to Landau in 1336 with Duke Otto
for Emperor Louis of Bavaria against King John of Bohemia and
Duke Henry of Lower Bavaria. The two opposing camps were
close together on the banks of the Isar. According to the
Königshofen Chronicle Otto and Louis had 5,500 knights and many
soldiers and John and Henry 4,400 knights.[257] Skirmishes took
place daily; Hans von Traun "...vocht...als ein frecher helt"
and was knighted by the Emperor along with young Burkhard von
Ellerbach (IX,56). The two armies stood ready to fight for
twelve days, banners flying, but neither side dared to begin
the real battle. On the thirteenth day finally Louis and Otto
gave up and left for Linz and King John hurried back to Bohemia
to assemble an army at Budweis. In the *Ehrenrede* in honor of
Leutold von Stadeck the credit for no battle and no loss of
life is given to God:

> Got understünd ir streiten: XV,111
> Die her zu paiden seiten
> Tzogten haim mit eren.--

Hans then joined the Bohemian King John in 1345 against King
Casimir of Poland. King John undertook this campaign personally
since he had sworn to touch (he was blind) the walls of the city
of Krakow with his own hands. Despite a desperate shortage of
food, John was able to reach a truce with Casimir and to nego-
tiate a peace. Hans fought bravely against the overpoweringly
large number of enemy.

It is interesting to note that Hans von Traun fought or
at least stood against King John of Bohemia at Landau in 1336,
and then fought for King John in 1345 against King Casimir--thus
are the ways of a soldier of fortune in the fourteenth century.
Hans continually traveled to the place of action.

Hans' service for King Edward III of England and his son, the Black Prince of Wales, continued over a number of years; Suchenwirt enumerates the highlights in chronological order interspersed with other ventures in the service of other masters. The overwhelming talent of the English commanders and the supremacy of the English weapons (especially the long bow) attracted in the middle of the fourteenth century a horde of knights and nobles from many countries to the English flag. At one time in Calais, the assembly point, there was not enough food or lodging to accommodate the large number of foreigners. Froissart claimed that he could not honestly name all those gathered there: "Les Allemans et les messenaires d'estrainges pays ne poroie savoir tous nommer: si m'en tairay atant."[258]

About 1345, after the peace at Krakow, Hans von Traun traveled to England where the English were preparing for war against France. Hans joined King Edward III in the siege of Calais (from August 1345 to August 1347). The English had surrounded the city both on land and on sea. When the King of France attempted to bring provisions by ship, the English burned the ships. In these skirmishes Hans killed many Frenchmen:

>   Di schef mit speisung man verprant.   XVIII,108
>   Do vacht der degen [Hans] hochgemüt
>   Auf den schiffen, daz daz plüt
>   Tze tal must fliezzen in di se;
>   Von den veinden ward awe
>   Geschriern und gesprochen,
>   Durchhawen und durchstochen
>   Vil manger ward von seiner hant!

The city, defended by Jeane de Vienne, was forced to surrender because of a shortage of food. Suchenwirt gives a very vivid picture of the siege including the deplorable conditions where rats were considered a treat and everything made of leather was gobbled up with great joy:

>   In der stat der hunger spilt,   XVIII,125
>   Ein ratt di galt ein alden schilt,
>   Und hielten doch als piderlewt.
>   Si azzen schüch, sil, chünt, und hewt;
>   Allez, daz von leder was,
>   Daz suten si mit haizzem glas;
>   Vor hunger si daz têten!

The city remained in the hands of the English for over two
hundred years. Although Froissart mentions an attempt by the
King of France to free the city from the land side,[259] he does
not include the detail, described by Suchenwirt, of the French
attempt to bring provisions into the city by sea.

A two year cease fire was decided upon and Edward
returned to England. Edward recommended Hans to the Black
Prince with whom he set out for Guienne (in the poem
Gaschkonien) in September of 1355. The Prince's army broke
into Languedoc, conquered the flat land and many cities as far
as Narbonne, and returned to Guienne after eight weeks with
much booty and many prisoners.[260] According to Suchenwirt Hans
accompanied the Prince back to England with the prisoners.
However, Primisser maintains that he continued directly to
Prussia, returning after a few months to the battlefield of
Poitiers.

After his adventures against the heathens Hans von Traun
returned to England and was received with joy by the King who
was assembling an army to invade France. Suchenwirt mistakenly
claims that Edward accompanied his army against the King of
France (this he did ten years earlier at the battle of Crécy).
In fact it was his son, the Black Prince, who was given this
task.[261] Suchenwirt continually refers to the King when he
should have written the Prince. This seems to indicate that
Suchenwirt was writing from second-hand knowledge. The Prince
put Hans in command of eighty lancers:

> Der chünig von Engelant geporn [mistake for Black Prince] XVIII,227
> Schikcht dem degen [Hans] auzerchorn
> Achtzig gläsen stoltzer helt
> Di er dar tzu het auzerwelt,
> Daz er daz her besähe.

Hans fell upon the rearguard of the French which included five
hundred especially chosen men. He fought and scattered them.
On the third day the battle between the French and the English
took place upon a broad field. The Prince presented Hans with
the honor of carrying his banner:

> Von Engelant der chünig her [Prince]   XVIII,253
> Erpot dem gast [Hans] ein grozze er:
> Durch sein ritterleiche gir

```
Enphalich er im di panyr
Des tages mit sein selbes hant.
Sein hertz der mynne tzunder prant,
Da er di wirdichait ansach!--
```

At the end of the battle the Prince awarded Hans a life long
pension of one hundred marks per year:

```
Von Engelant der siges reich [Prince]    XVIII,317
Sprach tzu dem helt [Hans] gar tugentleich:
„Hundert march, di weil ir lebt,
Di mügt ir leihen oder gebt,
Wem ir welt, die habt vor mir,
All iar nach ewrs hertzen gir,
Wo ir seit, in welhem lant."
```

The battle of Poitiers on September 19, 1356, including this
incident, has been discussed above in connection with the poem
of the life of the Black Prince (see pp. 51-56). The two
similar accounts of the life of Hans von Traun by Preuenhueber
and Hoheneck maintain that this was the battle of Crécy which
took place in 1346, but the details clearly do not support
this assumption: instead they coincide with Froissart's account.

After the battle of Poitiers, Hans fought for about ten
weeks in the area between Pytschorel and Tol. Pytschorel is
Becherel, a city in Upper Brittany; Tol is the city now called
Dôle, also in Upper Brittany with a bishop's seat. On the
night of St. Martin's Day, when the people of Dôle were eating
and drinking, Hans and his men surprised and won the city which
had been occupied by the French. Then the King of England asked
him to guard the city of Calais were he remained for ten weeks
as captain. The battles between Bercherel and Dôle, the
storming of Dôle, and Hans' command of Calais probably took
place between 1356 and 1360 (the Peace of Brétigny). From
about 1359 to the following year the King of England roamed
through the eastern provinces of France devastating the country-
side--using Calais as his headquarters.

Hans returned home and did not appear with the English
again until 1369. Then while crossing the channel from Calais
he engaged in a battle with a French ship and was able to
bring the English king prisoners and booty as well as winning
fame and honor for himself. In this year (1369) the French
attempted to invade England. Froissart merely writes:

En ce temps faisoit li roys de Franche le plus bel et le plus
grant aupareil de navie que on euist oncques mès veu sus le
revière de Saine, mouvant de Roem jusques à Harflues, et avoit
li dis roys entention et désir très-grant que d'envoyer son
frère le ducq de Bourgoingne en Engleterre gaster et essillier
le pays.262

Hoheneck must have had more detailed information for he writes:

Da der Krieg zwischen Frankreich und Englland wider angieng/ zog
er dem König in Engelland zu mit viertzig Pferden/ der ihn darumb
ersucht hat/ der schickt ihne in Franckreich mit Volck/ Calais,
so die Frantzosen belagert/ zu entschütten/ da er der Stadt halff/
und den Frantzosen jagt. Und als er wider nach Engelland über-
fahren wolt/ ward er von der Frantzösischen Armada angesprengt/
der er sich nicht allein wehret/ sondern zehen Schiff mit Guth
und Leuth dem König in Engelland gefangen brachte. Da er weg
wolt, schenckt ihm der König ein goldene Ketten und 600 March
Silber/ der Printz auch/ sein zu dencken/ einen köstlichen Ring/
und andere Haab.263

Between the campaign to Guienne with the Black Prince
and the battle of Poitiers, between October 1355 and September
1356, Hans fought against the heathens. First he rode towards
Lithuania where he, with nine of his men, surprised the enemy,
killing seven and taking five prisoners. Then after choosing
the twenty-six best men he again attacked the heathens, killing
thirty-two. He accompanied the Teutonic knights to Livonia
against the White Russians where he was made captain under the
banner of St. George:

Der edel helt [Hans] ward haubetman   XVIII,187
Sand Görgen, und fürt seinen van
Mit den gesten an der weil.

After this he killed the Duke of the Russians with his own
hands. He and his army continued their successful venture as
far as the city of Eisenburg (modern Izborsk) in White Russia.
Since they were unable to capture the city, the army retreated
and Hans von Traun returned to England.

After the battle of Poitiers (ca. 1358/59), Hans
returned home to Austria and came to the aid of Ulrich von
Walsee against the Bohemian nobles of Neuhaus. Here the dates
are confusing. A dispute between Eberhard von Walsee and
Heinrich von Neuhaus took place in 1351. The *Zwettler Chronicle*
reports:

Anno D.MCCCLI. Factum est magnum disturbium in Dominis de
Walse, et Dominis de Nova Domo, ita quod tota Austria fere

vastata fuerit. Tandem Dominus de Nova Domo capitur, et pax
redintegratur.[264]

The Bohemians began the argument by plundering and burning the
markets and villages from Freystadt to Hellmonsee near Linz and
to Ottensheim. Eberhard von Walsee, with an army of nobles as
well as peasants, pushed the maurading Bohemians back across
the Austrian borders.[265] The *Salzburg Chronicle* suggests that
the dispute broke out again in 1386:

> Item Pataviensis, et Capitaneus in Lintza Rempertus de Walse,
> et aliarum civitatum Anasi et Wels Burgenses castrum Comitis
> de Schawmberg, Newnhaus nuncupatum obsidebant; sed postea per
> placita recesserung.[266]

Although neither of these dates corresponds with Suchenwirt's
chronology, it seems clear that the Austrian-Bohemian feuds
were continuous. From here Hans set off to Gynis (probably
in Bohemia) at his own expense. One day he and seven of his
men rode out into the field searching for adventure when they
came upon twenty of the enemy; they took seven with them and
killed thirteen. Suchenwirt describes this incident in terms
typical of the courtly epic:

> Gen Gynis er tze reiten phlag,   XVIII,381
> Da er tzwai gantze moneyd lag
> Auf seinen phennig, unvertzait.
> Eins tages er selb sybenter rait
> Tze veld durch abentewre,
> Di vand der gehewre:
> Ir tzwaintzich an in chamen,
> Der syben da mit namen
> Beliben auf dem velde tot,
> Di andern liten grozze not,
> Dreitzehen vie der mütes reich:
> Di abentewr was ritterleich!

Then Hans joined Duke Albert II (referred to here as
der alte) at Zurich:

> Darnach der helt für Tzürich rait   XVIII,393
> Mit hertzog Albrecht unvertzait
> Von Östereich, dem alten;
> Der hat sein lob behalten,
> Daz er nie prach der ern glid.

He was captain of the men of Bishop Gottfried of Passau. He
won praise and honor at Zurich and also at the storming of
Weissenhorn (a little town in the former Swabian Austria, not
far from Constance on Lake Constance). He was severely wounded,
even held for dead; on the next day the city gave itself over

to the Duke:

> An dem stürm tze Weizzenhorn   XVIII,402
> Ward er gewarffen ungefüg;
> Für tot man in von danne trüg!
> Des andern tags gab man di stat
> Hertzog Albrecht mit weisem rat.--

Duke Albert's campaigns to Zurich took place in 1351 and 1354, dates which do not quite coincide with the time sequences presented here by Suchenwirt.

As the Bishop's captain Hans aided the Austrians against the Bavarians at Salzburg, at Mühldorf, and at Dornberg. The *Salzburg Chronicle* states for the year 1358:

> Eodem anno in Adventu Domini, in die Barbaræ Dux Stephanus adversabatur Metropolitano Salzburgensi, et fundavit castrum in Lichtentann, et castrum in Dornberch, et multa mala intulit suis hominibus. Tandem Metropolitanus cum fratre suo Episcopo Pataviensi se vindicavit in quantum potuit, Dornberch devastando expugnavit, et villas combussit.[267]

This dispute was settled the next year by the Duke of Austria in Passau. A defense of Mühldorf against the Bavarians is described in the *Salzburg Chronicle* in the year 1364, but Ulrich Weissenegger is named as defender, not Hans von Traun:

> Duces etiam Bawariæ circumvallaverunt civitatem Muldorf circiter tres menses cum civitatensibus et copioso popula: nec machinis, nec impugnationibus poterant quidquam proficere, quia Ulricus Weisenekkarius vixmet quadragesimus armatus, Capitaneus dictae civitatis, unacum belligeris civibus eis viriliter et animose repugnavit. Tunc Archiepiscopus et Muldorfenses continuo supplicabant Duci Austriæ, quantenus eis subveniret, sicut sponderat.[268]

The report of mistreatment of merchants in Friuli induced Duke Rudolf IV to undertake a campaign into Aquileia in 1361 accompanied by Hans von Traun. The Austrians captured Meussau, Haunberg, and Rosatz before the animosities were halted. The Patriarch was persuaded to travel to Vienna where he compromised and accepted Rudolf's mediation. However, since the two sides could not unite, the war broke out anew. The *Zwettler Chronicle* describes this affair as follows:

> Item Dux Rudolfus juxta portum Naonis invasus a Patriarcha Aquilegiensi, collecto exercitu de Austria occurrit ei contra gradum se viriliter defendens, et eundem, ad instantiam Cæsaris, in gratiam, recepit, satisfacturum ei de omnibus expensis in duplo, ut dicitur. Obierunt etiam Marchio de Branburck, Dux Bavariæ circa fest um S. Dionysii, et Purckhardus

de Maidburck circa festum S. Martini, et Dux Mediolanensis.
Partiarcha Wiennam veniens cum Duce, Capellam S. Mariae in
Ottenhaym renovatam consecraert.[269]

Suchenwirt describes this campaign similarly:

Er [Hans] für mit dem von Östereich   XVIII,421
Hertzog Rüdolf mächtichleich
In Frigaul, da auf der vart
Meusau von erst gestürmet wart,
Daz sich dem fürsten tugenthaft
Ergeben müst durch seine chraft;
Haunwerch ergab sich auch da pey
Und Rosatz; der schanden frey,
Des lob nach hohen ern ranch.
Den patrierch man dartzu twanch
Mit chrieg, daz er gen Wienn rait.

In 1364 while the Bavarians were besieging the Salzburg
controlled city of Mühldorf, Duke Rudolf rode against Ried.
According to the *Salzburg Chronicle*:

Tunc primo ascendit Dux Austriæ obsidens Ried, quod per placita
[i.e. by treaty] sibi tradebatur; at tamen Johannes, dictus
Meissawer, Ministerialis Australis ante placita ibi ictibus
interimebatur.[270]

Hans von Meissau was killed at the storming of Ried. Suchenwirt describes it thus:

Darnach der degen unvertzait [Hans]   XVIII,432
Mit hertzog Rüdolf tzoch für Ried,
Da man her Hans von Meyssaw schied
Mit werffen von dem leben.

The *Zwettler Chronicle* describes the death in somewhat more
detail: "...ubi ictu lapidis machinæ...interemtus est Q. de
Meissaw."[271]

Hans returned to his own lands which were being
ravished by the Bohemians. He managed to drive them away
inflicting many injuries upon the enemy, but also receiving
wounds himself. Nevertheless in 1367, again as captain of the
Bishop of Passau, he fought against the Bavarians. The *Salzburg
Chronicle* relates the following incident:

Eodem anno Stephanus Dux Bawariæ desponsavit sibi filiam Domini
Mediolanensis. Quo circa exegit a Plebanis, seu rusticis et
colonis in terra Bawariæ avenam multam; ab unox scaffas, ab
uno quinque secumdem majus et minus, quod fuit inauditum apud
antiquos Duces Bawariæ.[272]

Hans and his men drove the rebellious citizens of Passau into
the field where four hundred were killed, three hundred

captured, and the city finally surrendered. This was a very
bloody battle. Suchenwirt cleverly employs the term *spil* which
merely intensifies the terribleness (my italics):

> Darnach daz *spil* ward gar unfüzz,   XVIII,460
> Da gie ez durch einander,
> Waz ainer sucht daz vand er
> Mit schiezzen, slahen, stechen:
> Man sach den degen frechen
> Durch den hauffen dringen,
> Er *spilt* mit in „der chlingen",
> Daz ir do mit grimmer not
> Wol vir hundert bliben tot...

At the request of Duke Albert III Hans von Traun carried
the Austrian banner accompanying Emperor Charles IV to Rome in
1368. In 1369 Hans joined the Emperor, the Pope, the Patriarch,
the Dukes of Austria, and the Count of Görz against the
Venetians who were besieging Triest. Suchenwirt gives an
illuminating description of the difficulties of medieval warfare:

> Da stürmt ain her daz ander her   XVIII,480
> Gar mandleich sunder wanchen:
> Tieff gräben, und hoch planchen,
> Di vortail warn gar tze groz;
> Ainn man warf, den anndern schoz,
> Da mit erwert man di pastey!--

The Venetians won the city (bastion) by use of war machines,
lobbing missiles across the deep moats, while the defenders
shot at them from the inside.

After the defense of Triest, Hans appears again in
Calais and in England, and then in Prussia with Duke Leopold
of Austria in 1370. Duke Leopold, accompanied by the Grand
Master Martini, entered into Samogitia with four armies,
devastated the land far and wide. Again the purpose of the
campaign was to win knightly honor and fame. The warm
weather which kept the rivers from freezing made it necessary
for the knights to retreat (a frequent problem):

> Der chom da hin gedrungen   XVIII,502
> Mit mangem hoch getewertem helt,
> Di er dartzu het auzerwelt,
> Daz er wolt in di haidenschaft
> Ein rais mit ritterleicher chraft
> Erleich tziehen mit gewalt.
> Nu was der winder nicht so chalt,
> Da von di rais ward wenndich.--

This is the last military deed which Suchenwirt enumerates in
the life of Hans von Traun:

> Do tzoch der hoch genenndich   XVIII,510
> Tze lant, da er mit ern lebt.

Part II C consists of an elaboration of Hans' moral
characteristics--his loyalty, constancy, courage, honor,
honesty--as well as a general lament; normally this would fall
into part II A. Then Suchenwirt states that Hans served the
English against the French for three years minus twelve weeks.
This in no way corresponds to his entire service for the
English; perhaps Suchenwirt is only referring to the period of
his service from the campaign to Guienne in 1355 until after
the battle of Poitiers. The manuscript from which Hoheneck
copied appears more accurate:

> Hat in Kriegen zugebracht bey 30. Jahren nach einander/ allein
> in den drey Feldzügen auf des Königs von Engelland Seithen 9.
> Jahr/ und 30. Wochen in Schlachten/ Scharmützel/ Stürmen/ u.
> vil erlitten/ und grosse That begangen.273

Before Suchenwirt blazons Hans' arms, he indulges in a
typical humility formula and lament. In the subjunctive he
maintains that he *would* describe the coat of arms *if* he *were not*
incapable of such art:

> Wär ich der chünste nicht tze chranch,   XVIII,542
> Ich tät ew seine wappen chunt.

He then proceeds to correctly blazon (part III A) the arms of
the House of Traun (per pale argent and sable):

> Gar maisterleich so was der schilt   XVIII,546
> Von tzobel und von mer griezzen
> In blanch weiz, den nie liezzen
> Di manhait und die mynne
> Auz hertzen noch auz sinne.

Here the black and white symbolize manliness and love or
rationality and sentimentality--the two opposites which are so
vital to the happiness of man.

On the helmet is a pair of wings, joined--one white, the
other black:

> Auf seinem helm fürt der helt   XVIII,551
> Von den tzwain varben auzerwelt
> Zwo flüg gar ritterleichen.--

The poem concludes with an intercessary prayer (part II D) to

Christ and the Virgin Mary to protect him from the flames of
hell. Suchenwirt then names the hero (part III B), Hans von
Traun, and finally commends his soul to the protection of St.
George:

>Daz er der pest in Östereich   XVIII,564
>Vil manich iar gehaizzen hat,
>Der tewrist mit mandleicher tat.
>Sand Görg, du edler ritter güt,
>Hab di sele sein in hüt!
>Des pitt ich dich durch deine güt:
>Er het ye ritterleich gemüt!

These last seven lines could have been added on the occasion of
a ceremony, such as for the *Societas Templois*. The poem commences
with a reference to the order of knighthood and concludes with
a prayer to St. George. The only documentary information
pertaining to the *Societas Templois* is a list of members and of
donations made by some of the members (see p. 189). Many of
Suchenwirt's heroes were associated with the society; many of
them made pilgrimages to Prussia where they were knighted. It
is possible that this, as well as the other *Ehrenreden*, may have
been composed expressly for the *Societas Templois*. The grail
society may have performed ceremonies in which past members
were honored by the recitation of an *Ehrenrede*. Since both the coat
of arms and the name of the hero are not revealed until the conclusion of the poem, the audience must have been cognizant
of the subject by other means.

The four poems (III, IV, V, XVIII) discussed in detail
above illustrate the form and content of Suchenwirt's works
belonging to the broad genre of heraldic poetry. The death
laments (III, V) illustrate the transition from traditional
laments discussed in chapter III to the highly developed
formulaic *Ehrenreden*. The poem about Albert's Prussian campaign
(IV) is representative of the contents of both political-
historical poems and *Ehrenreden*. It indicates that Suchenwirt
was capable of chronicling a specific event in detail when not
restrained by the confines of the *Ehrenrede* formula. Finally
the *Ehrenrede* dedicated to Hans von Traun (XVIII) demonstrates
the manner in which Suchenwirt combines the various elements of
his prototypes into the highly formalized genre of *Ehrenrede*.

His competence in these diverse components is perhaps what differentiates his poetry from that of his predecessors; the combination of heraldry, history, and politics distinguishes the *Ehrenrede* from other types of poetry.

VI. PETER SUCHENWIRT AS HERALD

Although Suchenwirt was the first to employ the term
"herald" (erald) in German, he does not really elaborate upon the
position or duties of heralds. Presumably these were understood and taken for granted by his audience. However, information regarding heralds may be gleaned from passing remarks
made by Suchenwirt, and, of course, the prime example of a
herald's art is found in Suchenwirt's handling of heraldic
material.

Suchenwirt writes about the "order" of travelers which
is dependent upon the generosity of the nobility:

>   Als gerndem orden wol antzimpt,   XXIX,5
>   Der güt durich got, durich ere nympt.

He claims to belong to this "order" of *farende liute* which, like
other medieval orders (clergy, nobility, peasantry), was very
broad in scope:

>   ...„Ich nym durich er güt   XXIX,22
>   Und pin tze recht ein gernder man."

His membership in the "order" does not cast very much light on
heralds. Heralds and *gernde leüt* who accompanied Duke Albert
III and others on the campaign to Prussia enjoyed the gifts of
very generous patrons:

>   Eralden und gernde leüt   IV,139
>   Des fursten mild al da erfrewt.

One of the specific duties of the heralds (and also of the
pursuivants) was to announce the names of their masters:

>   Fürsten, grafen, freyen,   XV,119
>   Der namen hört man chreyen
>   Von den eralden, persewant.

Suchenwirt does not make a class distinction between heralds
and pursuivants, although, by naming them separately, he
suggests that he may not have considered them entirely
synonymous.

In the poem "Von der Mynn slaff" (XXX) Suchenwirt
expressly says that he is familiar with coats of arms. *Frau
Minne* wants to stage a tournament; she needs a man who can
distinguish among coats of arms and who will announce the
tournament far and wide:

„Und hiet wir einen chnappen,   XXX,169
Dem underschaid der wappen
Wær mit namen wol bechant,
Der solt verchunden in di lant
Der türnay in dew Vräudenaw."

Suchenwirt recommends himself for the task:

„Vraw, so nemt den Suechenwirt,   XXX,177
Der red mit worten schon florirt,
Den vindet man in Österreich
Pey den fürsten tugentleich."

Here again the close connection between heralds and tournaments
is asserted. In this case the purpose of the tournament is to
reinstate the lost courtly virtues:

Der turnay macht gesellen güt,   XXX,242
Er lert auch lewt derchennen
Ye nach der tat mit nennen.

At the beginning of the *Ehrenrede* dedicated to Burgrave
Albert of Nuremberg, Suchenwirt exhorts the nobility, the
fair ladies, as well as the *chnappen von der wappen,* to listen to
him extol the virtues of his hero:

Ir chnappen von den wappen hört,   VII,11
Tzung unde munt mit lieb erpört,
Dy von den wappen tichtens phlegen,
Nicht lat mit willen underwegen,
Ir übt den sin und auch den müt
Von dem, der dik sein edel plüt
In ritterschaft verreret hat,
Dem hat der tot gesprochen mat
An seines lebens sterke.

In the *Ehrenreden* Suchenwirt clearly states that
describing coats of arms is one of his talents, even duties:

Ach chunst, nu pin ich umbereit   XII,104
Tzu chunden hie der wappen sein.

Occasionally he appeals to God for help:

Ach got, wer ich der chunste rich,   XIII,202
Daz ich di edeln wappen sein
Verchundet nach dem willen mein,
Di er mit grozzen ern hat
Gefüret dik an maniger stat!

And frequently he overstates his case, protesting his modesty
too much:

Wær meiner zungen hamer   XVI,184
Werait mit rechter chunste,
So daz ich mit vernunste
Der hochgetewrten wappen grunt
Den edeln tæt mit worten chunt!

Suchenwirt's heraldic language is typical of fourteenth
century heraldry and indicates his careful attention to his
profession. He uses technical terms such as *vysiren, visieren,*
and *plasnieren* to describe and articulate a coat of arms
according to the proper heraldic terminology:[274]

> Des wappen ich vysiren wil.   VI,198

> Wer ich der chünsten nu berait,   VIII,236
> Daz ich visiert die wapen sein!

> Daz ich der wappen visament   VII,210
> Plasnierte....

Suchenwirt blazons correctly when he describes first the
surface or field of the shield and its colors; second, the
principal charge resting on the field; third, the secondary
charges resting on the field; and fourth, the objects resting
on the charges.[275]

Suchenwirt's choice of vocabulary to describe the
heraldic tinctures is limited, but effective. First he
recognizes the six basic colors--gold, silver, red, green,
black, and blue:[276]

> Der schilt der was quartiret rein   VII,216
> Mit den pesten varben tzweyn,
> Dy von den sechsen chomen sein.

Gold is referred to a simply gold or as the color of camels:

> Des goldes art gamillen var.   III,166

Silver is pearl, seasand or mother of pearl, ermine:

> Ain part di geit liechten schein   I,175
> Von perlein chlar und von rubein.

> Tzway quartir klar von perlen vein,   VII,219
> Dy ander tzway nach tzobl var.

> Der schilt in planchweis waz getailt   XVII,176
> Von zobel und von mirgriesse vein;
> Auch furt er auf dem helm sein
> Ein swann hals von perlein chlar.

> Gar maisterleich so was der schilt   XVIII,546
> Von tzobel und von mer griezzen.

> Den strauzzen hals hermleinen.   I,191

In one instance ermine *(harm)* does not seem to refer merely to
the color silver, but rather to the fur itself. Herdegen von
Pettau wore a helmet with an anchor made out of ermine fur:

> Dar auf ein ancher, also tzart   XII,121
> Von harm geswentzet nach seiner art.

Red is cited as ruby or as *chelenroth*. The latter term comes
from *gueules;* it is from the red throat or gullet of an animal:

> Den schilt man sach gehewre   XI,294
> Von chelen rot erscheinen,
> Den tzirt ich mit rubeinen.

Green is always emerald green:

> Den schilt man sach gar sunder spot   X,248
> Smaragden grün pei chlarem golt.

Black is referred to as sable:

> Dy ander tzway nach tzobl var.   VII,220
>
> Von zobel hat dar in ein wurm.   XII,108

Suchenwirt calls blue either sky blue, azure blue, or
sapphire blue:

> Lasur pla nach himel var,   XVI,199
> Darinn drey stern von golde chlar.
>
> Ein sameid, pla, saffirnvar.   XXIV,114

Suchenwirt employs a seventh tincture brown which he designates
by *ademas* and sapphire. Brown occasionally appears in other
German coats of arms as a seventh tincture. *Adamas* was considered to be a precious stone and was frequently identified with
the diamond; the diamond, in turn, was traditionally connected
with the tincture sable. Furthermore, brown was frequently
employed to mean dark. Thus Suchenwirt blazons the Carinthian
coat of arms as follows:

> Drey leben praün von ademas.   III,171
> In parre weis gelenket.

Had the black Carinthian lions not been so well known, one
might assume that Suchenwirt was referring to the "proper" color
of the animals as brown. In this case, however, the confusion
seems to revolve around the distinctions among brown, *adamas,*
diamond, and black. Similarly Suchenwirt blazons the arms of
the Walsee family as sapphire brown:

> Der schilt was chostper und reich,   XIII,207
> Saffirn brawn gar meisterleich
> Gereichet und geheret.

These arms also must have been quite well known to Suchenwirt,
and thus the misunderstanding must have to do with the nature
of the sapphire (does the term "sapphire" refer to the color
blue or to a brown stone?).

Generally Suchenwirt lets the colors speak for themselves; he describes the shield of Ulrich von Cilli as follows:

> Der schilt der glestet reicher art   XVI,192
> In rechter röt, als ein rubein,
> Dar inne zwo fasch von perla vein
> In parr weys gestrechet,
> In rechter mazz volrechet.

Occasionally, however, Suchenwirt adds his own opinions; he
maintains that the pearl (silver, argent) and the sable (black)
of the arms of Burgrave Albert of Nuremberg (House of Hohenzollern) are the best two colors among the six:

> Der schilt der was quartiret rein   VII,216
> Mit den pesten varben tzweyn,
> Dy von den sechsen chomen sein:
> Tzway quartir klar von perlen vein,
> Di ander tzway nach tzobl var.

The same tinctures in the arms of Hans von Traun represent
manliness *(manhait)* and courtly love *(mynne)* from the mind and
from the heart--discussed in the eighteenth century under the
rubric of "rationality" and "sentimentality:"

> Gar maisterleich so was der schilt   XVIII,546
> Von tzobel und von mer griezzen
> In blanch weiz, den nie liezzen
> Di manhait und di mynne
> Auz hertzen noch auz sinne.

Not only are the tinctures named after the most
precious materials and stones, but also the individual parts
of the shields and charges are polished, *polliret* or *purliert,*
made shining:

> Dar in leit manich edel stain   I,187
> Verworcht und auch polliret rain.

Suchenwirt describes the three cornered shield of the
time; the upper edge, the chief, was called the *ort,* the
opposite end, the base, the *spitz:*

> In blank weis chrichen gen dem ort   XIV,336
> Ein krebzen gleich dem zobl var.

> Der ort zu tal, der spitz enpor [i.e. inverted]   III,161

> Von tzobel hat dar in ein wurm   XII,108
> Den badel in den spitz gepogen.

Only in one case is Suchenwirt's terminology somewhat
confusing: he uses *di par* to indicate a horizonzal division
(Latin *fascia,* English fess). However, there is also a

French heraldic term *barre* which designates a diagonal bar
from left to right which is not to be mistaken for Suchenwirt's
par:

>   Des rot unertik scheinet.   III,138
>   Di par, die ee gefeinet
>   Mit morgen-tau geperlt lak.

This passage blazons the Austrian arms (gules, a fess argent).
At the same time Suchenwirt employs the term *fasch* also to mean
a horizontal division. He then adds the term *parrweis* to
describe precisely several horizontal divisions:

>   Dar inne zwo vasch von perla vein   XVI,194
>   In parr weys gestrechet,
>   In rechter mazz volrechet.

>   In den rubeinen reichen   VI,208
>   Lag ein par in parrweis.

The fact that *parrweis* comes from *par* is certainly a pleonasm:

>   Drey leon, di so vraidikleich   VI,204
>   Sahen gen der veinde tyust,
>   In parrweis vor seiner prust.

Three horizontally aligned diamonds *(ruten)* are blazoned as
follows:

>   Der ruten glast ich meret   XI,298
>   Mit perlein vein getziret gar,
>   Di man ee sach von silber var
>   In parra weis di dreye.

A vertical division is called *part,* English pale. *Das partiren*
means a lengthwise division:

>   Den schilt man sicht getziret   I,173
>   In planchweis gleich partiret,
>   Ain part di gelt liechten schein
>   Von perlein chlar und von rubein,
>   Purliert, acht stukch sind dar gelait
>   In parraweiz und wol berait,
>   Di ander part ist hymel pla...

Planchweis, thus, refers to a vertical division, *parrweis* to a
horizontal.[277]

The expression *in pellunch* referring to parallel arches
is found only once in Suchenwirt's work, in the poem honoring
Hans von Chappel:[278]

>   den schilt man sleht geeziret   2,117
>   in pellunch gepogiret
>   sechs pogen geben liechten schein
>   uon perlein chlar und uon rubein.

Einen schild teilen means to divide a shield in half
horizontally (French *couper*, English per fess). For example,
the Austrian shield:

> Den schilt man sach geteilet   VI,199
> In plank weis ungemeilet.

Quartiren means to divide into four parts *(quadripertiri, écarteler)*,
to quarter; *ein quartir* is a quarter field:

> Der schilt der was quartiret rein   VII,216
> Mit den pesten varben tzweyn,
> Dy von den sechsen chomen sein:
> Tzway quartir klar von perlen vein,
> Dy ander tzway nach tzobl var.

The coat of arms of the Ellerbach family, gold and green
quartered, is thus blazoned by Suchenwirt:

> Der schilt gab zwayer varbe schein,   VIII,238
> Gar maisterleich quartieret,
> Daz golt smaragden zieret.

Other heraldic terms employed by Suchenwirt include the
rute, diamond or lozenge,

> Der ruten glast ich meret   XI,298
> Mit perlein vein getziret gar.

the *flüg*, a pair of joined wings,

> Ein flüg von chlarem golde reich   XV,212
> Des pesten her von orient.

the *quast*, a plume of hen or peacock feathers. The peacock
plume was the traditional helmet crest for the Austrian princes.

> Von hannevedern einen chwast   XVI,205
> Nach zobel var...

> Von phaben fedren einen quast.   III,151

> Do sich der quast in winde rürt   XI,304
> Gar hurtleich gen der veinde schar
> Von hannen vedern tzowel var
> Auf seines glantzen helmes dach.

The mantling or *lambrequins*, the flowing drapery which
fluttered about the helmet, is called *chobertewer (covertiure,
couverture)* by Suchenwirt whereas the usual German term was
Helmdecke. Suchenwirt only describes this appendage twice as
for example in the arms of Friedrich von Kreußpeck where the
relationship between the crest and the mantling is essential:

> Von tzobl ein krebz durch wirde stewer   XIV,339
> Pegriffen het daz chobertewer
> Mit den vodern schern tzwein;

> Als sust was er gestrechet rein,
> Als er tzu tal nach preises gust
> Kem geschozzen durch den luft.

Only once again does Suchenwirt describe the mantling, namely in connection with the coat of arms of Duke Albert II of Austria:

> der helm geit reiches glastes prehen,   -3,145
> helmdekch und chowertewer
> uon sameid rot alsam ein fewer.

The animals in the coats of arms often stare menacingly toward the enemy:

> Drey leon, die so vraidikleich   VI,204
> Sahen gen der veinde tyust.

> Von tzobel hat dar in ein wurm...   XII,108
> Den hals gepogn, nicht gestracht,
> Den munt nach grimmichleicher acht
> Fur sich geschikcht und auf getan...
> Sein augen zornichleichen sehen
> Und gebn nach dem schilde glast.

The shield of Leutold of Stadeck was not only frightening:

> Dar inn ein lew von perlein reich   XV,199
> In planch weis, den man vraidichleich
> Sach inn dem schilde chlimmen
> Und gen den veinden limmen,
> Recht als er lebt in tzornes pein.

It was also well known to the enemy:

> Der schilt den veinden was bechant   XV,196
> In sturm und auch in streites not.

Frequently animal charges are alluded to instead of the princes or states which they represent. Thus in the poem "Die red haizzt der umbchert Wagen" (XXXVI) Suchenwirt implores Emperor Wenceslaus (whose arms include both the lion, *Leb*, of Bohemia and the eagle, *Ar*, of the Empire) to wake up and settle the feuds in Italy: the "cart" of Carrara (Francesco Carrara who bore a cart, *il carro*, in his shield) and the "serpent" of Milan (Galeazzo Visconti with a serpent in his shield) had driven out the "dog" of Verona, in German *Bern* or *Pern* (Antonio Cane della Scala):

> Wol auf, her Leb und auch her Ar,   XXXVI,1
> Ir slaffet gar tze lange!
> Secht, wie ez in den landen var:
> Der Wag und auch die Slange
> Den Hund von Pern han vertriben.

Suchenwirt's interest in heraldry and his skill in the

art of heraldic description are not limited to the main parts
of the shield, but also include detailed descriptions of the
extremities of heraldic animals. For example, his blazon of
the ostrich neck on the helmet of King Louis of Hungary:

> Den strauzzen hals hermleinen,   I,191
> Sein augen von rubeinen
> Glesten gen der veinde schar,
> Der snabel ist von golde gar,
> Dar inn er fürt ze preisen
> Gestalt, als ein hüfeysen
> Gepogen chlar von golde vein.
> Gechrönet ist daz hawbet sein
> Mit golde reich.

On the shield of Herdegen von Pettau Suchenwirt describes the
worm (snake, serpent) of sable with a tongue of rubies, and

> Sein augen zornichleichen sehen   XII,118
> Und gebn nach dem schilde glast.

> (i.e. the eyes, like the shield, are of gold)

Leutold von Stadeck wears a shield with a pearl lion,

> Tzung, tzend, und chlaw von golde chlar.   XV,206

Friedrich von Lochen wears on his helmet a swan's neck of pearl:

> Über den hals so waz ein rant   XVII,182
> Nach zobelvar gestekchet
> Von hannveder gerekchet;
> Dez swannen augen gaben schein
> In rechter röt als zwen rübein,
> Die plikchten gen der veinde schar;
> Der snabel was von golde chlar.

When a shield had an indeterminate number of figures,
they were "strewn," *gestrewt,* as in half of the shield of King Louis
of Hungary (azure, semé of fleurs-de-lis or):

> Di ander part ist hymel pla,   I,179
> Dar auf reichlich getziret da
> Sind lilygen reich von gold erhaben
> Gestrewt, die dikche stewer gaben.

On the other hand, Suchenwirt blazons a shield with three stars
(two in the chief, one in the base):

> Darinn drey stern von golde chlar,   XVI,200
> Gen yedem ort geyt ayner glitz,
> Der dritt gesenchet den dem spitz.

In describing the condition or position of a charge or figure
the sterm "stretched," *gestreckt* is used, e.g. the crab on the
helmet of Friedrich von Kreußpeck was "stretched" vertically
from the base to the chief, looking toward the sky:

    Als sust was er gestrechet rein,   XIV,342
    Als er tzu tal nach preises guft
    Kem geschozzen durch den luft.

The two stripes in the arms of the Count of Cilli are
"stretched" horizontally:

    Dar inne zwo vasch von perla vein   XVI,194
    In parr weys gestrechet.

If the helmet includes the same figure found in the shield,
this is indicated by: *nach dem schilde*. Thus the helmet decoration of Ellerbach is blazoned:

    Do fürt der edel auzerchorn   IX,231
    Nach dem schilde reich tzwai horn.

    (i.e. two horns divided in half, horizontally, gold/green and
    green/gold)

Duke Henry of Carinthia wore a helmet with a brim:

    Auf dem helm ein chostleich sach,   VI,213
    Ein rundel, dem man wirde iach,
    Nach dem schilt getzieret schon.

Most of the coats of arms blazoned by Suchenwirt belong
to old families and are very simple--black and silver, red and
silver, and green and gold. Among the more complicated are'
shields which have obvious symbolic meaning based on the
bearers' names or family history known as rebuses or canting
arms: for Moriz von Haunfeld a red shield with a golden hoe
(Hauen):

    des schildes glast erscheinet   1,74
    rubeyn rot gefeynet,
    als man in wunschen solde,
    darin in plankh uon golde
    ein hawen man gecziret sach.

Friedrich von Kreußpeck (Krebsbach) bore a black crab *(Krebs)*
crawling toward the top of the shield:

    Der schilt der gab von golde schein,   XIV,334
    Dor in man sach durch preises hort
    In blank weis chrichen gen dem ort
    Ein krebzen gleich dem zobl var.

In the shield of Herdegen von Pettau there was a black serpent
(Wurm) with a red tongue and gold eyes reminiscent of the Wurm-
berg, property owned by the family:

    Sein schilt von golt gab lichten schein   XII,106
    In manigem streit und auch in sturm;
    Von tzobel hat dar in ein wurm...

> Dar in ein zung, der farbe man
> Sicht von rubein rote prehen,
> Sein augen zornichleichen sehen
> Und gebn nach dem schilde glast.

An inverted shield indicated mourning. The poem dedicated to Duke Albert II illustrates the trappings of mourning employed by princes and nobility in the fourteenth century. Suchenwirt describes three knights on horseback, each carrying a banner and an inverted sword; each knight wears the inverted coat of arms on his chest. The colors are dull and the peacock plume has sunken to the ground:

> Ein man, der lützel freude wielt,   III,125
> Auf einem ors nach streites litz,
> Daz swert daz hiet er pei dem spitz.

> Der rubein rot enplechet   III,135
> Mit stözzen het des todes hobel,
> Vorselbet als ein plaicher tobel,
> Des rot unertik scheinet.

> Von phaben fedren einen quast   III,151
> Der was zurütten und zerfürt,
> Des orses hüf der quast perürt.

Death has inverted the rays which should gleam forth from the shield of Ulrich von Walsee:

> Des glentzen ist vercheret   XIII,210
> Von des pittern todes slag.

The pearls in the fess shine sadly and palely:

> Dar inn ein vasch getzieret lag   XIII,212
> In parraweis von perlin vyn,
> Di gebent layder trueben schin;
> Ir glentzen ist verplichen gar.

Suchenwirt does not proudly acclaim himself as a herald, most certainly because he was not inordinately proud of his "order." Although heralds held positions of considerable responsibility, they still did not occupy a very high rung on the social ladder. Despite the use of the subjunctive when disclaiming ability and proclaiming his modesty in introducing coats of arms, Suchenwirt clearly proves his proficiency as a herald in his blazons of shields and helmets. His lively sense of humor and fanciful imagination sometimes make for interesting descriptions. For example, if one were to blazon the helmet of Burgrave Albert of Nuremberg in strictly technical terms

as seen in the *Zurich Roll* or in Gelre's *Wapenboeck*, the result
would be "a gold hound dog with red ears." But Suchenwirt
describes the hound dog from real life, its tongue panting
as though it had been chasing a stag through the woods:

> Von golde reich ein praken haubt   VII,223
> Sach man dar ob erscheinen,
> Tzway orn von rubeinen,
> Sein tzungen recht also gestalt,
> Als man vervahen in dem walt
> Den praken sicht nach edler art
> Mit suchen wildes hirtzen vart,
> Sein tzung fur slingen unde lehen
> Von lauf und haizzer sunne brehen.

This again emphasizes the difference between a strictly
heraldic approach to blazon, which is common to heraldic books
and rolls, and a poetic heraldic approach, which is primarily
concerned with imagery and action such as that employed by
Konrad von Würzburg and found in the *Ehrenreden* of Suchenwirt
and Gelre. Neither approach needs to sacrifice technical
accuracy to achieve its goals.

Suchenwirt's approach to history can best be understood
by examining what he has to say about specific historical
events within the framework of the *Ehrenreden*. In the *Ehrenreden*
he describes the deeds of a hero, generally in chronological
order. Although he does not include every event in the hero's
life, it is difficult to posit any definite criteria for his
selection, which may have been based simply on the material
available.

Many of the same events are touched upon by Suchenwirt
in several *Ehrenreden*. His heroes were mostly connected in some
way with the Austrian court and many were members of the *Societas
Templois* in Vienna. For the reader who wishes to have a complete description of an event, most of Suchenwirt's accounts
are frustrating. The specific details which he does include
are frequently related to the sizes of the armies (which are
inherently unreliable and often at variance with contemporary
chronicles) or to human interest sidelights about the particular hero (which are very interesting and usually not
included in contemporary chronicles).

Sometimes by looking at the same event or similar type
of expedition as described in several poems it is possible to
get a more complete picture of what Suchenwirt was attempting
to portray and also to determine the extent of his information.
Only in the case of Duke Albert's Prussian campaign does
Suchenwirt claim to have been an eyewitness. However, in other
poems he claims to have traveled extensively (e.g. see pp. 98-
99), and it is quite possible that he was present at other
occasions described in the *Ehrenreden*.

Practically no country in the world then known is left
out of Suchenwirt's poems. He writes of the adventures of the
Austrian Friedrich von Kreußpeck (XIV) in Seville, Granada,
Aragon, in a campaign against the heathens in Valencia, in
Majorca, even as far as Tunis in the Barbary, Sardinia, Sicily,
Calabria, Rhodes, and Cyprus. Suchenwirt describes the
activities of Hans von Traun in the service of King Edward

III and the Black Prince of England during the siege of Calais,
the campaign into Guienne, the victory at Poitiers, the encounter at Becherel, and the storming of the city of Dôle
(XVIII). More than once Suchenwirt's heroes--Burgrave Albert
of Nuremberg (VII), Friedrich von Kreußpeck (XIV), Margrave
Louis of Brandenburg and his followers including Friedrich von
Lochen (XVII), Moriz von Haunfeld (1)--set out for England,
Scotland, and Ireland to battle against the unruly Scots.
There are strange references to a battle at Trachtal (?) and a
sea encounter with the Spanish which still need to be investi-
gated (XIV). The disputes between the counts of Holland and
the counts of Cleve (1346) are merely alluded to (IX). Campaigns in Sweden, Russia, Norway (XIV), and Denmark (XVII, XVI)
make for fascinating reading.

Suchenwirt's heroes are frequently found in the lands of
the heathen Prussians and Lithuanians (I, III, IV, VII, IX,
XIII, XIV, XV, XVI, XVIII, 1, 2, 4, 5). Also the territories
of Hungary, Serbia, Bulgaria, Croatia, Bosnia provided oppor-
tunities for the Austrian nobles to prove their martial ability
(I, VII, VIII, IX, X, XVI, 2). Suchenwirt's descriptions of
the court of King Louis of Hungary remind one of the court of
Attila or King Arthur where the heroes of the world once
gathered.

In Italy Ulrich von Walsee, Duke Henry of Carinthia,
Friedrich von Kreußpeck, and Hans von Chappel (XIII, VI, XIV,
2) were active in the territories of Friuli, Dalmatia, Lombardy,
and Naples. Suchenwirt elaborates on the gruesome feud among
the lords of Verona, Cararra, and Milan (XXVII), the fate of
Bernado of Milan (XX), the battle of Altopascio (XIV), and the
magnificent march to Rome undertaken by Charles IV, including
his knighting ceremony performed from the Tiber river bridge
(VII, XVI, XVIII). The long trips to the Holy Land, to the
Holy Sepulcher, Mount Sinai, to Alexandria, to Babylon and
India with the return trip through Armenia, Cyprus, Constan-
tinople, Tatary (VII, XIV, VIII, 1) seem incredible for the
time, but constitute a typical medieval topos.

Finally the poet's homeland provides a source for

descriptions: the disputed imperial election between Louis the
Bavarian and Frederick of Austria (XII, XIII, XIV); the
military activities from the battle at Hasenbüchel in 1298 in
which Adolf von Nassau was killed (VI) to the battle of Sempach
in 1386 which cost the life of Duke Leopold of Austria (XX);
the many disputes and feuds along the Austrian and Moravian
border (VIII, XI, XIV, XV, XVIII); the expulsion of John Henry
of Moravia, the husband of the infamous Margaretha Maultasch,
and her new husband Louis of Brandenburg (XVI, IX).

Often Suchenwirt merely mentions a place or event without elaborating upon the details. Prussia, Italy, and the
numerous small countries bordering on Austria were most often
frequented by Suchenwirt's heroes, and these areas have thus
been chosen for a more detailed investigation. An examination
of references to these areas will illustrate how well Suchenwirt fulfills his role as historian.

Duke Albert's crusade to Prussia and Lithuania, although
typical and described in most detail, is not the only crusade
mentioned by Suchenwirt; since it was the "thing to do" many
young Austrian, as well as German, French, English and
Scottish nobles participated in similar adventures. Even after
the subjugation of Prussia, the Teutonic Order continued its
colonizing efforts, purchasing the Duchy of Estonia from
Denmark in 1346 and allying with Poland against the
Lithuanians.[279] The area of Samogitia between Prussia and the
Order's possessions in Livonia proved extremely difficult to
conquer, partially due to the wilderness terrain.[280]

St. George was adopted as the patron saint for the
Teutonic Order and thus it was common for the lay nobles also
to consider him as their own patron. Many of the lay nobles
belonged to societies or brotherhoods of St. George, also
carrying the white banner with a red cross. For example, in
1348 King Edward III of England founded the Order of the
Garter in honor of St. George and in 1337 Duke Otto the Jovial
of Austria founded the *Societas Templois* whose members were
known as *Tempelaise* or *Tempeloiser* (i.e. Templars).[281]

The earliest such *Preußenfahrt* described by Suchenwirt is

that of Ulrich von Walsee of about 1321. Suchenwirt is very
brief:

> In deinem dinst [the Virgin Mary's] ist mir gesagt,   XIII,90
> Rait er [Ulrich] gen Prewzzen lande,
> Do er gar sunder schande
> Den hayden schüf grozzen ungemach.

There are no other records of this campaign; the date is
calculated by events which occurred before and afterwards:
Ulrich was with Duke Otto of Austria in Lombardy in 1321 and
took part in the battle at Mühldorf on September 28, 1322.

Friedrich von Kreußpeck accompanied King John of
Bohemia on the first of his three crusades to Prussia and
Lithuania in December 1328, an undertaking which lasted until
May 1329. This campaign was in retaliation for the devastation of Brandenburg by the heathens.[282] King John was also
accompanied by his wife Elisabeth, his oldest son, Charles of
Moravia (the future Emperor Charles IV), and a splendid
following of nobles and knights, many of whom had connections
with the Teutonic Order. The army included 250 Teutonic
knights, 300 knights in the service of King John, and 18,000
soldiers.[283]

The army departed Königsberg on January 20, 1329, crossed
the Memel river at the castle or fort of Ragnit, and continued
to the castle of Medewagen which was besieged on February 1.[284]
The fort at Medewagen was defended by 5,000 men, who, upon
surrendering, were baptized.[285] Suchenwirt describes the mass
baptism:

> Der christen hertz di manheit lött,   XIV,129
> Daz man di haiden des ernöt
> Mit stürmes chraft, mit haufen,
> Daz sich do liezzen taufen
> Wol fünf tausent haiden.
> Si wurden auch geschaiden
> Von sechs vesten, als ich hab
> Vernom, di man in stürmet ab.

Since the King of Bohemia participated and also due to good
fortune, this crusade is especially well documented. Descriptions of the mass baptism from two contemporary chronicles
will illustrate the method of presentation typical for a
chronicle. The *Chronicon Aulae regiae* describes the event

as follows:

> Eodem anno in die beati *Urbani Johannes* Rex *Bohemie* et *Polonie*
> de partibus *Prussie* et *Littovie* felliciter reversus in *Pragensi*
> suscipitur civitate, strenua valde et magnifica contra *Litwanos*
> et paganos in bellicis actibus exercuit opera, ut communis
> omnium hominum preconizat fama: Ipse namque, ut dicitur, ad
> remotiores paganorum transivit terminos, quam aliquis ante
> ipsum Principum fecerit, cuius memoria apud modernos sit. Sunt
> per ipsum inibi multa millia trucidata, et circiter tria millia
> gentillium baptizata; ad hec omnia fratres *Cruciferi* de *Domo*
> *Teuthonica* sua auxilia prebuerunt, fideliter et consilia:
> procurando vehiculorum levium XLV. millia portantium pro
> exercitu necessaria, et pro Rege.[286]

Pulkavia describes the same expedition in his chronicle:

> Post hec VI, die Decembris cum maxima multitudine bellatorum
> *Prussiam* ingreditur, et interiores *Lithuanorum* terras infidelium
> intrans, plura eorum castra acquirit violenter, et diruit,
> innumeros infideles interfecit, et ex eis citra tria millia
> captivitate constrinxit, *Prussiam* secum adducit, et procurat
> singulos baptisari. Ac post multos actus, magnificos, quibus
> eum Deus Omnipotens specialiter preceteris honoravit, rever-
> titur ad propria. Preterea dum in civitate sua *Wratislaviensi*
> moram faceret, subscriptos Duces, et eorum Ducatus sibi Regno et
> corone Bohemie in vasallos et vasallagia in perpetuum applicavit,
> prout in subscriptis privilegiis continetur; que facta sunt
> anno Domini MCCCXXIX.[287]

None of the accounts, including Suchenwirt's, gives a complete
picture even though each presents the facts as its author
understood them.

After the siege of Medewagen, King John, despite the
fact that the cold had blinded one of his eyes, wanted to
press deeper into heathen territory, but he received word
that the King of Poland had broken the truce and invaded
Kulmerland with 6,000 men. The army hurried out of Samogitia
towards the Drewenz river, siezed the castle Dobryn which the
King presented to the Teutonic Order along with other captured
forts, and finally returned to Thorn after inflicting much
damage upon the heathens and collecting much booty.

King John of Bohemia undertook a second crusade, 1336 to
1337,[288] including in his army King Charles Robert of Hungary,
Margrave Louis of Brandenburg, Count Philip of Namur, a count
from Henneberg, Duke Louis of Burgundy, Duke Henry of Bavaria,
many knights from France and Austria, as well as Burgrave
Albert of Nuremberg.[289] This expedition also took place in the

winter, but the mild weather made it impossible to cross the many streams and rivers. Instead, the foreign nobles contented themselves with the building of border fortifications, completing Marienburg and commencing the building of Baierburg, named in honor of Henry of Bavaria. Suchenwirt describes Burgrave Albert's role:

> Dar nach der herr [Albert] gen Preuzzen rait, VII,77
> Do man in hohes lobes chlait
> Tzwen chunige wirdichleichen sach,
> Den man do milt und manhait iach,
> Von Pehem und von Ungerlant,
> Di do den haiden vol bechant
> Wurden auf derselben vart.
> Der herre da ze ritter wart.
> Den orden seit er edel trüg
> Vor schanden von vor ungefüg
> Mit ern stetichleich behüt,
> Mit leib, mit willen, und mit güt.

This is a vague account, probably due to the lack of action:[290] although there was much plundering and looting, there were no great decisive battles. However, Albert did become a knight on this crusade, and that was the main purpose as far as he was concerned. Voigt expresses the general sentiment: "Sie alle trieb die Lust zum Ritterdienste unter der Heerfahne des Deutschen Ordens und der Ehrenkampf gegen die Heiden in diese Lande."[291]

King John's third campaign against the Lithuanians took place in the winter of 1344 to 1345. With him rode the young King Louis of Hungary, Margrave Charles of Moravia (the future Emperor), Count William IV of Holland, the Burgrave of Nuremberg, Count Günther von Schwarzburg, Count Heinrich von Holstein, and among the more than two hundred "nonullos ex Alemania milites et nobiles" was Leutold von Stadeck.[292] Suchenwirt describes King Louis' participation in general terms. emphasizing the large size of the army:

> In Prewzzenlant mit wernder tat I,112
> Lie sich der edel [Louis] schawen
> Ze dinest unser vrawen
> Mit chünig, mit grafen hochgeporn,
> Vreyen, dinstman auzerchorn,
> Mit ritter, chnechten, mutes reich.

At the assembly point the heralds called forth and identified the names of the various knights:

> Fürsten, grafen, freyen,   XV,119
> Der namen hört man chreyen
> Von den eralden, persewant,
> Der wappen volger Tribliant,
> Man sach, da wer der geste vil
> Auz vremden landen ane tzil,
> Die in die Littaw raisten.

Leutold von Stadeck gave the sign of St. George and plunged into battle; the colors of the St. George banner were reflected in the red bands of blood pouring through the white armor of his victims:

> Der Littaw er [Leutold] vil wenig spart   XV,130
> Mit seines swertes straichen,
> Er gab sand Jörgen tzaichen
> Durch weizzes harnasch liecht gevar
> Mit roten bunden, daz ist war,
> Daz maniger vor im tot gelag.

Leutold achieved his primary goal and was knighted for his bravery:

> Der edel helt vil güter   XV,128
> Wart ritter auf der selben vart.

The campaign lasted for more than ten days--all for the honor of the Virgin Mary and the promulgation of Christianity:

> Man was mer wenn tzehen tag   XV,136
> In der Littaw lande;
> Man slüg, man vie, man prande
> Durch Mariam, die vil heren
> Und den gelauben meren
> Der hochgetewerten christenhait.

Again the winter was mild and wet. The army waited several weeks in hopes of cold weather. Finally the Grand Master, Henry Dusemer, led the army in a southerly direction toward Lithuania, planning to overtake the capital of Wilna. He received a report that the Grand Prince of Lithuania had invaded eastern Samland with a mighty army and was in the process of completely devastating the land. The Grand Master then rushed the army toward Samland, while in the meantime the Lithuanians continued on toward Livonia where they robbed and burned from Mitau, Riga, Neuermühlen to as far as Segevold. Suchenwirt points out the many orphans produced by such a hit and run method of warfare:

Man sach, da wer der geste vil   XV,123
Auz vremden landen ane tzil,
Die in die Littaw raisten,
Der undiet vil verwaisten
Von vater und von müter.

When they found Samland empty of the enemy, the kings of
Bohemia and Hungary advised the Grand Master to follow the
Lithuanian army to Livonia to prevent more destruction. But
the Grand Master thought it would be more useful to lead the
army to Lithuania; this would bring the Lithuanian army back
from Livonia and would not only free the Order's territory
from the enemy army, but also put the war on the enemy's own
ground. Since the Order had many times before been successful
in similar ventures, the kings let themselves be persuaded.
Led by the Grand Master they entered Lithuanian territory at
the beginning of 1345 and devastated it by plundering and fire;
the few remaining people who had not fled into the woods they
took prisoner. There was an atmosphere of dissatisfaction in
the failure of the expedition to perform its primary mission,
i.e. the destruction of the Lithuanian army. For over ten
days this army of several thousand men had scoured the almost
empty land while at the same time in Livonia they could have
prevented devastation by the heathens. The foreign members of
the army placed the blame for the failure upon the stubborn
attitude of the Grand Master who would not give up his own
plan. They blamed him for the deaths of thousands of his
subjects. They were disappointed to have to return home
without a fight, without fame, and without profit. Only those
like Leutold von Stadeck who were privileged to be knighted on
the campaign could say that the crusade was a success.[293]

Burkhard von Ellerbach, the Younger, made two trips to
Prussia. The first was probably in the summer of 1346 where
he quickly proved his mettle:

Der edel [Burkhard] ist in Prewzzen lant   IX,81
Dreistund worden wol bechant,
Der verte tzwo geraiset sind
Ze schaden groz, daz muter chind
Der haidenschaft bedwungen wardt.
We im, wem er ze widerpart
Auf streite chumt geschiket!

None of the contemporary chronicles mentions Burkhard's name in this connection. It is possible that he joined King Waldemar III of Denmark, his brother Otto, and Duke Eric von Sachsen-Lauenburg whose ostensive purpose was a crusade against the heathen Lithuanians, but whose real purpose was to determine the relationsip between the Teutonic Order and Estonia which Denmark had just sold to the Order.[294] Several other campaigns, which the young Burkhard von Ellerbach easily could have joined, took place between 1346 and 1347.[295]

The second Prussian crusade by Friedrich von Kreußpeck was in conjunction with an involved itinerary, from the Crimea to Russia (Galicia), to Prussia via Masovia and Poland:

> In Tatrey hin gen Kaffa,   XIV,218
> Von Tatrey hin gen Reuzzen,
> Von dan rait er den Preuzzen,
> Durch die Masaw und durch Polan:
> Er tet di haiden lebens an
> Mit seiner ellenthaften hant.

From Prussia Friedrich went to Livonia, to White Russia, and fought in a battle at Eisenburg, modern Izborsk near Pskow on the southern arm of Lake Peipus:

> Von Preuzzen hin gen Eyflant   XIV,224
> Mit stoltzen helden heuzzen,
> Dar nach gen Weizzen Reuzzen
> Fur Eysenburk für der gehewer,
> Da ein grozze schumphfentewer
> Geschach, da wol ist von ze reden.--

According to the chronology established in the poem the battle at Eisenburg must have taken place before 1348; thus it cannot be the same battle of Eisenburg in which Hans von Traun participated in 1356 (XVIII,205, see p. 156). The Livonian chronicles do not mention a crusade in either of these years. There was fighting between the Germans and Livonians at Eisenburg in 1342 and 1367 and at Pskow in 1343 and 1362.[296]

The campaign which Hans von Traun undertook between October 1355 and September 1356 is described above (p. 156). Karl Heinrich von Busse[297] explains the lack of corroborative material for this campaign as well as others that Suchenwirt mentions by the simple fact that expeditions against the heathens were so very common and many were not considered important enough to record. In the introduction to the

Livonian Chronicles Johann Gottfried Arndt makes the following observation:

> So trocken die alte Historie an ausführlichen Begebenheiten ist; so fruchtbar wird sie nach der Zeit des Ordens an Feldzügen, Belagerungen, Streifereien, Scharmützeln, berühmten Personen und merkwürdigen Veränderungen; nicht als ob es vorher an der- gleichen Vorfällen gefehlet, sondern weil die Mönche zu ge- mächlich und neidisch gewesen, die häufigen Siege der Ordens- herren und ihrer Ritterschaft umständlich und rühmlich zu melden. Was auch von Möncharbeiten noch zu Papier gebracht worden, hat nicht immer Gedeihen gehabt. Vermuthlich ist mancher Aufsatz von dem Orden unterdrückt, weil mehrenteils die Geist- lichen, als der beleidigte Theil, ihr Unrecht und die erlittenen Bedrängnisse zu lebhaft beklagten.[298]

The crusade undertaken by Ulrich von Cilli fits the pattern of a typical Prussian campaign. The army spent more than ten days in the wilderness fighting against the heathens; Ulrich was knighted in the field:

> Darnach der edel [Ulrich] cherte   XVI,75
> Als in di manhait lerte
> In Preüssen gein der haidenschaft,
> Da man mit grozzer hereschraft
> In di Lytaw zogte
> Und in dem lande progte
> Mer wann tzehen gantzer tag,
> Da manig haiden tot gelag
> Von der christen handen;
> Man sach aus manigen landen
> Vil werder geste ane zal.
> Der edel zu dem selben mal
> Enphie den ritters segen,
> Den trueg der stoltze degen
> Mit ern alle seine tag.

This crusade must have taken place sometime between 1349 and 1351 according to other events in Ulrich's life (the activity mentioned preceding this crusade was Ulrich's participation in the conquest of Brandenburg for Margrave Louis which was completed in 1349; he fought with Ulrich von Walsee at Neuhaus in 1351). Neither the Cilli family chronicle from the fifteenth century nor contemporary chronicles mention Ulrich's name in reference to a Prussian campaign.[299]

Both King Louis of Hungary and Burkhard von Ellerbach, the Younger, made a second expedition against the Lithuanians in 1351. They were accompanied among others by Friedrich von Kreußpeck (his third campaign) who was making his way from Hungary to Sweden:

> Dar nach die dritten rais er [Friedrich] tzogt   XIV,273
> Gen Preuzzen, do er werleich progt
> Der haidenschaft ze ungewin.

John the Archdeacon sets the date in his chronicle and describes the crusade as follows:

> Ceterum contra Lithwanos, Christianis et maxime regno suo
> Rusciae insultantes, personaliter cum exercitu copioso et
> militia sua propria, nec non aliis nationibus, ad eum con-
> fluentibus, proficiscens, terris ipsorum seu tenutis in magna
> parte deuastatis, duce eorum capto, sed in continenti, sibi
> promissionem de fidelitate et obedientia faciente, liberato,
> feliciter ad Hungariam est reuerfus.[300]

The Lithuanian king, typical of his heathen ways, had broken his oath of allegiance sworn to the King of Hungary. This prompted the military campaign:

> Daz er der Litaw schaden mert,   I,106
> Dem chünig er dar ze laide für,
> Und den bedwanch, daz er im swür
> Noch haydenischem siten.
> Di trew di ward versniten,
> Daz er an im geprochen hat.

Suchenwirt repeats the allegation of faithlessness in the *Ehrenrede* honoring Burkhard von Ellerbach:

> In Lytaw für der mütes [Burkhard] früt   IX,136
> Von Ungern mit dem chunig wert,
> Des hertze trew und manhait gert,
> Dem sich der Lytaw chunik geporn
> Ergab, der ayde het gesworn
> Auf dem plüt noch seiner art.

The mighty army entered Prussia in the name of the Virgin Mary and fought gallantly:

> In Prewzzenlant mit wernder tat   I,112
> Lie sich der edel schawen
> Ze dinest unser vrawen
> Mit chünig mit grafen hochgeporn,
> Vreyen, dinstman auzerchorn,
> Mit ritter, chnechten, mutes reich.

Suchenwirt only briefly describes the second trip of Hans von Traun into Prussia in 1370[301] with the nineteen year old Duke Leopold of Austria:

> Darnach der helt gen Preuzzen rait   XVIII,499
> Mit hertzog Lewpolt unvertzait
> Von Östereich dem Jungen,
> Der chom da hin gedrungen
> Mit mangem hoch getewertem helt,
> Di er dartzu het auzerwelt,
> Daz er wolt in di haidenschaft

Ein rais mit ritterleicher chraft
Erleich tziehen mit gewalt.
Nu was der winder nicht so chalt,
Da von di rais war wenndich.--

Leopold was accompanied by the Dukes Frederick and Stephan of
Bavaria who also hoped to win honor and fame during the crusade.
Others included the two dukes from Poland, the Landgrave of
Leuchtenberg, a count from Hals, and Otto von Brandenburg.
Altogether there were 1,500 knights on horseback, "multos
principes, qui omnes in exercitium milicie et fidei protectionem
venerunt."[302] The army was graciously received by the Grand
Master; it then advanced to Königsberg where the new Marshal of
the Order, Rüdiger von Elner, led the army to Ragnit. Grand
Master Winrich divided the army into two divisions; he took
one along the Memel river to Leibgirren where he advanced upon
the area of Pomedien and devastated it. The other division was
commanded by the Marshal, and advanced toward the Jura in the
area of Koltinjany. The inhabitants had been warned and
managed to hide much of what the invaders had hoped to take
back as booty. The two divisions met at Wayken and together
devastated the area from Rossiene and Eragola to Geswo. They
spent six days in enemy territory, plundering, murdering, and
burning before returning to the territory of the Order with
many prisoners. Nevertheless it was not considered a particularly successful campaign. There were very few oppor-
tunities for the knights to display their bravery, and the
foreigners were forced by the warm weather to retreat back
to Königsberg (a similar situation hindered the campaign of
King John of Bohemia in 1377).

Not only were crusades against the heathens undertaken
because they were fashionable, but also because of the close
connection between the Vienna-based *Societas Templois* and the
Teutonic Order, both of whom regarded St. George as their
patron saint. It is possible that one of the conditions of
membership in the *Societas Templois* was a Prussian crusade.
Suchenwirt, who was possibly the official herald of the society,
may have joined the 1377 crusade precisely for the purpose
of gaining inside information about one of the most important

initiation rites of the society--namely a *Preußenfahrt*.

There are very few documents pertaining to the *Societas Templois*, "die halb gesellschaftlichen, halb religiösen Charakter hatte und vielleicht auch politische Ziele verfolgte."[303] The documents include a list of members (Vienna, ÖNB MS 3321, ff. 42^r-48^v) and several donations of money (from Ulrich and Friedrich von Walsee in 1377, from Rudolf von Liechtenstein in 1341, from Leopold of Austria in 1378).[304] The members were *milites* (knights), protectors of the grail-- the grail being the holy vessel from which Christ served his disciples the Last Supper. According to the German version the blood of Christ was collected in this vessel by Joseph of Arimathea and brought to Munsalvæsche (wild mountain) in Spain where it was guarded by an order of knighthood, the *Templeisen*. Finally it disappeared into India where Prester John was named the Grail King.[305] Members of the *Societas Templois* included not only Austrian dukes and nobles, but also foreign ruling lords and princes, including a duke of Saxony and a burgrave of Nuremberg. One of its first activities was to construct the St. George's chapel next to the church of St. Augustine in Vienna. The chapel was used for burials not only of members of the society, but also of outsiders such as Countess Sophie von Ortenburg. However, it is possible that members of the society were given honorary funerals here. It is also possible that Peter Suchenwirt recited his *Ehrenreden* at these memorial services.

Hermann Maschek maintains that the *Societas Templois* originated as an imitation of the *Templeisen* in the Bavarian monastery of Ettal which Louis IV of Bavaria had founded in 1330. He also suggests a possible connection between the farce about the priest of Kahlenberg and the *Societas Templois*. The Kahlenberg poem not only concludes with a prayer to St. George, but also contains references to the church of St. Augustine and the chapel on the Kahlenberg dedicated to St. George.[306]

Joseph Feil raises the question of Suchenwirt's connection with the society:

Nehmen wir noch darauf Rücksicht, daß wir in den Schilderungen
Suchenwirt's über jene Kreuzzüge vielfach den Heil. Georg anrufen
hören, daß öfter von St. Georgs Banner, von St. Georgs Seegen und
St. Georgszeichen, dann von einem St. Georgs-Hauptmann die Rede
ist, so möchte vielleicht vermuthet werden können, daß jene St.
Georgsgesellschaft, deren Besprechung Gegenstand dieser Zeilen
war, eine ritterliche Vereinigung zur kriegerischen Unterstützung
des deutschen Ordens in Preußen bei der Bekehrung der dortigen
heidnischen Völker gewesen?[307]

The following subjects of Suchenwirt's *Ehrenreden* were
members of the *Societas Templois:* Duke Albert III of Austria,
Burgrave Albert of Nuremberg, Ulrich von Walsee, Herdegen von
Pettau, Ulrich von Pfannberg, Albert von Rauchenstain,
Friedrich von Kreußpeck, Hans von Chappel, as well as members
of the Stadeck and Cilli families. Thus Suchenwirt describes
the military column following the flag of St. George as Duke
Albert III of Austria entered the heathen land (IV,240, 563);
Ulrich von Walsee received the blessing of St. George as he
became a knight (XIII,56); Leutold von Stadeck made the sign
of St. George as he launched into battle against the
Lithuanians (XV,132); Hans von Traun was named St. George's
captain in White Russia (XVIII,188, 282), and Suchenwirt
implored St. George to protect Hans' soul in heaven (XVIII,
567); the good knight entered battle in the name of St.
George (XXVIII,234).

The paucity of information about the *Societas Templois* is
probably due to its secret nature. Documents pertaining to
other similar societies are equally scarce. Hugh Clark lists
seventeen different Austrian orders of knighthood (from 1106
to 1757) but does not include this one.[308] There were also
other Austrian orders dedicated to St. George: Emperor Frederick
III founded the Order of *Saint Georgen Schilts* in 1448, a
military order for the defense of Hungary, Styria, and
Carinthia.[309] A contemporary of Duke Otto's, Count Amadeus
VI of Savoy, founded two orders of knighthood, the Order of
the Black Swan and the Order of the Collar. Both of these
served the practical purpose of winning loyal support and
financial aid for the Count.[310] The English Order of the
Garter, also founded in the fourteenth century and also
dedicated to St. George, has had a long and distinguished

history. Although many documents list the rules of organization of these various orders, the membership rolls, even the order of the initiation ceremonies, there is almost no information regarding their regular ceremonies.

Just as Suchenwirt records the Prussian campaigns of his heroes (possibly for the purpose of establishing their connections with the *Societas Templois*), so he also chronicles the events in which these same heroes played important roles on the peninsula of Italy. Here the purpose of the military campaigns was strictly secular. For example, the city of Padua, threatened by the Cane della Scala, Lord of Verona (known in German as the *Hund von Bern*), requested protection from Duke Frederick of Austria. In January 1320 Frederick appointed the elder Ulrich II von Walsee as governor of Padua. Ulrich returned to Austria with Duke Frederick but left his son Ulrich III and his brother-in-law Count Ulrich von Pfannberg behind as deputies. In the meantime the restless Cane built a strong castle near the city from which he directed a siege. Ulrich von Pfannberg and the young Ulrich von Walsee took one hundred Germans and successfully attacked this castle. But soon the lack of supplies became desperate; the bravest soldiers declared they would rather die of hunger than to dishonor the Duke of Austria. In August 1320 the garrison at Padua was rescued by Count Heinrich von Görz and the elder Ulrich von Walsee with eight hundred soldiers.[311]

The Austrians immediately set out against the Cane who was prepared with one thousand men to receive them. Young Ulrich von Walsee sprang to the front with umpremediated haste and jumped the enemy moat, but soon the overpowering odds brought him down: "Et quia inhabilis, terga dedit."[312] The Count of Görz and the elder Ulrich von Walsee once again came to his aid. The Cane was wounded and only barely escaped.

The *Leoben Chronicle* tells the same story but incorrectly places the date in 1314, a mistake which is perpetuated by Hanthaler in the nineteenth century:

Altero deinde Anno 1314. Paduanos oppressos à Veronensibus auxilium à FRIDERICO Austriaco Duce flagitasse: qui eisdem rursum cum exercitu submiserit *Ulricum de Walsee*, cum filio *Ulrico*, itemque Genero ULRICO *Pfannenbergico*. Atque hunc posteriorem, cum *Ulrico* juniore Walseano, praesidium urbis Paduae suscipientem, acerrimam Veronensium obsidionem eousque magnanimiter sustinuisse, donec *Ulricus* Senior de Walsee, collecto exteriùs milite, hostes ad muros gloriosè caeciderit. Quo facto Comites nostri ex Italia cum multa fama et celebritate suum ad Principem redierint.[313]

Not until 1321 does the Cane submit to peace. Suchenwirt's account of these affairs is very brief, but it does conform to the chronology established in other contemporary sources.

The death of Count Heinrich von Görz in 1323 provided another excuse for an Austrian campaign into Friuli as far as Padua. Duke Albert II took over the government of Görz as regent for the one year old son of the deceased governor, Johann. Even though the city of Treviso recognized Johann's claim, Duke Henry of Carinthia, Duke Otto of Austria, Friedrich von Kreußpeck and others came to Friuli under the leadership of Ulrich von Walsee to secure the inheritance and to straighten out the affairs of the province. Their terrible wasting of the countryside forced the native inhabitants to flee to Treviso. On July 11, 1324 the army arrived in Padua and on the next day Duke Henry marched to the stronghold of Monselice. Suchenwirt merely touches upon the highlights of the campaign through Friuli, from Belgrade to Monselice:

> Man sach den fursten [Henry] lobes palt   VI,148
> Vor Belegrat nach ern streben
> Mit swertes slegen (merchet eben),
> Daz er di veinde machte schiech,
> Daz maniger wart der manhait siech
> Von seiner ellenthaften hant:
> Des Veryaul vil wol enphant.
> Der Patriarch im siges iach.
> Vor Munttzili man in sach
> Preisleicher ern walden.

The Cane della Scala managed to get out of the trouble posed by the Austrians by negotiations and payment of ransoms. The two dukes went away leaving Ulrich von Pfannberg in Padua as deputy. In 1328 Padua fell again into the hands of the wiley Cane and in the following year Treviso also capitulated.[314]

The two campaigns mentioned by Suchenwirt involving
Ulrich von Walsee, the Younger, and Friedrich von Kreußpeck
must have taken place in 1320 and 1324. Suchenwirt claims,
for instance, that Friedrich fought with Duke Otto in
Lombardy:

> Mit hertzog Otten er [Friedrich] do rait   XIV,43
> In Lamparten unvertzait.

Suchenwirt also maintains that Friedrich fought twice
against Cane della Scala:

> Do man dem Hunt von Pern   XIV,36
> Tzwir angesigt tzway vechten güt.

The military activities of Ulrich von Pfannberg at Padua
took place, according to other events in his life, between
1316 and 1328.

A third campaign to Friuli was undertaken after the
murder of Bertrand, the Patriarch of Aquileia, in 1350.
Duke Albert II of Austria and Mastin della Scala were allied
against the Luxemburgers whom Bertrand had favored. Therefore Duke Albert quickly came to Friuli, with his wife and
son, accompanied by Ulrich von Walsee, in order to govern the
province personally until a new friendly Patriarch could be
elected. The people of Friuli were forced to swear allegiance to Austria:[315]

> Gen Friaul der edel [Ulrich] fuer,   XIII,145
> Do er der Walchen Luxemburgers schaden swür
> Tzu dienest dem von Östereich,
> In des dinst er willichleich
> Hat gewagt leib unde guet,
> Und twang Fryaul mit chechem muet,
> Daz seu den fürsten swürn.--

A final campaign into Friuli is mentioned in the poem honoring
Hans von Traun. Hans accompanied Duke Rudolf of Austria to
Aquileia in 1361, again for the purpose of securing peace
and loyalty.

Suchenwirt glorifies Friedrich von Kreußpeck in his
activities in Italy which took place after the capture of
Padua in 1325. Friedrich appears to be in the service of
the Florentines who as Guelphs were forced by Castruccio
Castracani, the Lord of Lucca, to go to war over the city of
Pistoja. Raymondo of Cardona, the commander of the

Florentine army had three thousand knights on horseback and
20,000 foot soldiers.[316] He overtook Articino, pushed toward
Pistoja, conquering castles along the way including the castle
of Altopascio, and even threatened Lucca. Then, however,
Castruccio, who was superior to Raymondo in talent as an army
commander, held up Raymondo and his army with limited strength
until reinforcements arrived in form of eight hundred men from
Azzo Visconti, the son of Galeazzo, the Lord of Milan. Raymondo
retreated back to Altopascio where he was attacked by Castruccio.
A distastrous battle took place on September 23, in which
many of the Florentines were killed and most of the rest,
including Raymondo and Friedrich, were taken prisoner.
Friedrich von Kreußpeck is not mentioned in the contemporary
chronicles; nevertheless Suchenwirt describes his role in the
battle:

> Tzu dem Alten Pazt er [Friedrich] strait   XIV,47
> Mit ellenthafter wirdichait.
> Tzway tausend gwappent stritten,
> Fümf hundert schaden litten
> Mit todes pein gar pitter,
> Dar wart der edel ritter.

As usual the numbers vary from account to account. Suchenwirt claims that the Castruccio received reinforcements from
Mantua rather than from the Visconti of Milan (apparently
a mistake on Suchenwirt's part):

> Do besammet sich von Luk   XIV,60
> Der Chastrutsch unbesundert,
> Dem komen vol tzwelf hundert
> Hauben durch der wirde schaw
> Tzu hilf von dem von Mantaw,
> Do ward gestriten al so vast
> Mit manheit an Alten Past,
> Daz mer den virtzig tausend man
> Würden alle lebens an.
> Florentzer fluren do den streit.

Suchenwirt describes the capture of Friedrich in some detail
while omitting that of Raymondo who appears prominently in
the chronicles. Friedrich's horse was wounded, he himself
covered with fifteen wounds, finally he gave himself over
to the enemy. For his bravery he was named the "best of
the day:"

```
Slüg er dy arm wol gespart,        XIV,77
Untz im sein ross erstochen wart;
Dy panir mit im nider gie
(Ich sag nür di warhait hie!)
Er ward in di ar e m wunt
Fümftzehen wunden tzu der stunt
Von nageln in der stangen:
Erst gab er sich gevangen.
Des tags man in den pesten hiez!--
```

The prisoner Friedrich von Kreußpeck, who was, after
all, a soldier of fortune, went over to the side of the same
Azzo Visconti who had helped capture him. Azzo had returned
home after the victory at Altopascio. Then Passerino
Buonacossi, Lord of Mantua and Modena (also a Ghibelline)
invited Azzo to take part in a feud against the Guelph city
of Bologna. Azzo and Passerino, united with Rainald of Este,
were victorious at Monteveglio on November 15, 1325. The
victors pressed up to the walls of Bologna and there held
three running contests to celebrate their victory. Three
thousand enemy soldiers were killed, 1,500 captured; the
baggage and booty was worth about 200,000 gold gulden.[317]
Bologna would surely have fallen if Passerino had not arranged
a peace. Suchenwirt describes the event as follows:

```
Fur Polony er do für     XIV,87
Mit dem von Mailan, da man swür
Dem von Mantaw ze helfen,
Da Gibling unde Gelfen
Mue and arbait litten,
Do ward so ser gestriten,
Daz fünftzehen tausent stürben tot.
```

Suchenwirt's figure of 15,000 dead is probably somewhat
distorted; all figures quoted by Suchenwirt and his contemporaries are suspect since they were generally motivated
by reasons other than historical accuracy. Again Friedrich
was named the "best of the day:"

```
Daz man in für den pesten tzalt    XIV,96
Des tag auf paiden tailen.
```

In 1326 the Cardinal legate of Bologna, Bertrand du
Pol'et, declared war against the Buonacossi. He attacked
Modena with papal assistance and overpowered the cities of
Parma and Modena. Landi, the Cardinal's captain, set fire
to three suburbs of Modena and burned over six hundred

houses in Carpi. Finally Modena fell into his hands because
of intrigues among the nobles.[318] It appears that Friedrich
was among the besieged in Modena. His brave deed took place
during an attack on one of the suburbs:

> In der vorstat er do sach   XIV,105
> Tzu ross sechs hundert, als man iach,
> Und wol tzway tausent man ze fuz;
> Uber einen graben er unfuz
> Selb ander sprangt mit keker tat,
> Und rante in di vorstat
> In di veint, stich und slach!

He rushed into the city ahead of his men, jumped the moat,
and held back the enemy until his men arrived. The enemy
was forced to retreat to the bridge and Praun von Reinach
was killed:

> Di veint di kerten da den ruk,   XIV,113
> Si iagten nach untz auf di pruk:
> Praun von Reinach war erslagen.

This Praun (Bruno ?) from Reinach does not appear in the
chronicles.

Finally Friedrich von Kreußpeck won more fame and honor
in tournaments *(schumphfentewer)* outside the castle Sandanin
and outside of Lucca:

> Er schumphentewert auch durch gewin   XIV,117
> Mit ernst vor Purk Sandaninn:
> Vor Luk ein grozze schumphfentewer
> Geschach durch hoher wirde stewer,
> Do seinen veinden misselank
> Und er nach hochen ern rank.

Suchenwirt refers to several campaigns into Italy
undertaken in the retinue of King Louis of Hungary. Upon
the request from the beleagured city of Zara (old German
Saders) on the Dalmatian coast Louis brought his army in
1345 to aid the rebellious Zaratines against Venice.
Contemporary accounts agree that Louis' army, including
many Germans such as Ulrich von Cilli, was sizable--as large
as 120,000 men.[319] Suchenwirt claims the army was larger
than 60,000:

> Er [Ulrich] für sein erst geverte   XVI,24
> Für Saders mit dem chünich reich
> In Unger lant, der mæchtichleich
> Vor der stat zu velde lag

> Mit hereschraft vil manigen tag
> Mit sechtzig tausent oder mer
> Durich lobez preis und auch durich er.

Reports of the engagement describe the war machines, especially
the sophisticated equipment employed by the Venetians. The
citizens of Zara received the Hungarians with great joy, but
a number of different events occured to make the freeing of
the city impossible: the gold which the Venetians had
distributed among the foreign leaders; the lack of siege
material and the lack of knowledge of its use by Louis and
his men; above all the report received that Louis' brother
Andrew had been murdered by mutineers, causing Louis to
think of nothing but revenge.[320]

The Hungarian army returned home after sustaining
great losses. Suchenwirt avoids the most umpleasant parts
of this affair, emphasizing rather the bravery of Louis and
his men:

> Sein [Louis'] hertze sich nicht reidet   I,124
> Von manhait mit dem willen sein,
> Dem tet er wol vor Sader schein,
> Do er besaz ein grozzes her,
> Und daz mit ritterleicher wer
> Wolt gern han bestanden.

This first attempt was disastrous, neither famous nor
successful.

In the meantime King Louis of Hungary had been
declared standardbearer of the Church by the Pope, and
Imperial Vicar by Emperor Charles IV for the war against
Venice. Among his allies were the Count of Görz and the
Patriarch of Aquileia. Thus with great power and astonishing
speed King Louis again invaded the territory of the Venetians
in 1356, defeating the enemy at all points, in Istria, Friuli,
and Treviso. He was accompanied by Ulrich von Cilli, Ulrich
von Walsee, and young Burkhard von Ellerbach (I,145; IX,146;
X,103; XIII,163; XVI,111). The most complete account is
found in the poem honoring Burkhard von Ellerbach, the
Younger. Suchenwirt describes the complicated war machines,
the number and weapons of the enemy, as well as the bravery
of Louis' army. At Treviso the battle was particularly

fierce; Burkhard emerged from the struggle covered with
arrows, and because of this his heroism was widely aclaimed:

> Sach man in var der selben stat [Treviso] ,   IX,157
> Daz harnasch, wappen unde wat
> Mit pheilen was besteket.
> Er [Burkhard] chünet unde cheket
> Manigen ungeübten tzagen,
> Der heldes hertz müz tragen,
> Wenn er in sicht so vraysleich
> Gen veinden wirken aysleich.

Again at Seravalle he proved so strong that both Ghibelline
and Guelph were forced to recognize his bravery:

> Daz Gibling unde Gelfe   IX,192
> Im müsten manhait iehen.

At Vicenza Burkhard swam the river Brenta and allegedly
overtook six hundred men:

> Ze Vitzentz uber di Prente   IX,196
> Swemt er (schol man gelauben?)
> So er sechshundert hauben
> Ubervil und tet den chunt,
> Daz maniger ward mit schaden wunt,
> Gevangen und erslagen.

King Louis again stormed Serravalle; the defenders shot many
a stone and many an arrow so that the river flowed red with
knights' blood. The chronicler Johann von Thurócz emphasizes
the daring military tactics of the "Germans" i.e. Louis army:

> Item tertia vice circa fluuium Brentham nauigabilem contra
> Tuetonicos et stipendiarios Venetorm, transpassato flumine
> super equos, cum magno periculo propter fluminis profundi-
> tatem, de mane subito irruentes, eosdem stipendiarios
> deuicerunt et captiuos abduxerunt, quos secundem moren sti-
> pendiariorum, equis et armis receptis, libere abire
> permiserunt.[321]

Upon the admonition of the Pope, King Louis agreed to a five
month cease fire and returned home. But Louis' commanders
remained in Italy and continued the war in 1357.

After this Burkhard went to Dalmatia where he took part
in the second invasion of Zara in 1357. Burkhard led the
attack upon Zara accompanied by two hundred marksmen and
sixty-five lancers:

> Tzway hundert schützen sicherleich   X,180
> Und fümf und sechtzk hauben
> (Di red schol man gelauben)
> Gewunnen do di werden stat

Saders, der man ere hat:
Do was er [Burkhard] öbrist haubtman.

There was no question of taking prisoners. Shouting "Hie
Ungerland!" the invaders attacked Zara from the Adriatic as
well as from the land side. Burkhard was killed by a lance:

Do war der edel [Burkhard] laider   X,197
Gechlait in todes chlaider:
Mit einer lantzen man in schoz.

According to Venetian chronicles the city was lost through
treachery and treason by the native citizens rather than by
a gallant attack from the outside.[322] However, Johann von
Thurócz agrees with Suchenwirt:

Iterum autem dictus Thomas [one of Louis' field commanders]
illuc [onto the Terra Ferma of Venice] est transmissus, et
viriliter ac potenter castra et terras acquisitas sub dominio
regis conferuauit tamdiu, donec, expugnata et recuperata
ciuitate Iddrensi, quae per strenuum militem, Elderbol
[Burkhard von Ellerbach] nomine, Teutonicum, cum gentibus
domini regis quadam nocte muros ciuitatis ascendendo, per
pugnam maximam, cum gentibus Venetorum armigeris, Teutonicis
et Gallicis, durissime commissam, vbi idem miles letaliter
exstitit vulneratus, ex quo vulnere vitam finiuit temporalem,
comite Venetorum seu capitaneo, in eadem constituto, eum suis
gentibus deuictis et fugatis, capta fuit et expugnata et in
partibus maritimis, in Dalmatia, regia potestas firmata
exstitit.[323]

Twice King Louis undertook campaigns to Apulia (the
Kingdom of Naples) accompanied by many noble knights including
Burgrave Albert of Nuremberg (VII,107) and Burkhard von
Ellerbach, the Younger (IX,132; X,64), for the purpose of
revenging the death of his brother Andrew. On September
18, 1345 Andrew had been strangled at Aversa under suspicious
circumstances involving his wife, Queen Joan of Naples. The
report of the murder reached Louis at Zara; Louis returned
home to plan his bloody revenge. At the beginning of 1348
he led a mighty army of Hungarians and Germans via Verona,
Aquila, and Benevento to Aversa. He carried a black banner
of mourning displaying the portrait of his murdered brother,
even depicting the murder in detail, which put fear and
terror into the hearts of the populace along the way. Queen
Joan, who had a guilty conscience, fled. Her brother-in-law,
Charles Durazzo, at first had taken terrible revenge upon
the murderers, then reconciled himself with Joan and took

up arms against King Louis. Thus, when Louis arrived, Charles greeted him in a friendly, but treacherous, manner; for his treason Charles was subsequently executed in the same gallery in which Andrew was murdered. After attempting to secure the throne for Andrew's oldest son, Charles Martel, King Louis left the conquered land in the hands of his commanders. It was necessary for Louis to return in 1350 to put down the rebellious followers of Queen Joan.

Neither campaign is described in much detail by Suchenwirt who appears to be more interested in the fact that such a campaign took place and its effect upon the local population:

> Er [Albert of Nuremberg] wolt gen Pullen [Apulia] raisen   VII,111
> Do witten unde waisen
> Wurden traurig unde vro;
> Der chunig [King Louis] rach sein pruder also,
> Da von man singet unde sagt.

It is extremely difficult to construct accurate historical accounts since the medieval sources are so erratic. Suchenwirt's accounts generally coincide with the chronicle versions. Frequently, however, he introduces material which is omitted from the chronicles--probably because the chroniclers were not as familiar with the individuals as was Suchenwirt. Suchenwirt does not appear to rely upon contemporary written sources which would necessarily be too recent. On the other hand, it is impossible to determine whether the chroniclers base their accounts on Suchenwirt since they do not mention his name.

It is clear from his political poems that Suchenwirt was concerned with German imperial problems; however, in the *Ehrenreden* he does not deal with these problems in a concise manner but instead refers to them in connection with the deeds of his heroes.

Suchenwirt states that Duke Henry of Carinthia and Burkhard von Ellerbach, the Elder, attended the double election of Louis the Bavarian and Frederick the Fair of Austria in Frankfurt on October 19 and 20, 1314:

> Tzu Franchenfurt, da man erbelt   VIII,34
> Tzwen chünig tzu dem reich:
> Der ain waz chunig Fridereich

Von Österreich genennet,
Der ander wart erchennet
Chunig Ludweig genant
Geporen fürst in Payerlant.

Burkhard von Ellerbach, the Elder, was knighted on this occasion:

Da wart dem stoltzen degen [Burkhard]   VIII,41
Geordent riters segen
Mit swerten und auch mit schilde.

Suchenwirt's account involving Henry of Carinthia is similar; in neither case does he comment on the advisability of such a double election or on the possible consequences thereof.

The Austrian party was camped at Sachsenhausen in sight of Frankfurt; on the other side at the ancient place of election in the suburbs of Frankfurt were Louis' followers. The Austrians chose Frederick and the Luxemburgers chose Louis. The city of Frankfurt opened its gates to Louis who was crowned in the cathedral; Frederick tried in vain to enter the city, attempted a siege but ran out of supplies, and then went to Bonn where he was crowned by the Elector of Cologne. The Pope recognized neither Louis nor Frederick.

The next few years were spent in a succession of combats in which both the Germans and the Austrians were equally exhausted and much of Germany was devastated. For example, a battle took place at Eßlingen on September 19, 1315. The Austrian dukes Frederick and Leopold fought against the Bavarian controlled city which was bravely defended by its citizens. Emperor Louis finally won after receiving reinforcements at the last minute. The two armies were camped on opposite sides of the Neckar river for five days without any action. Finally a disorderly battle took place, strangely enough, in the middle of the river. Many knights and soldiers were killed or wounded, a few taken prisoner, and many horses were killed. According to the *Königshofen Chronicle:*

Ludowici itaque exercitus, opitulante Deo, pervaluit et ex hiis, qui cum *Friderico* fuerant, XII. Comites cum aliis centum et quadraginta militibus, et viris militaribus captivavit et ex hiis, qui cum *Friderico* fuerant; mille vero, et quingenti dextrarii in eodem prelio sunt occisi in acie.324

Suchenwirt probably exaggerates when he claims that eight
hundred knights and *knechte* were killed:

> Der nach so vacht der milde [Burkhard, the Elder] VIII,44
> Tzu Ezzelingen, daz sein hant
> Den veinden mandleich wart bechant.
> Er ritert in der veinde schar,
> Do wol acht hundert (nemmet war!)
> Riter und chnecht wart erslagen.

Hans von Chappel was among those who lost their horses:

> vor Ezzeling der werde [Hans] strait   2,63
> mit chekchen mut gar unuerzait,
> des maniger also ser engalt,
> der uon dem rosse wart geualt.
> daz wag er ringer alsam ein per.

Ulrich von Pfannberg and Ulrich von Walsee were also present
at this battle on the Austrian side, but Suchenwirt does not
elaborate on their roles. King John of Bohemia was knighted
after the battle.[325]

The Austrians prepared for the final subjugation of
Bavaria and thus Frederick entrenched himself with a huge
army of 18,000 foot soldiers, 4,000 archers, and 7,000
horsemen on the plain between Mühldorf and Oettingen to wait
the arrival of his brother Leopold with a force from Switzerland. King John of Bohemia was allied with Emperor Louis,
Charles Robert of Hungary with Frederick. The battle took
place on September 28, 1322 before Leopold arrived with
reinforcements despite the recommendation against an attack
by Frederick's commanders, Dietrich von Pillichdorf and
Ulrich and Heinrich von Walsee.

An eyewitness account of the battle is found in the
Klosterneuburg Chronicle. The anonymous author paints a colorful
picture when he describes the Austrian knights divided into
four divisions prepared for battle:

> Des morgen frue waren sie beraitt mit vier rotten Pannier;
> Chunig Friedreich unter des Reichs Pannier; Hertzog Hainreich
> von Oesterreich sein Bruder unter dem Pannier von Oesterreich,
> die der Marschalich Dietreich von Pilichdorff furtt: dew
> dritt Herr Ulreich und Herr Hainreich die Brüder von Wallse,
> und ir Sun; die vierd unter dem Ertzbischolff von Salczpurk
> Pannier: alle die Herren, die da waren, die vachten mandleich.[326]

Frederick was named most brave: "Da straitt Kunig Fridreich

so Ritterleich, das man im gab den preiß, das in allem dem
streitt nie besser Ritter gewesen were: der vacht so maind-
leich, das nie khain Man chueneren Man in streitt ye gesechen
hiett."[327]

The battle was long and hard, from sunrise to sunset
without intermission. The course of the battle seemed to be
going in favor of Frederick when the Burgrave of Nuremberg
secured the victory for the Germans by a stratagem. He
galloped at the head of four hundred horsemen from the rear
of the Bavarian army bearing the Austrian colors as though he
were the reinforcement from Leopold. The Austrians mistook
him for Leopold and were soon thrown into confusion and
dispersed. Frederick maintained his position until his
horse was killed under him and he was forced to surrender
to the Burgrave of Nuremberg. Louis received his prisoner
in a most chivalrous manner and then confined him in the
fortress of Trausnitz in the Upper Palatinate.[328] Among the
prisoners were Friedrich von Kreußpeck[329] and Ulrich von
Walsee who had also fought with bravery and honor:

> Dar nach man in [Ulrich] mit ern sach   XIII,94
> In Payerlande an der Ysen,
> Da man enn unde disen
> Sach sterben um daz reiche,
> Do strait er ritterleiche
> Mit ern an der selben stunt:
> Er ward gevangen und wunt,
> Pei seinem herren daz geschach,
> An dem sein trew er nie geprach.--

The devastating loss at Mühldorf was to have repercussions
for many years among the Austrians.

The two Burkhards von Ellerbach brilliantly defended
the city of Burgau against the army of Emperor Louis. Several
contemporary chronicles describe this struggle which lasted
many months. For example, the *Leoben Chronicle* states:

> 1324. Interea Ludwicus castrum Burgaw obsidens, nil profecit;
> qui Burchardus de Hellerbach, qui id nomine Ducum Austriæ
> tenuit strenue resistens Leupoldi exsolutionem expectavit:
> qui cum exercitu copioso veniens, Ludwicum de campestribus
> abigebat.[330]

According to Suchenwirt the defense of Burgau deserves special
praise because there was no wall around the city:

```
Dar nach der wol vermezzen [Burkhard, the Elder ]    VIII,71
Tzu Purgaw wart besezzen
Mit starcher hers chrefte:
Vil edler riterschefte
Must leiden arbait sawre.
Umb Purgaw waz chain mawre,
Die vest ein zawn het umbevang,
Den wert der edle also lang
Mit pideben leuten riterleich,
Piz man in rett von Östereich.
```

The defenders were finally rescued by the dukes Albert
(despite his painful lameness) and Leopold, who forced the
enemy to capitulate and flee:[331]

```
uor Purgaw, da er [Albert II] ritter wart,    3,157
da was er leibs und mutes frut,
seid hat der edel furste gut
mit chrankchem leib geraiset,
der ern unuerwaiset
ist sein hochgelobtes adel,
des nam ist sunder falschen tadel.
```

In 1325 Frederick was liberated. According to the
terms imposed upon him, he renounced the crown and exhorted
his brothers and allies to pay allegiance to Louis as
Emperor. His brothers, especially the fiery Leopold, rejected
the articles pertaining to them and made vigorous preparations
for the prosecution of the war. Since it was impossible for
Frederick to live up to his promises alone, he surrendered
himself to Louis. Louis was affected by this unusual probity
and treated his captive with generosity and affection, finally
agreeing to share his reign with Frederick. The death of
both Frederick and Leopold resulted in peace between Austria
and Germany for some years. King John of Bohemia, the head
of the House of Luxemburg, had supported the interests of
Louis, but when the House of Habsburg, under Otto and Albert,
no longer posed any threats for the Empire, he began to cause
difficulties for both the Germans and the Austrians, forcing
Louis to form more intimate ties with Austria.

When the new Emperor Charles IV was crowned in Metz
in 1354 both Albert of Nuremberg and Ulrich von Cilli were
present; they then accompanied Charles to Rome where he was
crowned Roman Emperor on April 5, 1355. In both accounts
Suchenwirt emphasizes the pomp and ceremony of the occasion

and portrays Emperor Charles standing on the Tiber river
bridge where he knighted many of his followers:

> Do man mit stoltzen kreyen   VII,164
> Hort manigen lauten widerdoz
> „Rom und Reich mit ern groz!"
> Drang man fur sich und nicht ze ruk.
> Der edel auf der Teyfer pruk
> Machet stoltzer ritter vil.

He then rewarded them with gifts of silver, gold, and horses--
a sign of his generosity *(milte)*.

No exploits appear more frequently in Suchenwirt's poems
than those referring to the numerous and wasting disagreements
which took place in the border areas of Austria, Bohemia, and
Moravia between the years 1328 and 1332. It is difficult to
locate every one in time and place because Suchenwirt and
also the contemporary chronicles are vague and imprecise.

Several battles took place on the border of Moravia and
Austria in the area of Ulrichskirchen. Ulrich von Walsee, for
example, fought there, as well as at Steteldorf, and at
Deslsen (Ölsnitz in the poem) where he swam the river Mur:

> Vor Ulreichschirchen er [Ulrich] do vacht   XIII,119
> Mit chechem muet gar wol bedacht;
> Do schuef sein ritterleicher muet,
> Daz maniger sach sein aygen pluet
> Durch liechte ringe rern;
> Der veinde schaden mern
> Chund er mit ritterleicher tat.
> Vor Steteldarf gevochten hat...
> Pei Ölsnitz swemt er uber di muer,
> Und eylte da den veinden nach.

These events fit into the correct time sequence since
immediately thereafter the battle of Konstel is described.
Accounts reported in chronicles from 1329 and 1336 describe
the Hungarian-Bohemian confederation:

> Karolus Ungarorum Rex, Johannes Boemorum Rex insimul confœderatei,
> mirabiliter discordant, cum Alberto et Ottone Ducibus Austriæ
> proterea tota fere Australis provincia graviter est incendiis
> et rapinis devastata.[332]

Suchenwirt mentions the battle of Konstel in Moravia in
connection with the deeds of Leutold von Stadeck, Friedrich
von Pfannberg, and Friedrich von Kreußpeck who fought on the
Austrian side. The battle in which the Austrians were
victorious took place some time between 1325 and 1335,

possibly in 1330 (the chronicles are not specific and differ
from one another). Suchenwirt demonstrates his ability at
battle portrayal (fifty lines to describe Leutold's role).
Both sides shouted their battle cry to bolster their morale:

> „Hie Östereich! hie Ungerlant!"   XV,55
> Der paider chrey wart wol bechant.--
> Die rott sach man verwerren,
> Die orss begunden cherren
> Von hurtichleichen stozzen:
> Gewin und schaden grozzen
> In paiden hauffen da geschach.
> Hie gefang, dort stich und slach,
> Da ainer auf dem andern lakch
> Mit mezzern chitzeln umb den nakch;
> Swert und ar^embrust, pogen, phfeil
> Sach man an der selben weil
> Gar lutzel wenig rasten;
> Man sach gar veintlich tasten
> Under gollier, under schozz,
> Mit scharffen swerten-spitzen plozz.

Finally God awarded the victory to the Austrians:

> Tzu paiden seiten her und dar,   XV,90
> Pis daz got genedichleich
> Den sig gab den von Östereich
> Mit hochgetewerter wirdichait.

Suchenwirt excells again when describing the role of the
wounded Friedrich von Kreußpeck, who noticed the enemy was
fleeing and pursued it across the bridge on his wounded horse:

> Er [Friedrich] eylt den veinden allez nach,   XIV,160
> Er über di pruk ze Kötsse rant;
> Sein ross erstochen wart ze hant
> Dem edlen ritter zu der stunt
> Und auch er selbe sere wunt;
> Doch Östereich den sig behilt.

In 1331 King John of Bohemia hurried to Laa with an
army of 2,000 knights and 40,000 foot soldiers. However,
despite the size of the army, King John did not feel con-
fident against the Austrians reinforced by Hungarians and
thus he remained in the city. Duke Otto of Austria challenged
the Bohemians to a fight and finally besieged the city of
Laa. In the meantime other Bohemian knights began robbing,
plundering, and burning along the Bohemian-Austrian border
until in the spring of 1332 the situation came to a climax.
Two brothers from the Lippa family, Johann and Heinrich der
Eiserne, the commander of Laa, were taken prisoner.[333]

Dar nach vor Lo er [Burkhard, the Elder] mandleich vacht,   VIII,115
Da her gen her mit hauffen gacht.
Von Östereich, von Pehem lant
Sach man vil manges heldes hant
Nach hohen preise werben:
Genesen unde sterben
Di payde lagen auf der wag.
Gevangen wurden auf dem tag
Der hoch geteurete Hainreich,
Sein prüder Hans gar riterleich,
Die von der Leipen sint genant;
Da wart der mütes reich bechant,
Daz man noch von im saget mær,
Er macht mangen satel ler,
.Die orss man ledick laufen sach,
Vil manger im dez siges iach
Durch sinene ellenthaften müt.

The Austrians were commanded by Ulrich von Polheimer and Otto
von Walsee. In the account involving Hans von Traun,
Suchenwirt claims that over six hundred men took part in the
actual battle:

Ein vechten resch vor La geschach,   XVIII,43
Da man tze paiden seiten sach
Sechs hundert werleich under mer.

Laa, Weitra, Egenburg, and other cities again came into the
hands of the Austrians. Peace reigned for a short time.

The events elaborated upon above represent a good
sample of those mentioned by Suchenwirt in the *Ehrenreden*.
They illustrate his approach to historical events as well as
his poetic style. The mystery of his sources is intriguing:
usually he presents an accurate account of an event; sometimes he confuses the reader or makes outright mistakes; and
often he introduces new material not found in other accounts.
He gives no clues regarding his own sources. Only in the 1377
Prussian campaign is it certain that Suchenwirt was an eye-
witness. But he frequently reminds his audience that he is
telling the truth, a typical medieval topos:

(Ich sag nür di warhait hie!)   XIV,80

Wer adel hab, der merke,   VII,20
Ob ich hie di warhait sag
Von dem, den ich mit trewen chlag
Auz meines sinnes phorten.

Ja chünd ich allergerenst,   XV,30
Daz ich di warhait von im sagt.--

Suchenwirt's description of King Louis entering Naples, of the battle of Mühldorf, the election of Frederick and Louis in 1314, and the crowning of Emperor Charles IV coincide with chronicle accounts of the same events. In many cases I have quoted the appropriate chronicle to illustrate this. However, there still remains the question of source. Did the chronicles provide the source for Suchenwirt or vice versa? The eighteenth century accounts by Hoheneck and Preuenhueber regarding the career of Hans von Traun show how ambiguous the situation is and the difficulty of resolution. Did Suchenwirt rely upon eyewitness accounts reported to the court at Vienna by messengers, ambassadors, heralds? Did the information come from the participants themselves? Did Suchenwirt exchange information with other heralds while on his many travels? The most probable answer is that all these sources were used by Suchenwirt--except possibly chronicles which were too contemporary and often recorded years later. In other words, Suchenwirt used the same nebulous, undefinable sources as did the chroniclers, the "true historians."

The variety of sources also explains the confusion and mistakes found in Suchenwirt's poems. Suchenwirt claims that Hans von Traun carried the English banner at the battle of Poitiers and was rewarded with a life pension of one hundred marks. Unfortunately on the spot chroniclers, such as Froissart, were not interested in the exploits of Austrian knights, and Austrian chroniclers were not sufficiently close to the battle to make an accurate report. It is probably safe to say that Hans fought bravely against the French. Certainly stories of his deeds filtered back to Vienna. Whether these particular incidents took place during the battle is difficult to confirm. It is possible that they represent incidents which took place in similar circumstances at another time, after the campaign to Guienne, for example. The account of Burkhard von Ellerbach, the Younger, at the battle of Crécy in 1346 is similarly intriguing. The battle can be identified as Crécy because Suchenwirt mentions it as the occasion of the death of King John of Bohemia. According

to Suchenwirt Burkhard was left for dead, covered with blood
and grass, for many critical hours (IX,66-80).

Most of the confusion involves chronology. The various
battles which took place at Zurich are difficult to place in
relationship to the many other activities of the knights.
When Suchenwirt lists a number of battles in succession it
is often difficult to identify each one. Some of the
Prussian crusades are not mentioned in other sources, much
less their dates. The battle of Eisenburg mentioned in
connection with Friedrich von Kreußpeck and Hans von Traun
does not appear in any other sources within the time framework of the heroes' other deeds. The storming of Memming and
Munich in connection with Ulrich von Walsee cannot be
convincingly identified. Suchenwirt appears to make a mistake
when he writes that the lord of Mantua came to the aid of the
Castruccio in 1325 when other courses claim it was the lord
of Milan.

Clearly the confusion and mistakes perceived may also be
the result of new historical information which is presented
solely by Suchenwirt. Karl Heinrich von Busse claims that
the Livonian crusades were so common that chroniclers were
not interested in recording them.[334] There is no account of
the campaign by Ulrich von Cilli to Prussia ca. 1350 and very
little information about that of Duke Albert III. Very little
is known about Friedrich von Kreußpeck, especially his
escapades in Italy, fighting first for the Ghibellines, then
for the Guelphs. The adventures of Friedrich von Lochen in
Denmark and his role in the episode with the "false Waldemar"
appear in fragmentary form in contemporary chronicles. Finally
the extent of the travels of many of Suchenwirt's heroes would
be unknown were it not for the *Ehrenreden*.

Did Suchenwirt consider himself a chronicler, a
historian? The answer is probably negative. Chroniclers of
the fourteenth century such as Nicholaus von Jeroschin,
Wigand von Marburg, Thomas Ebendorfer von Haselbach, Leopold
Stainreuter, Johann von Posilge, Jacob Twinger von Königshofen,
Johann von Victring, Guglielmo and Albrigeti Cortusi, Hermann

von Wartberge, to name a few, appear very self-conscious in
their work. Even where they follow a party line, they strive
for an aura of objectivity. Their accounts are terse, to the
point, with very few human interest type details. The reader
finds them cold and unmoving.

Naturally Suchenwirt was influenced by this type of
writing. Even though he could not read Latin (most of the
chronicles were in Latin, only a few in the vernacular), he
was aware of the style involved. His accounts also tend to
be terse. However, Suchenwirt approaches the events which
he describes from a different perspective. He does not claim
to be writing a chronicle but rather a poem about an individual; thus his version of history is hero-oriented, not
event-oriented. Chronicles dealing with the great European
noble houses tend also to emphasize the actions of the
leaders of the houses, but the specific events are national
rather than individual in scope. For example, the
Österreichische Chronik von den 95 Herrschaften[335] written by
Leopold Stainreuter (1340-ca. 1400) is most similar in
attitude and mood to Suchenwirt's works and also in the
author's relationship with Duke Albert III. Nevertheless,
only major figures are the subject of chapters, and minor
figures such as Burkhard von Ellerbach, Friedrich von Kreußpeck, and Ulrich von Walsee are mentioned only in connection
with specific events. Suchenwirt is more interested in
stressing the bravery of his heroes than in describing an
actual event for posterity with historical accuracy. For
example, the siege of Belz in Galicia, ca. 1350, undertaken
by King Louis of Hungary is mentioned in connection with
Burkhard von Ellerbach, the Younger, and Albert of Nuremberg.
None of Suchenwirt's three accounts of this siege is very
illuminating:

> Vor Wels in stürmes herte,   X,59
> Do man mit ernst werte
> Daz chastel do vor dem gewalt
> Mit würffen, schüzzen manikvalt,
> Daz es plaib unbedwungen gar.

> Vor Pels, do maniger stürms phlag   IX,123
> Daz man in auf den selben tag

Tzalt tzu der pesten ainen:
Mit pheilen und mit stainen
Ward im ertzaigt der veinde haz;
Sein werleich müt sich nie vergaz
Gen alten noch gen iungen:
Doch plaib gar unbedwungen
Daz chastell von der veinde chraft.

Wi mandleich under schilde   VII,126
Vor Wels man in do stürmen sach
Fur ander leut, piz daz geschach
Ein würf mit swinden ungefüg,
Daz man in unversunnen trug
Von den planken laider dan!
Dar nach der edel sich versan,
'Der stürm nam ein ende,
Das chastel so behende
Des males ungewunnen wart.

The heroes were brave; the storming of Belz was unsuccessful.
Suchenwirt's hero-orientation is obvious.

It is interesting to note that this same hero-orientation
is present in the work of two other fourteenth century heralds--
Gelre and the Chandos Herald.   It is clear that heralds were
connected with tournaments, that they acted as ambassadors,
that they were related in class to the *farende liute*, and that
they frequently compiled heraldic books or rolls. No specific
reference is made to their duties as poets or historians.
And yet, Suchenwirt, Gelre, and the Chandos Herald wrote poems
about specific heroes, illustrating not only their ability
as professional heralds, but also their skill at writing
poetic history. The *Vie et gestes du Prince Noir* by the Chandos
Herald is a historical account which emphasizes the glorious
deeds of the Black Prince of Wales. In this case the details
can generally be verified in other less poetic sources.
Gelre's chronicles of the dukes of Brabant and of the counts
of Holland are similar; in both cases, in the works of
Chandos Herald and Gelre, the individual is more important
than the nation. This is even more obvious in Gelre's
Ehrenreden, each of which, like Suchenwirt's, deals with one
particular hero; furthermore, these heroes do not appear
often in other sources.

Needless to say, documentary evidence from the
fourteenth century, much less, specific information about

heralds or individual heralds or even chroniclers, is
extremely rare. Three heralds wrote historical poems about
contemporary individuals. Were these activities part of
their recognized duties or were they merely sidelines, suited
to their particular abilities?

VIII. PETER SUCHENWIRT AS POLITICAL COMMENTATOR

Suchenwirt's perspective toward politics is closely connected to what he regards as the best interests of the House of Austria. His attitude is frequently patronizing: he calls the young dukes *pippel* (children) and admonishes them to guard their prerogatives. His close relationship with the royal family as court herald is indicated by his rather presumptuous attitude. Suchenwirt's politically oriented poems appear to be written later in his life according to Seemüller's chronology; they clearly represent the position of a mature, well-informed man.

Suchenwirt's continuous disapproval of a division of the Habsburg territories appears again and again. When Rudolf IV died in 1365 his brother Albert III was seventeen and Leopold II was fifteen. The family treaty based on the privilege of 1156, reestablished by their father, and confirmed by Rudolf, left the sole administration of their possessions vested in Albert. However, the discordant natures of the two brothers were ill calculated to maintain the family union which had been religiously preserved: Leopold quickly overthrew the system established by his ancestors for securing undiminished the power and possessions of his family. At first Leopold was entrusted with the administration of the Swabian territories and divided with Albert the government of Tyrol; but, ambitious for power and impatient for control, Leopold extorted a new family compact by which he left only Austria to his brother, and acquired (in addition to the territories in Alsace and Swabia) Styria and Carinthia, with their dependencies, and the exclusive possession of Tyrol, together with the city of Neustadt and the neighboring district. Since not only the family pact but also the imperial investiture established the indivisibility of the Austrian territories and vested the administration in the eldest brother, Leopold applied for the consent of the Emperor to the new arrangement. Naturally Emperor Charles IV was happy to give his sanction, observing

at the time that the dukes of Austria had humbled themselves
where the Emperor himself had failed.

After the death of Leopold in 1386, Albert resumed the
administration of affairs as head of the family, but when the
young princes, his nephews, reached maturity, they extorted
from him the dominions which had been held by their father.[336]

On the death of Albert III in 1395, William claimed the
administration of Austria as the eldest member of the family,
but, being opposed by young Albert IV, his cousin, violent
dissensions arose between the two cousins, until it was at
length settled that both princes should exercise a joint
administration during their lives, and after their deaths,
the government was to be vested in the eldest surviving
member of the family.

The poem "Die red haizzt der new rat" (XXII) appears
to refer to the division of land among the sons of Albert II
after his death in 1358. Suchenwirt holds the advisers and
greedy vassals responsible for the unfortunate division.
Suchenwirt's admonition, however, is veiled in allegory. The
poet loses his way in the woods, comes upon a spring where
he is received by a friendly hermit. They introduce themselves
and the hermit tells of his fate--how he was once a respected
man at court and the tutor of the young prince whom he taught
fear of God and love of virtue: "Ich riet im chewsch, ich
lert in zucht." But then a courtly adviser expelled him and
through flattery turned the young prince away from virtue.
He himself was forced to flee to this monastery in the wilderness. He compares the education of youth with the taming
of a falcon. The falcon is tamed by a birdhouse, a harness
or line, and by the clipping of its long feathers. A youth
is educated at home, by his tutors and advisers, and by the
withholding of money and possessions which cause arrogance.

In the poem "Von der fürsten tailung" Suchenwirt again
disguises his advice, this time in a fable told by a father
to his two sons. It is the old story of the bundle of sticks
tied together which cannot be broken while a single stick is
easily split. The father carefully explains the moral, a

united land remains powerful, undefeatable:

> Der vater sprach: „Hört, waz ich main,   XXXIV,83
> Und mercht di abentewre.
> Ir habt land und lewt weit
> Mit güter ritterschefte;
> Di weil ir ungetailet seit,
> So habt ir vil der chrefte,
> Daz euch chain fürst gepiegen mag.
> Er werd von euch gechrenchet."

But a divided land will quickly be overtaken by enemies:

> „Ez mag noch chomen wol der tag,   XXXIV,91
> Daz ir an mich gedenchet!
> Tailt ir di land, also daz holtz,
> Ir müzzt ew lazz pukchen,
> Wärt ir an chreften noch so stoltz,
> Di herschaft wirt tzu stukchen....
> Purg und stet pei einander schol
> Beleiben; ez pringt iamer,
> Wo man auz güten landen weit
> Wil stukch und drümer machen.
> Da müz schier in chürtzer tzeit
> Gwalt und herschaft swachen."

Since the poem is directed to two brothers *(tzwen prüder)* it probably refers to the pact of July 7, 1379 between Albert III and Leopold II. However, it could also apply to the pact of November 22, 1395 between the cousins Albert IV and William. In both cases the division of territories proved disasterous.

Once again in the poem "Das ist der getrew rat" Suchenwirt advises the young princes:

> Ich han ew, pippel, vil gesait,   XXXIII,117
> In trewen ich daz maine:
> Chrieg tzwischen frewnden bringet laid
> Und affterrew nicht chlaine;
> Wo neid und haz in hertzen swiert,
> Da mues di ere chrenchen.

Suchenwirt illustrates his advice by quoting from the Bible--Lucifer, Adam and Eve, King Herod--and by relating the parable of the war among the elements. He climaxes his remarks with the more immediate example of the unfortunate fate of the princes of Brunswick who, after reigning for more than a century, lost their power through family feuds and division of property. This was apparently the prime example for Suchenwirt since he mentions the fate of the Brunswicks also in "Von dem Phenning." Despite the allegory,

parables, fables, and Biblical illustrations Suchenwirt is
very explicit in his warnings:

> Wo herren untailet sind,   XXXIII,97
> Den solt man frewntlich raten,
> Is möcht der landesherren chind
> Noch chomen wol tzu staten.
> Wer hewer machet widertail,
> Tzu iar ez sich vercheret;
> Hat er nicht gelukches hail,
> Sein schad wiert gemeret.

Suchenwirt clearly states that Albert III is already dead and
that the territories have not yet been partitioned; thus this
poem was probably written between August 1395, the death of
Albert, and November 1395, when a new treaty was approved
which divided the lands among the young dukes.

In a similarly "familiar" vein Suchenwirt suggests
that the young princes repeal the tax on wine and other drinks
known as the *Ungeld*. This tax was promulgated under Rudolf IV
as a means of raising revenue; it consisted of a ten per cent
levy on all drinks sold in public bars. It was considered
oppressive by all classes of society. Leopold Stainreuter,
writes that it was continued by Duke Albert in 1383:

> Des jar slueg man ain stewr auf die wein in der stat ze Wienn,
> auf yegleich fueder ain phunt und auf ain dreiling VI ßdl.
> Auch uberhueb man nyemant, weder phaffen, münich noch nunnen,
> ritter noch chnecht, noch des herczogen hofgesind.[337]

Suchenwirt begins the poem by flattering the young dukes
Albert and Leopold and by appealing to their desire to virtue
and good deeds. First he establishes their noble lineage.
They are fresh sprigs from a noble tree (Albert II) which was
cut down by the gardener, God himself. (This establishes the
date of the poem between 1365, the death of Rudolf IV, and
1386, the death of Leopold II.) The two young dukes are
directed to pay attention to the example of their father in
the execution of law and justice, to appoint true and loyal
advisers, to accept true advice, to forbid slanderers
entrance to the court, and finally to repeal the *Ungeld:*

> Lat tugent an euch scheinen,   XXVII,55
> Daz nert euch dort vor peinen:
> Den ungelt auf den weinen
> Lat ab durch ewer edel tzucht,

> Daz pringt euch selde mit genucht;
> Der gemeine flüch pringt lützel frucht.

They are admonished to listen to the pleas of the poor, for
whom the tax was especially difficult:

> So hört der armen lewte chlag   XXVII,77
> Und endet snelle nach der wag.
> Lang peiten und vertziehen
> Chan von den eren vliehen
> Recht als di tugende-schiehen.

They will not go unrewarded:

> Ir seit geherret weiter lant,   XXVII,85
> Welt ir nu werden hoch genant,
> .So macht mit tugenden euch bechant,
> Vrawen-preis in hertzen übt,
> Priesterschaft mit nicht betrübt.

Although Suchenwirt is modest in his request (convention and
his position necessitate modesty), his message is clear.[338]

    In another political poem, "Daz sind Aristotiles rêt"
(XXXVIII) Suchenwirt clothes his instruction to contemporary
princes in the form of a letter from Aristotles to his pupil,
Alexander the Great. The year 1394 is mentioned as well as
the source for the poem, the *Secreta secretorum*. Suchenwirt
appears to be admonishing Duke Albert III for the part he
may have played in the imprisonment of King Wenceslaus:
on May 8, 1394 Margrave Jobst of Moravia attacked his nephew
Wenceslaus, as Wenceslaus was returning to Prague from his
favorite castle Bettlern; Jobst imprisoned Wenceslaus in his
own castle for several months. Suchenwirt's advice to
preclude a recurrence of a similar outrage is subtle, no
names are mentioned:

> Hiet ain chünig die rêt gelesen,   XXXVIII,333
> Es wêr im paz ergangen,
> Und wêr auch ordenleich gewesen,
> Er wêr nie gevangen!

    Suchenwirt again identifies with the plight of the poor
in the poem "Von der füursten chrieg und von des reiches
steten." The war which is in progress is detrimental to
all involved:

> Ain chrieg hat sich gehebet an,   XXXVII,1
> Den schatzet man gar chlaine;
> Ich fürcht, daz in weib und man
> Noch chlæglich bewaine.

Suchenwirt asks: if there were no more peasants, how would
they who call themselves lords live? The nobles will not
bother with plows and the bourgeoisie of the cities are too
proud to farm:

> Wenn gepawrn nicht mer ist,   XXXVII,21
> So wirt der schimph entrennet:
> Wez denn lebent die selben frist,
> Die herren sind genennet?
> Die fürsten nicht mit phluegen gan,
> Die purger sich sein schamen,
> So müzz man underwegen lan
> Auf ækcher werffen den samen.

The coffers of the rich are full, those of the poor empty.
The poor watch their wives and children grow pale from
hunger. Finally they cry:

> „Den reichen schrotet auf die tor,   XXXVII,47
> Wir wellen mit in ezzen;"
> ‚Pazz tzimpt, wir werden all erslagen,
> Ee wir vor hunger sterben,
> Wir wellen daz leben frischleich wagen
> Ee wir also verderben."

The result is a terrible bloodletting in which all are
involved:

> So wirt ein plutvergiezzen groz   XXXVII,53
> Von arm und von reichen,
> Von ritter, chnechten, widerdos:
> Daz stet gar chlêgleichen!

Suchenwirt insists that cities and princes are the two main
components of a country and must remain united. When they
are against each other, they only make the Jews and heathens
happy. He names the year 1387--possibly the year of the
composition of the poem--as especially difficult and
depressing.

The treaties of confederacy among imperial cities
were increasing. Neither the united nobility, nor the
frequently broken *Landfrieden* (1384, 1385, 1387) could solve
the problem; individual princes tended to vacillate from one
side to another. Duke Leopold stood at the head of the
imperial cities united against the nobility; the Archbishop
of Salzburg fought with the powerful Swabian cities against
the Bavarian duke; even Emperor Wenceslaus came forward on
the side of the cities. Vienna, whose trade was frequently

disrupted by Bohemian nobility, also felt the results of the
generally widespread enmity among nobles, cities, and the
country population. Suchenwirt's solution seems somewhat
naive and ineffectual when seen today in retrospect, since
the difficulties continued for another century. He appeals
to King Wenceslaus to go to Rome to be crowned:

> In Pehem mawst der Adalar,   XXXVII,77
> Hat er icht schier gerekchet:
> Chunich Wentzla, dez nempt war,
> Ewr flug die strekchet,
> Habt ir gehertet tzu dem flug,
> Hebt ew auf die raise,
> Tzewcht ein chayserleichen tzug
> Gen Rom durch manig prayse,
> Seit ir ein römisch chunich seit,
> Und habt den nam auf erde.

He hopes that as emperor Wenceslaus will be able to exercise
his rights as supreme imperial judge and will be able to
settle the feuds between the princes and the imperial cities:

> So nennet man ewch weiten,   XXXVII,96
> Daz ir daz reich und auch daz recht
> Mit trewen so besorget,
> Daz stet und fursten pleiden slecht,
> Und nicht dem unrecht porget,
> Also daz ir guet richter seit
> Den arm und den reichen.
> Ob ew got die genade geit,
> So lebt ir wirdichleichen!

In this poem Suchenwirt acknowledges the basic economic
relationship between the countryside and the cities and the
dependency of both the cities and the nobility upon the
peasant. This is fairly unusual material for a poem.
Suchenwirt himself is clearly caught between his economic
allegiance to his employers, the nobility, and his class
allegiance to the city bourgeoisie.

For less specific reasons Suchenwirt urges Wenceslaus
to travel to Rome as quickly as possible in the poem "Von
tzwain päbsten." He maintains that there is one emperor too
few and one pope too many:

> Eins chaisers dez hab wir tzu chlain   XXXV,93
> Eins pabst tzu vil auf erden.

Wenceslaus, who was already named Emperor by his father
Charles IV in 1376, had not yet been crowned in Rome. (The

coronation took place in 1378.) Pope Urban VI, a Neapolitan,
had been elected Pope by the cardinals in Rome; at the same
time thirteen other cardinals had elected Count Robert of
Geneva to be Pope at Fondi. Robert called himself Clement VII
and chose Avignon as his place of residence:

> Pabst Urban ist von erst erwelt   XXXV,53
> Tzu Rom, dez hör ich iechen,...
> Darnach von Jeniff der graff Rubprecht
> Pabst Clemens ist genennet.
> Ist daz göttleich und recht?

Suchenwirt's allegiance is obviously on the side of the first
chosen Pope Urban. He lists the followers of each Pope. On
the side of the true Pope are the countries from Livonia to
Tuscany, from the Rhine into Hungary, plus the five kingdoms
of Naples, Norway, Denmark, Sweden and England:

> Von Leyfflant in Tuschkane,   XXXV,62
> Von dem Rein in Ungerlant
> Die sind mit pabst Urbane.
> Noch ist mit uns, daz wil ich reden,
> Fümf chünichreich bechennet:
> Püllen, Norbeg, Temmarch, Sweden
> Und Engellant genennet.

On the other side are Provence, France, Spain, Portugal,
Aragon, and others which Suchenwirt maintains he does not
want to name:

> Da wider Previntz und Franchreich   XXXV,69
> Die lant sind all tzu male
> Mit dem pabst Clemens geleich,
> Yspanien, Portigale,
> Arragun und dennoch mer,
> Dez ich nicht mag genennen.

Suchenwirt only errs in the allegiance of Naples and Portugal:
Queen Joan of Naples chose Clement and Portugal came to the
side of Urban. Suchenwirt cleverly, even slyly, declined
to mention all the followers of Clement which included Duke
Leopold of Austria, who, much to the despair of his brother
Albert, had joined other Lower Rhine families with the
opposition party, which was led by the French. Albert
remained true to the Church in Rome and to Urban, who in
1384 gave him permission to found a theological faculty at
the University of Vienna.

If God could make two human beings, Adam and Eve,

from one, why could he not make one pope from two:

> Du hast gemachet mit fürnunft   XXXV,99
> Even aws Adamen,
> Hast aws ainem gemachet tzway
> So mach aws tzwain uns aines:...
> Aws tzwain päbsten mach uns ainn.

Suchenwirt then restates the medieval theory of church and state:

> Tzway haubt gib der christenhait   XXXV,109
> Ainn pabst und ainn chayser,
> Dy in der werlt lankch und prait
> Daz unrecht machen haiser:
> So wirt die christenhait getzirt,
> Darumb süllen wir got flehen.

In this poem Suchenwirt again demonstrates his facility for handling geographical as well as political material. Although there was surely much interest at the court in Vienna regarding the allegiance of the major European powers, it was not typically a subject matter for poetry.

If Suchenwirt reveals part of his personality in his attitude towards the young dukes, he also reveals himself and his position as a fairly intimate observer, even participant, in the poem "Von dem Phenning." The poet (Suchenwirt) meets money personified as the *Phenning*, a wise well-traveled old man who accompanies him, commenting on their journey about various persons and places. The *Phenning* asks the poet: "Shall we travel to the left?" The poet replies, "No, it is well known that bad men live there."

> Tzu dem alten sprach ich do: XXIX,30
> „Well wir tzu der lenken hant?"
> „Nain! so wurden uns bechant
> Poser herren mer wenn vil.
> Die rechten strazz ich reiten wil."

This exchange not only refers to right and left--good and evil-- but more specifically alludes to the powerful leaders in party-torn Italy, on the left hand side of the road (i.e. western) when one is traveling north to Austria.

The *Phenning* claims that the Emperor loves and honors him: "Der chayser hat mich lieb und wert." Emperor Charles IV was well known for his love of money as well as for his parsimony. His brothers John Henry and Wenceslaus are also

characterized in an unflattering manner, overly concerned
with amassing wealth. The *Phenning* claims:

> „Gen Pravant hab ich snelle muet   XXIX,141
> Tzu seinem edeln pruder güt."

This refers to Wenceslaus who was the husband of the rich
heiress Joan of Brabant.

When asked about his own background the *Phenning* claims
that he comes from Saxony, the area of the oldest and richest
silver mines. The *Phenning* measures the goodness and badness
of noble families by their generosity to wandering poets and
other travelers. Frequently he enriches his comments by
allegorical remarks referring to the heraldic devices of the
nobles, for example the rising eagle of the Meissen family:

> „Sind euch die fursten icht bechant   XXIX,154
> In Meichsen, allez wandels vrey?"
> „Mainst du di fürsten alle drey?"
> Sprach der Phenning da tzu mir:
> „Die habent mein mit eren gir,
> Ir er nympt auf von iar zu iar,
> Recht als ein edel adellar
> Über ander vogel steyget,
> Ir wird nicht nyder seyget,
> Di chlimment auf von tag zu tag."

On the other hand, he is scathing in his denunciation of
evil or bad nobles:

> „Hertzog Otten in der Marckh   XXIX,169
> Chenn ich, der ward nie gutes charkch,
> Sein adel chlingt der eren steig."

He then especially praises the hospitality of Duke Rupprecht
from the Rhine and Duke Adolf of Heidelberg:

> „Tzu hertzog Rupprecht an den Rein;   XXIX,181
> Wann ich dem chum, der lat mich ein,
> Dez hof siecht man gar wirdichleich
> In schonn tzuchten fräudenreich:
> Mit herschaft und mit vrawen
> Mag man in chostleich schawen.
> Hertzog Adolf von Haidelberch,
> Dem pin ich lieber denn ein twerch,
> Der ist hübsch und chluger sit,
> Dem wil ich geren wonen mit
> Mit trewen und mit eren."

For the dukes of Bavaria, whom he had not visited for a long
time, the *Phenning* prophesied a dim future, the same fate as the lord
of Milan. The huge Bavarian family was reduced to poverty by
numerous feuds and wars; they negotiated with Charles IV and

sold him some of their cities; to the Austrian dukes they sold
the rights to Tyrol.

Finally the poet asks the *Phenning* whether he has been in
Austria. The *Phenning* replies that the princes are too young
and do not yet know him:

> Er sprach: „Da han ich chaine phlicht.   XXIX,213
> Die sind ze iunch und chenn mein nicht:
> Ir adel ist mir wol bechant,
> Grozz herscheft, weytew lant,
> Und chüm doch nicht in ir gewalt.
> Würden si ein wenig alt,
> Daz si mich erchanden paz,
> .Pey in so belib ich sunder haz."

However, he is acquainted with the nobility of Austria and
may yet have the opportunity of meeting the princes.

The poem ends with a eulogy in honor of King Louis of
Hungary, prompting the suggestion that Suchenwirt may have
served King Louis before coming to the Austrian court:

> „Der [King Louis] gevelt mir wol in sein tagen;   XXIX,224
> Die weil er hat die Dautschen wert
> So chlingt seins hohen lobs swert
> Durich alle lant den maisten tail,
> Er hat gelukch und siges hail;
> Daz er gewinnt pürg unde lant,
> Seit er mich mit so milter hant,
> Daz sein di chron hat ere:
> Er volget weiser lere
> Mit gantzer innerchleicher gir...."

Peter Suchenwirt would probably not have used the term
political commentator to describe his activities. Nevertheless,
he did not hesitate to express his personal opinions regarding political matters, even sensitive ones. His approach
to contemporary politics appears conscientious but not
cautious. On the other hand, he may well have considered
himself a type of court adviser--especially in his later years
when the dukes were very young. His attitude towards the
dukes is familiar, even paternal; his political position is
clearly partisan in favor of Austrian interests. Although
conditions had changed considerably since the time of Walther
von der Vogelweide, Suchenwirt still maintains the theory of
state requiring a strong pope and a strong emperor; in this
his poems are reminiscent of Walther's. Walther's prime
concern was for a government of laws and justice established

and maintained through an ordered hierarchy of leaders: king,
lords, and knights. Thus he maintained that if the king were
crowned with the proper symbols (i.e. with the *weise*, the
stone in the imperial crown) and in the right place, the kingdom would be in order. He implored: "Philippe setze en
weisen uf, und hiez si treten hinder sich!" (7,2,25)[339] Both
Walther and Suchenwirt were concerned with the coronation
ceremony which conferred upon the emperor the requisite
authority to govern in an orderly manner.

In the *sacerdotium-imperium* controversy Walther's enmity
for the Pope caused him to omit the office of the Papacy from
his scheme of things. Walther comes to the Emperor as a
fronebote bringing him a message from God:

> Her keiser, ich bin fronebote   13,3,1
> und bring iu boteschaft von gote:
> ir habt die erde, er hat daz himelriche.

He viewed God (not the Pope) and the Emperor as the two
supreme powers with a direct relationship:

> Er heiz iu klagen (ir sit sin voget),   13,3,4
> in sines sunes lande broget
> diu heidenschaft iu beiden lasterliche.
> Ir muget im gerne rihten.

The Emperor must set things right on earth which is overrun
by heathens (i.e. he must undertake a crusade).

Suchenwirt, on the other hand, displays a more sophisticated and less hierarchical view of the complex nature of
society. The intricate relationship among the various
classes and professions, which did not interest Walther who
lived in a courtly environment, intrigued Suchenwirt:

> Stet und fürsten sind tzwen tail   XXXVII,57
> In all der werlt die pesten,
> Halten die nicht frides hail,
> Wie get ez dann tzum lesten?

Though both were committed to the partisan politics of their
time, they advocated a grand harmonious theoretical system
of government.

CONCLUSION

As a herald Suchenwirt illustrates both the position of heralds in society and the state of the craft of heraldry in fourteenth century Austria. He clearly was not excessively proud of his status, his "order" as he calls it. He frequently regrets the necessity of living off the generosity of his patrons. He appears to have been closely connected with the Habsburg family, and he was a property owner. The latter is a modest indication of the upward mobility of his class during the late Middle Ages.

Suchenwirt's heraldic terminology is accurate and precise. It appears somewhat more descriptive than the heraldry of today (which is less technical in German than in English). Without sacrificing accuracy the poetic aspects are dominant in his heraldic descriptions. He is not interested in the legal problems of the right to bear arms or of disputes about arms which were gaining importance at the time. The purpose of Suchenwirt's blazon is not to identify his hero by his arms, but to honor the hero by describing his arms.

Suchenwirt appears to have taken his task as a chronicler very seriously even though the format of his poems indicates that he was concerned with more than just the cold facts of history. Some of Suchenwirt's accounts differ from those of his contemporaries, but since most of the details usually agree, there is no reason to believe that he was fabricating. Medieval source material is extremely erratic. Not only did the historians of the time have a narrow perspective of current events based on their own limited travels, but at the same time their concept of history was more cosmologically oriented than concerned with specific contemporary details. The great chronicles of the fourteenth century traced the ruling dynasties from the beginning of the world or the birth of Christ to Charlemagne and his successors. Suchenwirt, on the other hand, provides a different view of the Middle Ages, one centered upon individual heroes, not great ruling houses or decisive events. His heroes appear frequently in documents, occasionally in chronicles, but usually, except for those who were kings or dukes, their life history is not discussed in comparable detail in any other sources.

Although Suchenwirt does not appear particularly proud of his position as herald, he does exhibit an air of self-confidence when advising the young Habsburg princes; he feels secure enough to offer advice in a very familiar vein. The subject matter of his political comments is especially enlightening. He discusses the ramifications of a division of property, the political consequences of a tax on wine, and the interrelationship among the classes; these are not generally the subject matter for chronicles or historical songs.

Here only those parts of his works which relate to the subject of heraldic poetry have been considered; the examination suggests that Suchenwirt is as unique in German literature as Gelre is unique in Dutch literature; *Ehrenreden* such as those by Suchenwirt and Gelre which adhere to a strict formula do not appear elsewhere. However, the content of their poetry places them within a long and illustrious tradition which has its origins in the death lament, the political-historical song, and in "tournament and siege poetry."

Heraldic elements found in medieval epics tended to be symbolic in nature: the strong knight wore red armor, the pure knight white armor, the mysterious knight black armor. The author invented appropriate arms for his imaginary characters. Later the real coats of arms of real individuals became important to authors. Although "tournament and siege poems" were composed to commemorate a particular tournament or siege, one suspects that the authors merely chose this occasion to display their interest in heraldry--as it really existed. If the underlying symbolism in the original selection of the coat of arms was forgotten, the current honor and importance of the arms was not lost to the audience. The sight of the imperial eagle, the French *fleurs-de-lis*, or the English lions was enough to set medieval hearts aflutter. In the late Middle Ages these same hearts were more interested in the true exploits of

their contemporaries than in idealized fantasies of the past.
In the fourteenth century this realistic element is evident in
all the subgenres of heraldic poetry--in the political-historical song, in "tournament and siege poetry," in chronicles,
and in the *Ehrenrede*.

Society was changing rapidly, especially in the cities.
Court life, the duties of heralds, and heraldry itself was
changing. At the end of the fourteenth century the scope of
heraldry proliferated greatly; it became necessary to issue
Wappenbriefe proving a knight's right to bear arms. In England
Visitations aided in controlling and solidifying the expansion
of arms. The blazons of Suchenwirt and his contemporaries
tended to be factual rather than symbolic even though they
never lose sight of inherent symbolism. Changing times also
prompted Suchenwirt to comment on politics, to advise his
young masters in terms somewhat reminiscent of Walther von der
Vogelweide. He and his fellow heraldic poets had to maintain
a precarious liaison between the court society and the rising
middle classes.

Even though arms were inherited within families, heraldry
and specific arms were always associated with an individual--
in the epic, the death lament, popular songs, chronicles, and
the *Ehrenrede*. The connection between Suchenwirt's heroes and
the *Societas Templois* in Vienna strongly suggests that the
Ehrenreden served a ceremonial function within the society--
perhaps initially a private function and later a public function.

The interest in the fourteenth century was on the
individual and his deeds, and the poet and herald catered to
this interest. The heroes of the day used all of Europe as
their stage. Thus, for example, Suchenwirt, Gelre, the Chandos
Herald, and Jean Froissart wrote about the siege of Calais, the
death of King John of Bohemia, and the battle of Poitiers.
Except for Froissart they each centered their account around
one individual. Most probably Suchenwirt was not present at
the battle of Poitiers; I do not think he would have mistaken
the Prince of Wales for the King of England, an error which
could easily be made in a second-hand version of the battle.

Karl Helm's theory that Suchenwirt was familiar with Gelre's
chronicle of the counts of Holland and with the anonymous poem
lamenting the death of Count William of Holland cannot be
further substantiated.   Unfortunately, Helm does not provide
any proof and is merely suggesting a possibility which is
plausible.   The heroes of Suchenwirt's and Gelre's *Ehrenreden*
follow similar life patterns with crusades against the heathens
in Prussia, pilgrimages to the Holy Land, expeditions into
Italy, and numerous local campaigns in their homelands.

Interest in the individual and in realism also extended
into the area of the popular song where the subject matter
included not only love but also history.   Chronicles in both
Latin and in the vernacular were meticulously kept as were
historical records in the court archives (though, unfortunately,
many of them have since been lost or destroyed).   An interest
in history, in the deeds of contemporary heroes, and in heraldry
was a natural one in the fourteenth century, and an amalgamation
of these interests into the poetic genre of the *Ehrenrede* was
almost inevitable.   Those best qualified to write *Ehrenreden* were
the heralds: they were well-traveled, acquainted with the heroes
of the day, had good contacts for information, and were, of
course, thoroughly familiar with the rules of heraldry.

Heraldic poetry developed steadily throughout the centuries.   Since the end of the fourteenth century, mottos such
as the Black Prince's "Ich dene" were added to the inherited
coats of arms.   These emblems with symbolic (often animal)
charges and mottos first appeared in connection with princes
and nobles, then with cities and patricians, publishers, and
scholars.   During the sixteenth and seventeenth centuries
heraldic poetry changed to emblematic poetry.

In conclusion it appears most useful to maintain the two
definitions: heraldic poetry is poetry containing references
or allusions to heraldry, and the *Ehrenrede* is a narrowly defined
subgenre of heraldic poetry, consisting of poems adhering to
a definite formula.   The *Ehrenrede* appears in its true form
only in the works of Peter Suchenwirt and Gelre.   The literary
histories are incorrect, however, in confining heraldic

poetry to the fourteenth century. Both threads of heraldic
material, the broadly defined heraldic poetry and the narrow
Ehrenrede, have their antecedents in the pre-literary past;
both find their immediate predecessors in the twelfth and
thirteenth centuries at a time when heraldry was becoming
standardized throughout Europe. That heraldic poetry
manifested itself differently in the fourteenth century was
due more to the changing times and interests and composition
of the audience than to the emergence of such heraldic poets
as Suchenwirt and Gelre or to the emergence of a new genre.

APPENDIX I: REGISTER OF SUCHENWIRT MANUSCRIPTS

Poems in this register are arranged in the sequence in which they appear in MS A.

Primisser's Numeration	Page and Line in MS A	Title of Poem (according to Primisser's text)	Other MSS
--	1,1-17	title missing	B (see 5 below)
I	1,8-9,10	Von Chünik Ludwig von Ungerlant	B, 442^b–444^b
II	9,11-12,20	Von der Kayserin von Payrn	B, 444^b–445^b
XXIII	12,21-17,12	Ein red von der Minne	
IX	17,13-27,24	Von hern Puppli von Elrwach (dem jungen)	B, 445^b–447^a (incomplete)
XLV	28 (incomplete)	Ein red von hübscher lug	C, 27^b–29^b
XXIV	29,1-42,12	Die Minne vor Gericht (Primisser's title)	
XI	42,13-54,10	Von graff Ulreich von Phfanberg	B, 456^b–460^a
X	54,11-64,19 (lacunae)	Von hern Puppily von Elrwach (dem jungen)	B, 460^a–463^a
XII	64,20-70,19	Von her Herdegen von Petaw	B, 463^a–464^b
--	70,20-80,18	Von hern Ulrich von Walse	
III	80,19-89,14 (lacunae)	Von hertzog Albrecht von Östereich	B, 438^a–439^b
XIII	89,15-99,3	Von hern Ulrich von Walse	B, 464^b–467^a
XIV	99,4-114,3	Von hern Fridreichen dem Chreuzzpekch	B, 447^a–450^b (incomplete) s, 6 1/2 pages from middle of MS
VII	114,4-124,13 (lacunae)	Von purgraf Albrechten von Nurnberch	B, 470^a–472^b

VI	124,14-134,7	Von Kernden hertzog Hainreich	B, 473^a-475^a
XXI	134,8-142,20	Die red haist der brief	
XXV	143,1-156,22	Die schön Abentewr	m$_4^3$, 137-146
			m$_2^4$, 124^v-130^v
			g , 1-4rb
			t$_7$, 493-500
			d^2, 36-41^b
			d^2, 98^v-103^r
			W , 132^r-133^v
XXVI	157,1-159,16	Das geiaid	
XXVII	159,17-163,14	Der rat von dem ungelt	B, 475^a-477^b
XV	163,15-171,25	Von Leutolten von Stadekk	B, 477^b-480^a
VIII	171,26-182,5	Von her Pircharten Ellerbach dem alten	m$_2^4$, 107^v-114^r
XXVIII	182,6-193,28	Die red haist der widertail	b^2, 262^r-268^r
			d^2, 148^r-151^v
			l, 196-198
			st, 278^r-284^r
			n, 4^v-9^r
			f$_4$, 2ra-4ra
			m^5, 72^v-79^r
XVI	193,29-203,20	Von graff Ulreichen von Tzili	B, 480^b-482^b
XXIX	203,21-213,16	Von dem Phenning	
XXX	213,17-223,20	Von der Mynn slaff	a
XVII	223,21-231,25	Von hern Fridreichen von Lochen	B, 482^b-485^b
XXXI	232,1-241,20	Daz ist di verlegenhait	
XXXIX	242,1-252,20	Daz sind di tzehen gepot	w^1, 60^v-64^r
			w^2, 262^r-274^r
			m , 96-97
XXXII	253,1-255,20	Daz ist di geitichait	

XLVI	Gar ain schöne rede von der Liebin und der Schonin, wie sie kriegten mit ain ander	h^3_4, 228^r–230^v m^5, 68^v–71^r m^5, 31^v–43^r
Friess' Numeration		
1	Lobgedicht auf Moriz von Hawnfeld (title missing in MS)	B, 436^a–436^b
2	Von Hern Hansen von Chappell	B, 436^b–438^a
3	Von Herzog Albrechten von Oesterreich	B, 467^{a}–$470^{a)}$
4	Von Hern Albrechten von Rawchenstein	B, 439^b–441^a
5	Von Hern Sumolf Lappen von Ernwicht	B, 441^a–442^b
No Number	Was ψbels ainem yeglichem vsz Spil chom (Vom Würfelspiel)	p_2, 113^v–116^v b, 145^r–149^r r_8, 1^r–2^r m, 1^r–2^r k_8, 167^r–170^r w, 35va–36va

APPENDIX II: GLOSSARY OF HERALDIC TERMS

English, French, Middle High German, and Middle Dutch heraldic terms appear in the glossary in the same forms in which they occur in the text; the various spellings of the same word are often listed together. French, Middle High German, and Middle Dutch terms, so designated, are translated into English (no distinction is made between Old French and Anglo-Norman). The reader is referred to their English versions for a definition and explanation.

Adalar, adelar, adellar, Adler (MHG)--eagle.

ademas (MHG)--a precious stone, brown, referring to the tincture sable, see p. 167.

ancher, anker (MHG)--anchor. This is frequently used as a charge or crest, emblematical of hope, or of naval service.

Ar, aren, arn (MHG); aern (MD)--eagle.

argent--the tincture silver.

azure--the tincture blue. The name probably derives from the Arabic word for a blue stone, *lazura*.

badge or cognizance--a mark of distinction somewhat similar to a crest but not placed on a wreath nor worn upon the helmet. They were rather supplemental bearings quite independent of the charge of the original arms and were borne on the banners, ensigns, and even on the breasts and especially on the sleeves of servants and followers.

baner, baniere (Fr.); banir (MHG)--banner (see below).

banner--a kind of flag painted or embroidered with arms, and of the size proportioned to the rank of the bearer.

bar--resembles the fess in form, but occupies about one-fifth of the field. *In bar* or *barwise* signifies the horizontal arrangement of charges in two or more rows (*in fess* only when one row is placed across the fess point). The French term *bar* corresponds to the English bend.

barenstele, baresteel, barestele (MD)--see label.

barree (Fr.)--see barry.

barry--denotes that the field is horizontally divided into a certain even number of equal parts.

base--the lower part of the shield; hence *in base* means that the charge is so to be placed.

bend--an ordinary, a bend running slantwise from the left-hand corner of a shield; from the right-hand corner it is a bend sinister. It should not be less than one-fifth of the shield's width or, if charged, more than one-third. *Per bend* means a diagonal division of the field. *In bend* refers to an object or a number of objects crossing the field in the direction of and position of a bend.

bend embowed--a bend arched across the shield instead of straight diagonally.

berwiis (MD)--see in fess or fesswise.

black--see sable.

blanc (Fr., MHG); blonc (Fr.)--white, see argent.

in blanchweiz, in blankweis (MHG)--see pale, in pale.

blasineren, geblasunniert (MHG); blasinieren (MD)--see blazon.

blau (MHG)--blue, see azure.

blazon--to describe a coat of arms in such a manner that an accurate drawing may be made from the description.

blue--see azure.

bordure--a sub-ordinary, a border or band, one-fifth of the width of the shield which it surrounds. In old heraldry it was frequently used as a mark of cadency, i.e. to mark a younger branch of a family.

cadency, marks of--distinctions or differences, variations of the original arms of a family or marks attached to them for the purpose of pointing out the several branches, and the relation in which they stand to each other and to their common ancestor. See bordure and label.

çaintour (Fr.)--see saltire.

camel (MHG)--gold, see or.

canting arms--arms containing charges which are allusive to the name of the bearer. See also rebus.

charge--anything borne on a coat of arms, whether upon the field, or upon an ordinary or upon another charge.

chelen rot (MHG)--red, see gules.

checky, chequy, checquer-bearing--terms applied to a field or charge divided by perpendicular and horizontal lines into small squares of alternating colors. There should be at least twenty squares in the shield. If less, the number is named.

chief--1)an ordinary one-third of the width of the shield, occupying the uppermost section of the field; 2)all of the field above fess point--the line constituting the top of the shield. Charges blazoned *in chief* are disposed upward near the top of the shield.

chobertewer, chowertewer (MHG); covertuer (MD)--see mantling.

cognizance--see badge.

couped, coupy--cut off in a straight line, as is often the case with the heads and limbs of animals. It is sometimes applied to the extremities of ordinaries; thus a cross couped, known as *humetté*. The French *couper* means to divide a shield horizontally into two equal parts; English heralds would describe the same as *party per fess*.

crab--the common crab occurs on the coats of arms of several families.

crest--a figure or group of figures affixed to the helmet, usually heads
of men or birds, animals, or plumes of feathers.

crois (Fr.)--cross.

croissetes petites (Fr.)--a cross couped, *humetté*.

cross--an ordinary, the plain or Greek cross, which has four equal arms.
The cross should occupy one-fifth of the shield; when charged it
may occupy one-third of the shield. See also cross patonce and
saltire.

crosslet--two or more crosses borne in the same coat. They are drawn
couped.

cross patonce--a cross consisting of four arms concave on each side, and
at the ends convex and notched twice, thus having the appearance
of a very shallow *fleur-de-lis*.

crown--this word occurring in blazon without any addition usually implies
a ducal coronet without a cap.

device--a motto, emblem, or other mark by which those who entered the
lists were distinguished at tournaments, but especially a motto
affixed to the arms, having some punning allusion to the name.
It differed from a badge or cognizance only inasmuch as it was
an arbitrary and generally temporary distinction, whereas the
badge was often borne by members of the same house successively.

dexter--the right-hand side of the shield seen from the bearer's point
of view. A bend, if not otherwise blazoned, is supposed to be a
bend dexter.

dog--a charge which occurs very frequently in armorial bearings. The
ordinary position is passant, i.e. walking with three paws
on the ground, the head looking forward. The ears may be of a
different tincture, and it is frequently *gorged* or collared.

eagle--recognized as king of birds, is a favorite charge. The eagle
was borne by the German emperors (who claimed to be the successors of the Caesars of Rome) and hence the term frequently
applied to it is the imperial eagle.

eber (MHG)--boar.

engrailed--a term applied to the cutting of the edge of a border, bend,
or fess, etc. into small semicircular indents, the teeth or
points of which being outward enter the field.

engreellie (Fr.)--see engrailed.

ermine--see argent, the fur most frequently used in heraldry. It derives
its name from the ermine, a small white animal. The arms blazoned
here are tinctured white or silver to represent this fur; here
ermine appears to be synonymous with argent although in later
arms the distinction between the metal and the fur was carefully
maintained.

escutcheon--1)the shield itself whereon arms are emblazoned; 2)a small
shield of which more than one (generally three) are borne on the
shield. A single one is called an *inescutcheon*.

fasch (MHG); faes (MD)--see fess.

Felde (MHG)--see field.

fess--an ordinary crossing the field horizontally at the center of the
shield. *Per fess* refers to a horizontal division in the center of
the shield. *In fess* or *fesswise* pertains to a number of objects
ranged across the field horizontally at the visual center,
occupying the position of a fess.

fesse (Fr.)--see fess.

field--the whole of the surface of the shield.

fleur-de-lis--the conventionalized lily used in heraldic terminology.
It may be a rebus signifying "flower of Louis."

flory counter flory, fleury counter fleury--signifies adorned with
fleurs-de-lis alternately placed.

flüg, flügel, flugel (MHG)--see wings.

gamillen var (MHG)--gold, see or.

gescaectafelt (MD)--see checky.

gestrecket entwerhes (MHG)--see in fess, fesswise.

gestrewt (MHG)--strewn, see semé.

gold, golt (MHG)--gold, see or.

goude (MD)--gold, see or.

grifîn (MHG)--griffin, had the head, breast, foreclaws and wings of an
eagle, and the hindquarters and tail of a lion.

grün (MHG)--green, see vert.

gueles (Fr.)--see gules.

guldin, guldîn (MHG); guldiin (MD)--golden, see or.

gules--the tincture red. The name is probably derived from the Arabic
gule, a red rose just as azure comes from the Arabic *lazura*.
Heralds have claimed it to be derived from the Latin *gula*, old
French *gueule*, i.e. the red throat of an animal.

harm (MHG)--ermine, see argent.

hawen (MHG)--hoe.

helm (MHG)--see helmet.

helmdekch (MHG)--see mantling.

helmet--the covering for protection of the helm in warfare has varied
in form from the earliest ages onwards. In heraldry the helmet
assumed an important place as an appendage to the shield, for
on this was fixed the crest. The helmet sometimes has plumes of
feathers.

hermleinen, hermlî, hermîn (MHG); hermel (MD)--ermine, see argent.

himel var, hymel pla (MHG)--blue, see azure.

kelen, keln roit, kelen röt, rôten kelen (MHG); keel, root van kele,
van roider keyle (MD)--see gules.

krebz, krebzen (MHG)--see crab.

kru̇z (MHG)--see cross.

label--a charge generally considered to be a temporary mark of cadency,
a horizontal bar across the top of the shield with short vertical
bars, called points, hanging from it. A label of three or five
points is the distinction of the eldest son during the lifetime
of his father.

lasur pla (MHG); lasure, lasuer (MD)--see azure.

Leb, leben, lebârten, leon, lew, lewen, löuw, löuwen, Löwe (MHG); leeu,
lewen (MD); Lÿoun, lïoun (Fr.)--lion (see below).

lion--in early heraldry it is generally represented rampant, i.e. rearing
with the left hinder leg and the left fore leg lower than the
two right legs, always facing the right side of the shield. Lions
are frequently crowned. A lion may be armed or armed and langued
of a different tincture (i.e. with its tongue, claws, or teeth,
etc. of such tincture) also enraged or incensed, i.e. with fire
issuing from the mouth and ears. There was no distinction made
between lions and leopards except that the term leopard was
sometimes used to indicate passant guardant, i.e. walking past
towards the right with the head looking towards the observer.

liljen, lilygen (MHG)--lilies, see *fleur-de-lis*.

lozenge--this charge is of a diamond shape, the diameter being about
equal to each of the sides.

mantling--this device of the painter to give prominence to the coat of
arms and crest is considered in theoretical heraldry to represent
the *lambrequin*, or covering of the helmet, to protect it from the
sun or rain.

martlet--a bird resembling a swallow, with thighs but no visible legs.

merlos (Fr.)--see martlet.

mirgriesse, mer griezzen (MHG); mergriis (MD)--mother of pearl, see
argent.

mit morgen-tau geperlt (MHG)--see argent.

or--gold, the most important of the tinctures.

ordinaries--certain charges in common use in arms, and in their simple
forms are bounded by straight lines and thus form geometric shapes.

ort (MHG)--see chief.

ostrich--this bird charge does not occur very frequently although
ostrich feathers are common in the plume.

paerliin (MD)--pearl, see argent.

pale--1)an ordinary one-third of the width of the shield, vertical and
central; 2)a vertical central line, either real or imaginary,
by which the shield is parted. *Per pale* signifies a vertical
division of the shield down the center. *In pale* refers to an
object or number of objects in the center of the shield, occupying
the position of a pale.

panir, pannier, panyr (MHG)--see banner.

par (MHG)--see fess.

in parra weis, in parraweiz, in parre weis gelenket, in parr weis, in
  parr weys gestrechet (MHG)--see in fess or per fess.

part (MHG)--see pale.

partiren (MHG)--see per pale.

in pellunch gepogirt (MHG)--see bend embowed.

perla vein (MHG)--pearl, see argent.

perlein, perlen, perlin, geperlt (MHG)--pearl, see argent.

pla (MHG)--blue, see azure.

plankweis (MHG)--blank white, see argent.

in plank weis...geteilet, in plankh, in planchweis, in planchweis...
  partiret (MHG)--see in pale or per pale.

plasnieren (MHG)--see blazon.

plume--of feathers, one feather or usually three or more, affixed to the
  crest.

praün von ademas (MHG)--brown, see p. 167.

purprin (MHG)--purple, see gules.

quarter--an ordinary occupying one-fourth of the field and situated
  (unless otherwise directed) in the dexter chief.

quartered--when a shield is divided into four or more squares for the
  reception of *different* coats of arms.

quarterly--when a coat of arms is divided into four parts (party per
  cross). The divisions are numbered 1, 2, 3, 4 beginning at the
  dexter chief, and most frequently numbers 1 and 4 are alike as
  also numbers 2 and 3; when the quarter is charged, its number
  must be specified.

quartir (MHG)--see quarter.

quartirt, quartiret, quartieret (MHG)--see quarterly.

quast (MHG)--see plume

queue-forché--having a forked tail.

rant (MHG)--border, see tressure.

rebus--a word represented by a picture; a graphic pun or the presentation of a name by pictorial suggestion.

rot, röt, rôt (MHG)--red, see gules.

rubein, rubeyn rot, rebein rot, rubîn, rübein (MHG); robiin, root van
  kele (MD)--ruby, see gules.

ruten (MHG)--diamond, see lozenge.

sable--the heraldic term for black, the term being probably derived
  from the black animal known as the sable.

saffin brawn (MHG)--sapphire brown, see p. 167.

saffirnvar, safîre blâ, saphir (MHG)--sapphire, see azure.

safrin (Fr.)--saffron, see or.

St. Andrew's cross--see saltire.

saltire--an ordinary supposed to represent the cross whereon St.
          Andrew was crucified. The fusion of a bend and a bend sinister
          giving an X-shaped cross.

sarapandratest (MHG)--a dragon's head.

schâchzabeleht (MHG)--see checky.

schaprûn, schappern, schapperûne (MHG)--see tabard.

schilt (MHG)--shield, see escutcheon.

semé--means that the field is sown or strewed over with several of the
          charges named, drawn small and without any reference to the number.

serpent--and snake are snonymous in heraldry. This reptile occurs
          rather frequently in coats of arms.

silber, siluer (MHG)--silver, see argent.

sinister--pertains to the left-hand seen from the bearer's point of view.

slange (MHG)--see serpent.

smaragden, smaragden grün, smaragd (MHG)--emerald green, see vert.

spitz (MHG)--see base.

stern (MHG)--star, known in heraldry as *estoile*, usually of six points
          and wavy.

strauzzenhals (MHG)--ostrich neck.

strich (MHG)--see fess.

swan--this graceful bird has been a favorite charge in armorial bearings.
          They are generally blazoned white or argent, but they are
          frequently beaked and legged of other tinctures.

swannen augen (MHG)--eyes of a swan.

swann hals (MHG)--a swan's neck.

swarz, swartz, swarzgevar (MHG)--black, see sable.

tabard--a shirt-like coat worn by heralds emblazoned on the front, back,
          and sleeves with the arms of their masters.

tobel (MHG)--see sable.

tressure--a subordinary, in the form of a bordure, but detached from
          the sides of the shield.

tschabrûn (MHG)--see tabard.

tzobel (MHG)--see sable.

vasch (MHG)--see fess.

velde, velt (MHG)--see field.

vermoilles, vermoil, vermellettis (Fr.)--see gules.

vert--the tincture green.

visiert, vyseyern, vysiren (MHG); visieren (MD)--see blazon.

Wag (MHG)--cart.

wâpenroc, wapenrocch, wapenroch, wapincleit, wâpencleider (MHG);
      wapencleit (MD)--see tabard.

wazerperlein (MHG)--see argent.

weiss (MHG)--white, see argent.

wîz, wizgevar, wîz hermîn (MHG)--white, see argent.

wurm (MHG)--see serpent.

wings--occur frequently as heraldic devices. If no description is given
      or implied, the wing must be drawn like an eagle's wing with the
      tip upwards. Wings are borne single (Ger. *Flügel*, Fr. *demi-vol*)
      or two are conjoined (Ger. *Flug*, Fr. *vol*).

zilver (MD)--silver, see argent.

zobel, zobel var, zabel, zobl, zobelvar (MHG)--see sable.

FOOTNOTES

[1]Otfried Weber, *Peter Suchenwirt. Studien über sein Wesen und Werk*, Deutsches Werden, 11 (Greifswald, 1937).

[2]Hans Rupprich, *Vom späten Mittelalter bis zum Barock. Das ausgehende Mittelalter, Humanismus und Renaissance 1370-1520*, vol. IV/1 of *Geschichte der deutschen Literatur*, ed. Helmut de Boor and Richard Newald (Munich, 1970). Rupprich was chosen not only because his comments are typical of literary histories but also because his is the most recent literary history of the period mentioning Suchenwirt.

[3]Alois Primisser, ed., *Peter Suchenwirt's Werke aus dem vierzehnten Jahrhunderte. Ein Beytrag zur Zeit- und Sittengeschichte* (Vienna, 1827; rpt. Vienna, 1961).

[4]All well-known names of places and persons have been translated into their common English equivalents.

[5]Rupprich, pp. 205-212.

[6]Francis Pierrepont Bernard, *Mediaeval England* (Oxford, 1924), pp. 242-243.

[7]Donald Lindsay Galbreath, *Handbüchlein der Heraldik*, 2nd ed. (Lausanne, 1948), p. 15.

[8]Ibid., p. 14.

[9]Johann Christian Siebenkees, *Erläuterungen der Heraldik als ein Commentar über Herrn...Gatterers Abriss dieser Wissenschaft* (Nuremberg, 1789), pp. 13, 15.

[10]Anthony Richard Wagner, *Heralds and Heraldry in the Middle Ages* (London, 1939), p.12.

[11]Anthony Richard Wagner, *Historic Heraldry of Britain* (London, 1939), p. 31.

[12]Wagner, *Heralds and Heraldry*, p. 14.

[13]Erich Gritzner, "Heraldik," in *Grundriß der Geschichtswissenschaft*, ed. Aloys Meister, 2nd ed., I/4 (Leipzig, Berlin, 1912), 64: "Man schuf nämlich eine ,vorheraldische Zeit', um die man sich nicht weiter kümmerte, als daß sich aus dem sog. ,Urbrei' urplötzlich das Wappenwesen entwickelt hätte."

[14]Otto Höfler, "Zur Herkunft der Heraldik," in *Festschrift für Hans Sedlmayr*, ed. Karl Oettinger and Mohammed Rassem (Munich, 1962), pp. 134-200; also Höfler's "Vorformen der Heraldik," *Genealogica et Heraldica* 10 (1970), 363-370.

[15]Erich Kittel, "Wappentheorien," *SAH Archivum Heraldicum (Schweiz)*,

1971, Bulletin 2-3, 18-26, Bulletin 4, 53-59, discusses nine different theories of origin and supplies an extensive bibliography.

[16]Théodore de Renesse, *Dictionnaire des figures héraldiques,* II (Brussels, 1895), 33-49.

[17]The boar as a heraldic symbol was very cleverly employed by Gottfried von Strassburg; see Manfred Zips, "Tristan und die Eber-symbolik," *PBB* 94 (Tübingen, 1972), 134-152.

[18]Friedrich Maurer, ed., *Die Lieder Walthers von der Vogelweide, I, Die religiösen und die politischen Lieder,* 3rd ed., ATB, 43 (Tübingen, 1967), p. 42.

[19]Manfred Zips, "Einige Zeugnisse aus der mittelhochdeutschen Epik zur Beziehung zwischen dem ritterlichen Helden und seinem Wappensymbol," *Jahrbuch Adler* 8,3 (1971/73), 155-182.

[20]Medieval examples include Siegfried's sword "Notung," King Arthur's "Excalibur," Roland's "Durendal," and Charlemagne's "Joyeuse."

[21]Heinrich Rückert, ed., *Der Wälsche Gast des Thomasin von Zirclaria* (Berlin, 1965), pp. 284-285.

[22]George F. Timpson, "Heraldry in Wolfram's Parzival," *The Coat of Arms* 4 (1957), 278-281.

[23]Karl Lachmann, ed., *Wolfram von Eschenbach. Parzival,* 6th ed. (Berlin, Leipzig, 1926; rpt. Berlin, 1965), pp. 7, 31, 45.

[24]Gottlob Heinrich Friedrich Scholl, *Diu Crône von Heinrich von dem Türlîn,* SLV, 27 (Tübingen, 1852), pp. 120-121.

[25]Evan John Jones, *Medieval Heraldry. Some Fourteenth Century Heraldic Works* (Cardiff, 1943), p. 7. For a discussion regarding the true identity of John Trevor and his relationship to Johannes de Bado Aureo, Nicholas Upton, and others see Jones' "Introduction."

[26]Ibid., p. 19.

[27]Albert Leitzmann, ed., *Erec von Hartmann von Aue,* ATB, 39 (Halle/Salle, 1939), pp. 233-234.

[28]Friedrich Maurer, ed., *Der altdeutsche Physiologus,* ATB, 67 (Tübingen, 1967), p. 55.

[29]Otto Behaghel, ed., *Heinrich von Veldecke. Eneide* (Heilbronn, 1882; rpt. Hildesheim, 1970), p. 507.

[30]Friedrich Mess, ed., *Heinrich von Ofterdingen. Wartburgkrieg und verwandte Dichtungen* (Weimar, 1963), p. 82.

[31]Rückert, p. 381.

[32]Werner Wolf, ed., *Albrechts von Scharfenberg Jüngerer Titurel,* DTM, 45 (Berlin, 1955), pp. 472-473.

[33]The technical description of heraldic insignia is called blazon; the painting of arms on a shield is referred to as emblazoning. The technical heraldic terminology, i.e. blazon, is given here in parentheses after the arms are described in layman's English. These terms are again explained in APPENDIX II: GLOSSARY OF HERALDIC TERMS, pp. 233-240.

[34]Jacob Grimm and Wilhelm Grimm, *Deutsches Wörterbuch*, IV/2 (Leipzig, 1877), 1122-1123; Friedrich Kluge and Alfred Götze, *Etymologisches Wörterbuch der deutschen Sprache*, 14th ed. (Berlin, 1948), p. 247. See also: Johann Adrrian Eduard von Hoverden, "Wie ist das Wort ‚Heraldik' zu erklären?" *Der deutsche Herold* 9 (1878), 14-15; Arnold Robens, *Elementarwerkchen der Wapenkunden* (Düsseldorf, Aachen, 1790), pp. 7-8; Gritzner, p. 62; Gustav A. Seyler, *Geschichte der Heraldik*, Abtheilung A des Siebmacher'schen Wappenbuches (Nuremberg, 1885), p. 26.

[35]Wagner, *Heralds and Heraldry*, p. 46.

[36]Mario Roques, ed., *Les romans de Chrétien de Troyes, III, Le chevalier de la charrete*, Les classiques Français du moyen age, 86 (Paris, 1969), pp. 168-169.

[37]Leitzmann, p. 56.

[38]Friedrich Heinrich von der Hagen, *Minnesinger* (Leipzig, 1838; rpt. Aalen, 1963), III, 46.

[39]Otto Posse, *Heraldik und Spragistik der Wettiner* (Leipzig, 1893), p. 1.

[40]Franz Lichenstein, ed., *Eilhart von Oberge*, Quellen und Forschungen zur Sprach- und Culturgeschichte der germanischen Völker, 19 (Strassburg, 1877), p. 369.

[41]Friedrich Heinrich von der Hagen and Johann Gustav Büsching, *Deutsche Gedichte des Mittelalters*, I (Berlin, 1808), 48.

[42]Seyler, p. 20. Seyler collected the early German references to heralds and was unable to find any occurence of the actual word "herald" before about 1367, when Peter Suchenwirt wrote in his poem "Von Leutolten von Stadekk:"
> Fürsten, grafen, freyen,   XV,119
> Der namen hört man chreyen
> Von den eralden, persewant,
> Der wappen volger Tribiiant.

Seyler concluded that the same officers are certainly intended by the names of *garzûne, crogierer*, and *knappen von den wâpen*, or *wappenknaben*. The first two names appear as early as the twelfth century, but from about the third quarter of the thirteenth century are superseded by the latter two.

[43]Ibid., p. 21.

[44]Oskar Jänicke, ed., *Biterolf und Dietleib*, Deutsches Heldenbuch, 1 (Berlin, 1866), p. 174.

[45]Victor Junk, ed., *Rudolf von Ems. Willehalm von Orlens,* DTM, 2 (Berlin, 1905), p. 108.

[46]Julius Weiske, ed., *Der Sachsenspiegel (Landrecht),* 5th ed. (Leipzig, 1876), p. 97.

[47]Edward Schröder, ed., *Kleinere Dichtungen Konrads von Würzburg, II, Der Schwanritter, Das Turnier von Nantes,* 3rd ed. (Berlin, 1959), p. 69.

[48]Paul Gereke, ed., *Konrad von Würzburg. Engelhard,* 2nd ed. rev. Ingo Reiffenstein, ATB, 17 (Tübingen, 1963), p. 108.

[49]Alois Primisser, ed., *Peter Suchenwirt's Werke aus dem vier-zehnten Jahrhunderte. Ein Beytrag zur Zeit- und Sittengeschichte* (Vienna, 1827; rpt. Vienna, 1961). All quotations from Suchenwirt's work from Primisser's edition are followed by a roman numeral and the line number. Other poems by Suchenwirt are denoted by arabic numerals and come from Godfried Edmund Friess, "Fünf unedierte Ehrenreden Peter Suchenwirts," *WSB* (1877), 99-126.

[50]Valentin Ferdinand Gudenus, *Codex diplomaticus anecdotorum,* III (Frankfurt, Leipzig, 1751), 282.

[51]Seyler, p. 25.

[52]Hagen, *Minnesinger,* III, 59.

[53]Raymund Duellius, *Excerptorum genealogico historicorum* (Leipzig, 1725), p. 255.

[54]Marx Wirsung, *Wann und umb wellicher ursachen willen das loblich Ritterspil des turniers erdacht und zum ersten geübet worden ist* (Augsburg, 1518), pp. Diiii, Dii.

[55]Erich Gritzner, "Ein Bericht über das Turnier der vier Lande zu Eisenach 1480," *Der deutsche Herold* 37 (1906), 67-68.

[56]Maurice Delbouille, ed., *Jacques Bretel. Le tournoi de Chauvency,* Bibliothèque de la Faculté de Philosophie et Lettres de l'Université de Liège, 49 (Paris, 1932), p. 18.

[57]Wagner, *Heralds and Heraldry,* p. 29.

[58]August Scheler, ed., *Dits et contes de Baudouin de Condé et de son fils Jean de Condé* (Brussels, 1866), I, 169-170.

[59]Adelbert von Keller, ed., *Karl Meinet,* SLV, 45 (Tübingen, 1858; rpt. Amsterdam, 1971), p. 439.

[60]Kervyn de Lettenhove, ed., *Œuvres de Froissart publiées avec les variantes des divers manuscrits,* III (Brussels, 1867), 38.

[61]Wagner, *Heralds and Heraldry,* pp. 37-38.

[62]Lettenhove, II, 7.

[63] Ibid., XV, 123.

[64] Michael Richard Buch, ed., *Ulrich von Richental Chronik des Constanzer Concils 1414 bis 1418*, SLV, 158 (Tübingen, 1882), p. 183.

[65] Ibid., pp. 202, 215.

[66] Duellius, p. 255.

[67] Seyler, p. 44.

[68] Primisser, p. XIII; Siebenkees, p. 33.

[69] Lettenhove, XVII, 566.

[70] Charles Boutell, *Heraldry*, rev. by J. P. Brook-Little (London, New York, 1970), p. 247.

[71] Maximilian Pankraz von Freyberg, *Sammlung historischer Schriften und Urkunden* (Stuttgart, Tübingen, 1827-1836), III, no. 34.

[72] Seyler, p. 27; Karl von Bahder, "Der König vom Odenwalde," *Germania* 23 (Vienna, 1878), 213-216.

[73] Joseph Chmel, *Regesta chronologico-diplomatica, Friderici IV. Romanorum regis (Imperatoris III.). Reichsregistraturbücher vom Jahre 1440-1493* (Vienna, 1838), p. 465.

[74] Johann Burchard Menken, *Historia vitae Imp. Sigismundi*, Scriptores rerum Germanicarum praecipve Saxonicarum, I (Leipzig, 1728), 1144.

[75] Heinrich Christian Senckenberg, *Collectanea manuscripta de judicus Westphalius*, I (Regensburg, 1762), no. 87.

[76] Franz Pfeiffer, ed., *Wirnt von Gravenberg. Wigalois*, Dichtungen des deutschen Mittelalters, 6 (Leipzig, 1847), pp. 40-41.

[77] Johann Benedict Carpzov, *Neueröffneter Ehren-Tempel merckwürdiger Antiquitæten des Marggrafftums Ober-Lausitz* (Leipzig, 1719), I, 163.

[78] Wagner, *Heralds and Heraldry*, pp. 48-55, suggested this classification.

[79] Theodor von Liebenau claims the *Clipearium Theutonicorum* was compiled between 1244 and 1273. See *Das älteste Wappengedicht Deutschlands* (Luzern, 1880), p. 26. The original manuscript is preserved in Master Felix Hemmerlin's work *De nobilitate*.

[80] Paul Ganz, *Geschichte der heraldischen Kunst in der Schweiz im XII. und XIII. Jahrhundert* (Frauenfeld, 1899), pp. 174, 180.

[81] Walther Merz and Friedrich Hegi, eds., *Die Wappenrolle von Zürich* (Zurich, Leipzig, 1930).

[82] Victor Bouton, ed., *Wapenboeck ou armorial de 1334 à 1372 par Gelre, héraut d'armes,* 4 vols. (Paris, Brussels, 1881-1886).

[83] Wagner, *Heralds and Heraldry,* pp. 54-55.

[84] Richard Leicher, *Die Totenklage in der deutschen Epik von der ältesten Zeit bis zur Nibelungen-Klage,* Germanistische Abhandlungen, 58 (Breslau, 1927), believes that the death lament was originally a common cult performance which was practiced by all Germanic tribes. As a result of the migrations, it developed peculiar characteristics in various regions before dying out completely in order to make room for the individual lament *(Einzelklage).* Ernst Robert Curtius, *Europäische Literatur und lateinisches Mittelalter* (Bern, 1948), pp. 161-173, discusses the connection between the classical panegyrical tradition and medieval poetry.

[85] Leopold Heinemann, "Über Quellen, Entwicklung und Gestaltung der lyrischen Totenklagen deutscher Dichter bis zum Ausgang der mittelhochdeutschen Zeit" (Diss. unpubl., Marburg, 1923).

[86] Leicher, p. 167.

[87] Heinemann, pp. 50-52.

[88] Carl Wesle, ed., *Das Rolandslied des Pfaffen Konrad,* 2nd ed., ATB, 68 (Tübingen, 1967), ll. 1490-1558; Ludwig Wolff, ed., *Hartmann von Aue. Iwein,* 7th ed. (Berlin, 1968), ll. 1454-1475.

[89] Philipp Strauch, ed., *Jansen Enikels Werke,* MGH, Deutsche Chroniken, III (Hannover, Leipzig, 1900), 636-638, ll. 2001-2096.

[90] Weber, p. 113.

[91] Leicher, pp. 160-167.

[92] Hagen, *Minnesinger,* III, 53, 66.

[93] Ludwig Ferdinand Clauss, "Die Totenklage der deutschen Minnesänger: Herkunft und Wesen ihrer Form" (Diss. unpubl., Freiburg, 1921), pp. 50-51.

[94] Maurer, *Die Lieder Walthers..., I, Die religiösen und die politischen...,* pp. 37-38.

[95] Friedrich Heinrich von der Hagen, "Klagegedicht auf Herzog Johannes von Brabant aus der Würzburg Handschrift," *Germania* 3 (Berlin, 1839), 116-130. Duke Johann spent his life in continuous strife, strengthening his dukedom to a leading position in the Netherlands. He had contacts with Church and lay leaders from the Netherlands to the cities of the Lower Rhine. In a dispute between the Archbishop of Cologne and the citizens of Cologne, Johann took the part of the citizens; the victory at Worringen on June 5, 1288, emanating from this dispute made him famous. He died on May 5, 1294 from wounds received at a tournament at Bar. Duke Johann was a patron of poetry and composed nine songs in the *Manesse Songbook,* accompanied by the following illustration: six knights on horseback are fighting with swords, each is wearing a

recognizable, but not always completely correct, coat of arms. According to Hagen, *Minnesinger*, IV, 42, this scene obviously refers to Johann's famous victory over Henry of Luxemburg. For a discussion of Johann's dialect and the problems of translation of his poetry see: Anton Kalla, *Über die Haager Liederhandschrift, Nr. 721*, Prager deutsche Studien, 14 (Prague, 1909), pp. 10-13; Heinrich Hoffmann von Fallersleben, "Lieder Herzogs Jan I. von Brabant," *Germania* 3 (Vienna, 1858), 154-161.

[96]Joseph von Laßberg, *Lieder-Saal: Sammlung altteutscher Gedichte* (1822; rpt. Hildesheim, 1968), II, 266-287.

[97]Clair Hayden Bell and Erwin G. Gudde, *The Poems of Lupold Hornburg*, University of California Publications in Modern Philology, 27 (Berkeley, Los Angeles, 1945).

[98]Konrad Zwierzina, "Lupold Hornburgs Gedichte," in *Festschrift des k.k. Erzherzog Rainer-Real-Gymnasium im II. Gemeinde-Bezirke in Wien* (Vienna, 1914), pp. 115-136.

[99]Weber, p. 115.

[100]Zwierzina, p. 125; Weber remarks, pp. 115-116: "Eine kunstgerechte Blasonierung der Wappen bringt Lupold allerdings nicht; dazu reichten die Kräfte des Laien nicht aus, wie er in der Einleitung selbst zugibt (5 f.). Er zeigt aber wenigstens die Stelle an, wo er hätte von den Wappen reden sollen, in V. 51 vor der Bekanntgabe der *krey: sine wöppen laz ich ligen*. Man sieht daraus, wie notwendig dem Dichter diese Erwähnung schien, und kann mit Sicherheit schließen, daß die Wappenschilderung durchaus zum Typ der Klagerede im 14. Jh. gehört haben muß und von heraldisch vorgebildeten Dichtern auch wahrscheinlich gepflegt wurde."

[101]Friedrich Heinrich von der Hagen, "Graf Wilhelm von Holland aus der Berliner Handschrift von Gottfrieds Tristan," *Germania* 6 (Berlin, 1844), 251-271.

[102] Ibid., p. 264, Hagen discusses the identity of the Count William of the poem: it could be William III (†1337) or William IV (†1345). A poem by "Vruodengher" laments the death of William IV, see: Ernst Ferdinand Kossmann, ed., *Die Haager Liederhandschrift. Faksimile des Originals mit Einleitung und Transskription* (The Hague, 1940), pp. 53-60.

[103]Laßberg, pp. 318-326. Karl Bartsch claims the author was Reinfried von Braunschweig, *Die Schweizer Minnesänger*, Bibliothek älterer Schriftwerke der deutschen Schweiz, 6 (Frauenfeld, 1886), p. CLXXXII.

[104]None of the historical documents mentions Werner's name in connection with his poetry; eight poems by a Count Werner of Honberg are found in the *Manesse Songbook*. The illustration in the songbook shows Werner storming a tower of a castle or city defended by footsoldiers and knights. The coats of arms seem to point to real friends and real foes of Count Werner. His coat of arms, gold with two black eagles, and the helmet with swan which are described in the lament are also portrayed in the miniature. According to Siebmacher (II,7; II,20) the shield had a silver field, but the helmet included two silver swans with golden rings

in their beaks, just as in the poem.

[105]Laßberg, p. 318.

[106]At the death of his father in 1286 Werner was made a ward of a cousin. His mother remarried Count Rudolf von Habsburg-Laufenburg in 1295. After Elisabeth's death in 1309 Count Rudolf married Countess Maria von Oettingen. Later, after the death of her first husband, Countess Maria married her step-son Werner in 1315. In the fall of 1304 Count Werner undertook a campaign to Lithuania with the knights of the Teutonic Order, "von den kristen zuo den Heiden" as he describes the occasion in a *Minnesang*: Friedrich Pfaff, *Die große Heidelberger Liederhandschrift* (Heidelberg, 1909), p. 114. He served Emperor Henry VII in Italy, was appointed governor in Thurgau in 1315 by Frederick the Fair of Austria, and died on March 21, 1320 (this date is according to Jakob Baechtold, *Geschichte der deutschen Litteratur in der Schweiz* (1892; Frauenfeld, 1919), p. 161).

[107]Josef Seemüller, "Deutsche Poesie vom Ende des XIII. bis in den Beginn des XVI. Jahrhunderts," in *Geschichte der Stadt Wien,* ed. Albert Starzer, III/1 (Vienna, 1907), 61.

[108]Weber, p. 115.

[109]Seemüller, p. 61.

[110]Erich Seemann, "Historisches Lied," *RL,* 2nd ed., I (Berlin, 1958), 688.

[111]For specific definitions and catagorizations see: Karen W. Klein, *The Partisan Voice* (The Hague, Paris, 1971); Hans Gille, *Die historischen und politischen Gedichte Michel Beheims,* Palaestra, 96 (Berlin, 1910); Wolfgang Mohr and Werner Kohlschmidt, "Politische Dichtung," *RL,* 2nd ed., III (Berlin, 1966), 157-220.

[112]Henry Furneaux, ed., *Cornelius Tacitus. De Germania* (Oxford, 1894), ch. 2, p. 40.

[113]Emil Levy, "Guillem Figueria" (Diss. unpubl., Berlin, 1880), p. 16.

[114]Friedrich Diez, *Die Poesie der Troubadours,* 2nd ed., Karl Bartsch (Leipzig, 1883).

[115]Klein, pp. 44-45.

[116]According to tradition Oswald von Wolkenstein also participated in this Prussian campaign. Since he was not born until 1377 (according to recent scholarship), such reports must refer to a similar crusade undertaken a decade later. See Norbert Mayr, *Die Reiselieder und Reisen Oswalds von Wolkenstein,* Schlern-Schriften, 115 (Innsbruck, 1961), pp. 34-37. For a complete discussion of these and other political poets see: Herta Gent, *Die mittelhochdeutsche politische Lyrik,* Deutschkundliche Arbeiten A. 13 (Breslau, 1938).

[117]Alfred Jeanroy, *La poésie lyrique des troubadours* (Paris,

1934), I, 226, designates the political *sirventes* a "campagne de presse;" Richard de Boysson, *Études sur Bertrand de Born* (Paris, 1902), p. 138, maintains "les sirventes des troubadours constituaient au XIIe-siècle, des véritables gazettes...;" Isabel Alpin, *Anglo-Norman Political Songs* (Oxford, 1953), p. xiii, observes, "Reading them, one can fancy one is reading medieval newspaper leaders;" Martin de Riquer, "La littérature provençale à la cour d'Alphonse II d'Aragon," *Cahiers de civilisation médiévale* X^e-XIIe *siècles* 2 (1959), 177, declares "...la poésie des troubadours est réellement une sorte de précédent de la presse de nos jours...."

[118] Walter Bulst, ed., *Martin Opitz: Das Anno-Lied*, 2nd ed. (Heidelberg, 1961), p. 44.

[119] Friedrich Maurer, ed., *Die Leider Walthers von der Vogelweide, II, Die Liebeslieder*, 3rd ed., ATB, 47 (Tübingen, 1969), p. 68.

[120] Very little is known about the Chandos Herald who is mentioned several times by Froissart, Lettenhove, XX, 536-640. It is possible that his birthplace was in or near the city of Valenciennes where the counts of Hainnault held court, Israel Gollancz, *Ich Dene* (London, 1921), p. I.

[121] Reginald Arthur Rye, *Catalogue of the Manuscripts and Autograph Letters in the University Library...with a Description of the Manuscript Life of Edward, Prince of Wales, the Black Prince by Chandos the Herald* (London, 1921), p. 5. The frontispiece of the manuscript includes a full-page illustration in two registers depicting the Trinity, to whom the Prince gave special reverence, and the Prince kneeling on a cushion, praying, "et hec tres unum sunt," (I John 5:7-8). On each side of the Prince is a large ostrich feather with the motto "Ich dene." There has been much discussion regarding the correct form of the motto, which means "I serve," and which is not entirely clear in the manuscript since it is neither High German nor Dutch. It points to a dialect of the southeastern part of the Low Franconian district, including Old Gelders Cleves. Thus it appears that the Black Prince deliberately and for political reasons used for the motto of his "badge of peace" the dialect of the Duchy of Gelders, which was closely identified with his father's interests in the Low Countries. For more discussion on this motto see Gollancz, p. II.

[122] All quotations from this work are from the edition by Francisque-Michel, *Le Prince Noir poêm du héraut d'armes Chandos* (London, Paris, 1883).

[123] In 1395 Froissart claimed that he had been away from England for twenty-seven years. The Chandos Herald may have seen the first part of Froissart's chronicles which had been presented to Queen Philippa before 1360.

[124] The exact numbers vary in different documents, but all approximate these figures.

[125] Primisser, pp. 270-271.

[126] *The Register of Edward, The Black Prince*, IV, 234, 236, December 9, 1357. See also Herbert James Hewitt, *The Black Prince's*

Expedition of 1355-1357 (Manchester, 1958), pp. 43-77, 162, 216.

[127]For other examples see Thomas Wright, ed., *Political Poems and Songs relating to English History,* Rerum Britannicarum medii aevi, Scriptores, XIV/1 (London, 1859; rpt. London, 1965).

[128]Rochus von Liliencron, *Die historischen Volkslieder der Deutschen vom 13. bis 16. Jahrhundert,* I (Leipzig, 1865), 109-118.

[129]Ibid., pp. 118-123.

[130]Ibid., pp. 123-145.

[131]Baechtold, p. 196; Ottokar Lorenz, "Die Sempacher Schlachtlieder," *Germania* 6 (Berlin, 1861), 169-173; Liliencron, pp. 124-145. The last strophe poses some interesting problems regarding the identity of the author:

Halbsuter unvergeßen   Str. 67
also ist er genant,
zů Lucern ist er geseßen,
und was gar wol erkant,
he er was ein biderman:
dis lied hat er gemachet,
als er ab der schlacht ist kan.

Documents from 1382 to 1434 refer to a Hans Halbsuter of Lucerne. Another Hans Halbsuter became a citizen of Lucerne in 1435 and was still living in 1480. The question of the true author remains unanswered today: the poem was written too late to be attributed to the earlier Halbsuter, but he may have composed a lost version. The battle mentioned in the last line may not refer to the Sempach battle but to one of the Burgundian battles in which the later Halbsuter took part. Theodor von Liebenau, "Hans Halbsuter und die Schlacht zu Sempach," *Festzeitung für das Zentralschweizerische Schützenfest in Luzern, 7. bis 14. Juli 1889* (Luzern, 1889), p. 40.

[132]There is much controversy regarding the veracity of this account since it does not appear in the earliest documents referring to the battle. For a discussion see: Gustav Schlatter, "Zu Halbsuters Sempacherlied und seiner Erzählung von der That Winkelrieds," *Anzeiger für Schweizerische Geschichte,* NS 1 (1870-1873), 14-15; Lorenz, pp. 180-185.

[133]This number also varies from account to account. See Lorenz, pp. 178, 182.

[134]Liliencron, pp. 11-21.

[135]Seyler, p. 36.

[136]Adolf Bach, *Die Werke des Verfassers der Schlacht bei Göllheim (Meister Zilies von Seine?),* Rheinisches Archiv, 11 (Bonn, 1930). There is some argument that the author may have been a knight, p. 184; the text, pp. 193-209.

[137]Ibid., p. 11.

[138] Ibid., text, pp. 210-219.

[139] Liliencron claims that the main thrust of the poem is to honor Eberhart von Katzenellenbogen, p. 7; Jan te Winkel, "Neue Bruchstücke des Gedichtes von der Böhmenschlacht," *PBB* 19 (1894), 491, disagrees, insisting that King Rudolf is the honored one.

[140] Schröder, *Kleinere Dichtungen,* pp. 42-75.

[141] Baechtold, p. 119.

[142] Ganz, p. 168. For more discussion on dating see: Baechtold, p. 118; Hans Lauden, "Die Chronologie der Werke des Konrads von Würzburg" (Diss. unpubl., Göttingen, 1906); Edward Schröder, "Studien zu Konrad von Würzburg," *Nachrichten von der Königlichen Gesellschaft der Wissenschaften zu Göttingen,* Phil.-Hist. Kl. (1917), pp. 117-128; Arnold Galle, "Wappenwesen und Heraldik bei Konrad von Würzburg. Zugleich ein Beitrag zur Chronologie seiner Werke," *ZfdA* 53 (1912), 253; Max Prinet, "Les armoriés Françaises dans le Tournoi de Nantes de Conrad de Wurtzbourg," *Moyen Age* 32 (1921), 232.

[143] Boutell, p. 135.

[144] This shield was only possible after the marriage of Alfonso IX, King of Leon to Bérengère, Queen of Castile: Ferdinand le Saint, their son, became King of Castile in 1217 and King of Leon in 1230, Prinet, p. 227.

[145] Ganz, p. 174.

[146] Seyler, p. 88.

[147] Ganz, pp. 167-168.

[148] Galle, pp. 211-212.

[149] Ibid., p. 213.

[150] Otfried Weber stretches the point when he hypothesizes a "lost model," p. 169: "Ich glaube, daß Such. auch in dieser Anordnung, wie im ganzen Aufbau der Ehrenrede, auf die Muster der Gattung zurückgeht, die er in seiner berufsmäßigen Ausbildung zum Wappensprecher kennen gelernt hat, die uns heute aber leider verloren gegangen sind und für eben Such.s Gestaltung Zeugnis geben muß."

[151] The editor, Maurice Delbouille, pp. XXVIII-XXIX, believes that Bretel, the author, "eut un collaborateur chargé de noter les armoires," and that this is Bruiant, "qui accueille J. Bretel au château et l'aide à identifier les seigneurs présents, grâce à la grande compétence dont il dispose en fait 'd'armes et de chevalerie'." The only information anywhere about Jacques Bretel (sometimes referred to as Bretex, i.e. Breteus or Bertiaus) is contained in very general references in the text. There are documents, however, referring to two Jehan Bretels who died in 1230 and 1272 respectively and who may have been Jacques' grandfather and father. Jacques seems to suggest in the text that he was a well-traveled

and mature man when he wrote the poem. The manuscript of the poem (Oxford, Bodleian Library MS Douce 308) is from the fourteenth century, but it is possible that the delightful accompanying miniatures represent a tradition coeval with and independent of that of the text, since they correct two incorrectly blazoned arms and add several coats of arms referred to but not blazoned in the text.

[152] Bach, text, pp. 227-229.

[153] Gerard J. Brault, ed., *Eight Thirteenth-Century Rolls of Arms in French and Anglo-Norman Blazon* (University Park, Penn., 1973). All quotations are from this edition.

[154] The poem (London, British Museum MS Cotton Caligula A. XVIII) was composed shortly after the siege, possibly by a herald who accompanied King Edward's army, Thomas Warton, *History of English Poetry* (London, 1774; rpt. New York, London, 1968), I, 335. Sir Harris Nicolas, ed., *The Siege of Carlaverock* (London, 1828), the first editor of the manuscript, claims that the work was written by a monk named Walter of Exeter, who was the author of the French romance *Guy of Warwick*. Thomas Wright, *The Roll of Arms of the Princes, Barons, and Knights who attended King Edward I. to the Siege of Caerlaverock, in 1300* (London, 1864), p. vii, disagrees with this, basing his view on his own translation of the text and on a stylistic comparison of the manuscript of the poem with that of the romance. Wright believes this manuscript represents the earliest roll of arms.

[155] Victor Bouton, ed., *Wapenboeck ou armorial de 1334 à 1372 par Gelre, héraut d'armes,* 4 vols. (Paris, Brussels, 1881-1886). All quotations are from this edition, Vol. I. For a summary in French of the contents of Gelre's poetic works see pp. 175-265. Also Bouton translates the poems into French.

[156] Lettenhove, III, 38.

[157] Paul Adam-Even, "L'armorial universel du héraut Gelre (1370-1395)," *SAH* 78 (1961), 50-53. See also Willem Adriaan Beelaerts van Blokland, *Beyeren quondam Gelre, armorum rex de Ruyris. Eene historische-heraldische studie* ('s-Gravenhage, 1933).

[158] Seyler, p. 538.

[159] Bouton, p. 111.

[160] See Donald Lindsay Galbreath, "La Suisse féodale d'après l'Armorial de Gelre," *SAH* 46 (1932), 1-5, 68-73, 124-128, 149-158; Joseph Klemme, "Proben aus Gelre's Wappenbuch," *Jahrbuch Adler* 11 (1884), 159-168; Merz and Hegi, especially the "Introduction."

[161] Hellmut Rosenfeld, "Gelre," *VL* 5 (Berlin, 1955), 252.

[162] Hellmut Rosenfeld, "Nordische Schilddichtung und mittelalterliche Wappendichtung," *ZfdPh* 61 (1936), 248-250.

[163] Bouton, p. 142.

[164]Karl Helm, "Zu Suchenwirts Ehrenreden," *PBB* 62 (1933), 383-386.

[165]Rosenfeld, "Nordische Schilddichtung...," pp. 232-269.

[166]Joseph Seemüller, ed., *Seifried Helbling* (Halle/Salle, 1886), pp. 14-21.

[167]Schröder, "Studien zu Konrad von Würzburg," pp. 122-128.

[168]Richard Groner, *Wien wie es war,* 5th ed., rev. Felix Czeike (Vienna, Munich, 1965), p. 530; Paul Harrer, "Wien seine Häuser, Menschen und Kultur," I/2 (Vienna, 1951), 341-343, IV/3 (Vienna, 1955), 611.

[169]Franz Staub, *Die ältesten Kaufbücher (1368-1388),* vol. III/1 of *Quellen zur Geschichte der Stadt Wien,* ed. Anton Mayer (Vienna, 1898), 244, 252, 277-278; by the same author, *Gewerbuch B (1370-1419)--Verbotbuch (1373-1399),* vol. III/2 of *Quellen zur Geschichte der Stadt Wien,* ed. Anton Mayer (Vienna, 1911), 71, 91, 132-133, 230-231, 236-237, 262.

[170]Josef Lampel, *Regesten aus dem k. und k. Haus-, Hof- und Staatsarchive in Wien,* vol. I/2 of *Quellen zur Geschichte der Stadt Wien,* ed. Anton Mayer (Vienna, 1898), 148-149; Richard Müller, "Wiens räumliche Entwicklung und topographische Benennungen vom Ende des XIII. bis zum Beginne des XVI. Jahrhunderts," in *Geschichte der Stadt Wien,* ed. Heinrich Zimmermann, II/1 (Vienna, 1900), 170-172.

[171]Weber, pp. 28-29.

[172]Ludwig Schönach, "Zu Peter Suchenwirt," *AfdA* 36 (1913), 199.

[173]Karl Bartsch, ed., *Hugo von Montfort,* SLV, 146 (Tübingen, 1879), p. 33.

[174]Weber, pp. 7-29.

[175]Franz Kratochwil, "Über den gegenwärtigen Stand der Suchenwirt-Handschriften," *Germania* 34 (Vienna, 1889), 203-244, 303-345, 431-487.

[176]Kratochwil, pp. 204-230, lists twenty different scribes and discusses their contributions to MS A; Hermann Menhardt, *Verzeichnis der altdeutschen literarischen Handschriften der österreichischen National-bibliothek,* Veröffentlichungen des Instituts für deutsche Sprache und Literatur, 13 (Berlin, 1961), p. 1304, counted seventeen scribes.

[177]Kratochwil, pp. 203-244, 303-345, 431-487.

[178]Weber, pp. 30-62.

[179]Joseph von Laßberg, *Lieder-Saal: Sammlung altteutscher Gedichte* (1825; rpt. Hildesheim, 1968).

[180]Carl Haltaus, ed., *Liederbuch der Clara Hätzlerin*, Bibliothek der gesammten deutschen National-Literatur, 8 (Quedlinburg, Leipzig, 1840); rpt. Deutsche Neudrucke, Reihe: Texte des Mittelalters (Berlin, 1966).

[181]Alois Primisser, *Peter Suchenwirt's Werke aus dem vierzehnten Jahrhunderte. Ein Beytrag zur Zeit- und Sittengeschichte* (Vienna, 1827; rpt. Vienna, 1961). An anonymous review appeared in the *Göttingische gelehrte Anzeigen* 2 (1827), 841-848.

[182]Haltaus, pp. 203-205.

[183]Godfried Edmund Friess, "Fünf unedirte Ehrenreden Peter Suchenwirts," *WSB* 88 (1877), 99-126.

[184]Erduin Julius Koch, *Kompendium der Deutschen Literatur-Geschichte von den ältesten Zeiten bis auf Lessings Tod* (Berlin, 1798), II, 73, 361-382.

[185]Friedrich Adelung, *Altdeutsche Gedichte in Rom oder fortgesetzte Nachrichten von Heidelbergischen Handschriften in der Vatikanischen Bibliothek* (Königsberg, 1799), pp. 248-249, 305-306.

[186]Bernhard Joseph Docen, "Versuch einer vollständigen Literatur der älteren Deutschen Poesie, von den frühesten Zeiten bis zu Anfange des XVI. Jahrh. Erste Abteilung," in *Museum für Altdeutsche Literatur und Kunst,* ed. Friedrich Heinrich von der Hagen, Bernhard Joseph Docen, and Johann Gustav Büsching, I (Berlin, 1809), 126-237, especially p. 210.

[187]Bernhard Joseph Docen, "Beiträge zu einer Bibliothek der ältern einheimischen Literatur," *Neue oberdeutsche allgemeine Literaturzeitung,* II/2 (Munich, 1810), 101-104, 109-112, 117-120, especially p. 102.

[188]Friedrich Heinrich von der Hagen and Johann Gustav Büsching, *Literarischer Grundriß zur Geschichte der deutschen Poesie von der ältesten Zeit bis in das sechzehnte Jahrhundert* (Berlin, 1812), pp. 341-342, 408-409.

[189]Bernhard Joseph Docen, "Die Schlacht bei Sempach, 1386. Von Peter Suchenwirt," in *Sammlung für altdeutsche Literatur und Kunst,* ed. Friedrich Heinrich von der Hagen, Bernhard Joseph Docen, Johann Gustav Büsching, and Bernhard Hundeshagen, I/1 (Breslau, 1812), 152-160. These poems are from MS m^2, Munich Staatsbibliothek, MS Cgm. 1113.

[190]Julius Max Schottky, "Ueber Heinrich Teychner, einen Wiener Spruchdichter des 14ten Jahrhunderts," *Jahrbücher der Literatur* 11 (1818), Anzeigeblatt, 26-40.

[191]Alois Primisser, "Nachricht von einer neuentdeckten Handschrift mit deutschen Gedichten aus dem vierzehnten Jahrhundert, verfaßt von Peter Suchenwirt, aus Oesterreich," *Jahrbücher der Literatur* 14 (1821), Anzeigeblatt, 10-51.

[192]Julius Max Schottky, "Hertzog Albrechts III. von Österreich Kreutzzug gegen die heidnischen Preussen," *Archiv für Geographie, Historie, Staats- und Kriegskunst* 13 (1822), 444-447.

[193] Laßberg, III, 57-67.

[194] Primisser discusses his editorial methods on pages XLIII-XIV.

[195] Eberhard Gottlieb Graff, *Diutiska. Denkmäler deutscher Sprache und Literatur aus alten Handschriften zum ersten Male theils herausgegeben, theils nachgewiesen und beschrieben* (Stuttgart, Tübingen, 1827; rpt. Hildesheim, New York, 1970), II, 77-111. Graff describes for the second time the MS st, Stuttgart Codex poet. et philol. Q 69.

[196] Heinrich Niewöhner, "Suchenwirt-Handschriften," *ZfdA* 68 (1931), 273-274.

[197] August Koberstein, *Über die Sprache des österreichischen Dichters Peter Suchenwirt, I, Lautlehre* (Naumburg, 1828); II, *Quaestiones Suchenwirtianae, Deklination* (Naumburg, 1842); III, *Über die Betonung mehrsilbiger Wörter in Suchenwirts Versen* (Naumburg, 1843); IV, *Abhandlung der Conjugation* (Naumburg, 1852).

[198] Karl Heinrich von Busse, "Peter Suchenwirt's Sagen über Livland," in *Mittheilungen aus dem Gebiete der Geschichte Liv-, Esth- und Kurland's,* ed. Gesellschaft für Geschichte und Alterthumskunde der russischen Ostsee-Provinzen, III (Riga, 1845), 5-21.

[199] Cf. Ottokar Lorenz, *Deutschlands Geschichtsquellen im Mittelalter seit der Mitte des dreizehnten Jahrhunderts* (Berlin, 1886), I, 236-240; August Potthast, *Bibliotheca historica medii aevi. Wegweiser durch die Geschichtswerke des europäischen Mittelalters bis 1500* (Berlin, 1896), II, 1038.

[200] Franz Kratochwil, "Der österreichische Didactiker Peter Suchenwirt, sein Leben und seine Werke," in *Jahresbericht des k.k. Ober-Gymnasiums in Krems am Schlusse des Schuljahres 1871* (Krems, 1871), pp. 3-54.

[201] Kratochwil, "Über den gegenwärtigen Stand...."

[202] Julius Pölzl, "Der gegenwärtige Stand der Suchenwirt-Hss.," *Blätter des Vereins für Landeskunde von Niederösterreich* 24 (1890), 184-185.

[203] Ewald Frey, *Die Temporalconjunctionen der deutschen Sprache in der Uebergangszeit vom Mhd. zum Nhd.,* besprochen im Anschluss an Peter Suchenwirt und Hugo von Montfort, Berliner Beiträge zur germanischen und romanischen Philologie, Germanische Abteilung, 4 (Berlin, 1893).

[204] Wilhelm Uhl, "Peter Suchenwirt," in *ADB,* XXXVII (Berlin, 1894), 774-780.

[205] Joseph Seemüller, "Chronologie der Gedichte Suchenwirts," *ZfdA* 41 (1897), 193-233.

[206] Seemüller, "Deutsche Poesie...," pp. 1-81, especially pp. 52-63.

[207] Albert Morey Sturtevant, "Zur Sprache des Peter von Suchenwirt. ,Der Widertail'," *MLN* 25 (1910), 47-51.

[208] Felizitas Freiberger, "Die geblümte Rede bei Peter Suchenwirt" (Diss. unpubl., Vienna, 1913).

[209] Schönach, p. 199.

[210] Albert Leitzmann, "Suchenwirtiana," *PBB* 44 (1919), 312-315.

[211] Niewöhner, pp. 273-274.

[212] Gustav Ehrismann, *Geschichte der deutschen Literatur bis zum Ausgang des Mittelalters, II/2, Die mittelhochdeutsche Literatur* (Munich, 1935), 490-491.

[213] Otfried Weber, *Peter Suchenwirt: Studien über sein Wesen und Werk,* Deutsches Werden, 11 (Greifswald, 1937).

[214] Rosenfeld, "Nordische Schilddichtung...," pp. 232-269.

[215] Helm, pp. 383-390.

[216] Hans Friedrich Rosenfeld, "Suchenwirt, Peter," *VL* 4 (Berlin, 1953), 310-315.

[217] Hans Blosen, "Überlegungen zur Textüberlieferung und zur Textgestaltung bei einem Gedicht von Peter Suchenwirt," in *Probleme altgermanistischer Editionen,* ed. Hugo Kuhn, Karl Stackmann, and Dieter Wuttke, Forschungsberichte, 13 (Wiesbaden, 1968), pp. 232-269.

[218] Rupprich, pp. 205-212.

[219] Seemüller, "Chronologie der Gedichte Suchenwirts," pp. 213-214.

[220] Hans Blosen, "Philologische Studien zu Suchenwirts ‚Widertail'" (Staatsexamenarbeit unpubl., Bonn, 1966), "Anmerkungen," pp. 6-10.

[221] Sturtevant, pp. 47-51, refers to the poet as Peter von Suchenwirt. The evidence points more strongly towards Suchenwirt as a professional name since there is no locality by that name.

[222] "After" does not necessarily mean soon after. For example, events referred to in VI indicate that the *Ehrenrede* was written at least twelve years after Henry's death in 1335. Since Suchenwirt was still alive in 1395, it is unlikely that any of the poems were written before 1350.

[223] Hagen, *Minnesinger,* II, 356-357.

[224] Seemüller, "Deutsche Poesie...," pp. 62-63.

[225] Hagen, *Minnesinger*, III, 354.

[226] Uhl, pp. 779. Unfortunately Hugo von Montfort is the only contemporary who mentions Suchenwirt's name.

[227] Hieronymus Pez, ed., *Scriptores rerum Austriacarum,* II (Regensburg, 1725), 796. Thomas Ebendorfer's *Chronicon Austriacum*

embraces the time span from the first century A.D. to the year 1400.

[228]Primisser, *Peter Suchenwirt's Werke,* p. 194.

[229]Pez, II, 792.

[230]Joseph Seemüller, ed., *Österreichische Chronik von den 95 Herrschaften,* MGH, Deutsche Chroniken, VI (Hannover, Leipzig, 1909), 210. Pez mistakenly identifies the author as Gregor Hagen, I, 1151. This chronicle is from the beginning of the world to the year 1398.

[231]Pez, II, 812.

[232]Kaspar Schütz, *Historia rerum Prussicarum,* 2nd ed. (Leipzig, 1599), p. 82.

[233]William Guthrie and John Gray, *Allgemeine Weltgeschichte,* trans. C. G. Heyne et al., XV (Brünn, 1788), 85.

[234]Docen, "Versuch einer vollständigen Literatur...," p. 186.

[235]Schottky, "Herzog Albrecht III. von Österreich Kreutzzug...," pp. 444-445.

[236]Erasmus Froelich, *Genealogiae Sounekiorum comitum Celejæ, et comitum de Heunburg specimina duo* (Veinna, 1755), p. 100.

[237]Winrich gained the position of Grand Master in 1351 and ruled until June 24, 1382. He was known for his great tenacity and wisdom and for thirty victories over the Lithuanians.

[238]Theodor Hirsch, Max Töppen, and Ernst Strehlke, eds., *Scriptores rerum Prussicarum,* II (Leipzig, 1863), 163, 167.

[239]For more information regarding the *Ehrentisch* see: Johannes Voigt, *Geschichte Preussens,* V (Königsberg, 1832), 712-719. The establishment of a *Hochmahl am Ehrentisch* is usually said to have been instituted during the reign of the Grand Master Wallenrod (1391-1394), but this poem proves that the custom was well established much earlier.

[240]Ibid., p. 279.

[241]Primisser, *Peter Suchenwirt's Werke,* p. 202.

[242]Busse, p. 19. Busse's "miles" are the measurement common in 1845 and are somewhat larger than our miles.

[243]Ibid., pp. 17-21.

[244]Friedrich Benninghoven, "Zur Technik spätmittelalterlicher Feldzüge im Ostbaltikum," *Zeitschrift für Ostforschung* 19/4 (1970), 633.

[245]Ibid., p. 635.

[246]Hirsch, Töppen, and Strehlke, pp. 101-102. The so-called *Hochmeister-chroniken* are made up of a number of writings connected with the Teutonic Order including the following: the *Livonian Chronicle* (1358-1378) by the Livonian commander's chaplain, Hermann von Wartberge; the Latin chronicle of Prussia (1360-1405) by Johann von Posilge (†1405); the rhymed *Die Kronike von Pruzinlant* (1331-1335) by the Grand Master's herald, Wigand von Marburg, who translated from an unknown Latin source in 1464.

[247]Ibid., pp. 115-116.

[248]Benninghoven, p. 650.

[249]Pez, II, 810.

[250]Seemüller, "Deutsche Poesie...," p. 63.

[251]Bartsch, *Hugo von Montfort*, pp. 33-34.

[252]The chart and comments following it are based on Seemüller, "Chronologie der Gedichte Suchenwirts," pp. 216-224. During the revision errors contained in the original were corrected. For summaries of and bibliographies for Suchenwirt's *Ehrenreden* see: Primisser, *Peter Suchenwirt's Werke*, pp. 173-276; Ulrich Müller, *Untersuchungen zur politischen Lyrik des deutschen Mittelalters*, GAG, 55/56 (Göppingen, 1974), pp. 190-201.

[253]Bouton summarizes the *Ehrenreden* and translates them into French, pp. 175-265; Müller summarizes the *Ehrenreden* and provides a bibliography, pp. 185-190.

[254]Valentin Preuenhueber, *Annales Styrenses samt dessen übrigen Historisch- und Genealogischen Schriften* (Nuremberg, 1740), p. 416.

[255]Johann von Hoheneck, *Die Löbliche Herren Herren Stände, von Herren und Ritterstand in dem Erzhertzogthum Oesterreich ob der Ennß. Dero Familien abgestorben, und völlig erloschen oder Genealog- und Historische Beschreibung*, II (Passau, 1732), 686-691.

[256]Seemüller, "Chronologie der Gedichte Suchenwirts," pp. 207-208.

[257]Gelasius Dobner, *Monumenta historica Boemiae*, V (Prague, 1784), 492. The Latin chronicle by Jacob Twinger von Königshofen (1346-1420) was compiled before 1382, continued to 1419.

[258]Lettenhove, VI, 210.

[259]Ibid., V, 188-192.

[260]For a complete description of this campaign see Hewitt.

[261]Lettenhove, V, 421-424.

[262]Ibid., VII, 414.

[263]Hoheneck, p. 690.

[264]Pez, I, 542. The *Zwettler Chronicle* records history from the birth of Christ to 1343, with continuations to 1386. The many authors who kept this chronicle up to date from the twelfth century to 1386 are unknown.

[265]Franz Kurz, *Oesterreich unter H. Albrecht dem Lahmen* (Linz, 1819), pp. 287-292.

[266]Pez, I, 429. The *Chronicon Salisburgense* covers the years from the first century A.D. to 1398.

[267]Ibid., I, 414.

[268]Ibid., I, 415-416.

[269]Ibid., I, 1000.

[270]Ibid., I, 416.

[271]Ibid., I, 544.

[272]Ibid., I, 419.

[273]Hoheneck, p. 690.

[274]Primisser maintains that Suchenwirt makes a distinction between *visieren* and *plasnieren;* however, Primisser does not adequately define the two terms. I do not perceive any difference and consider them interchangeable in Suchenwirt's work. For example, they do not seem to distinguish the difference between blazon and emblazon, or between a technical and a general description.

[275]See APPENDIX II: GLOSSARY OF HERALDIC TERMS.

[276]Suchenwirt and his contemporaries do not make the strict distinctions among metals, colors, and furs which concern modern heralds. Furs, for example, do not occur very often in German heraldry. Suchenwirt and the compilers of heraldic books and rolls appear most interested in the overall color scheme of the shield taken as a whole.

[277]Primisser translates *planchweis* as *Blankweiß, Silberweiß* (blank, pure, or silver white) instead of a vertical positioning. Even in the arms of Friedrich von Kreußpeck where the position of the crab and its claws is all important, i.e. vertical, Primisser does not recognize his mistake. He may have been led astray by the arms of Leutold von Stadeck where the presumed *Blankweiß* coincidentally corresponds to the color of the heraldic animal. See Seyler, p. 223.

[278]This relatively unusual expression also appears in a *Wappenbrief* from 1399 in which Hans Eberstorffer confers the arms of Streitgreun:

ain Schilt von zobel und von gold mit zwain Flügen aus dem Schilt genommen auch von zobel und von golt getailt in pellunkh. A *Wappenbrief* of Duke William of Austria (Graz, 1401) describes the same arms without the expression *in pellunch:*

einen Schilt von Zabel vnd von golde gelegen in fazz vnd
zwo flüg auf dem Helm.
See Seyler, p. 224.

[279]Walther Hubatsch, *Quellen zur Geschichte des Deutschen Ordens*
(Göttingen, Frankfurt, Berlin, 1954), pp. 140-149.

[280]Despite the vast amount of literature pertaining to the Teutonic
Order, there is very little material regarding the *Preußenfahrten* or
crusades made by laymen knights. The reason appears to be that they did
not have very significant impact either upon the Teutonic Order itself
or upon the settling and conversion of heathen lands and peoples.

[281]This society, also known as *societas capellae St. Georgii
dominorum* or *militum Templois*, was active until 1379.

[282]For the best discussion of this crusade, including a more
complete list of the participants see Voigt, IV, 423-437; Nicolaus von
Jeroschin gives an interesting rhymed account, "Wî Medewagen sich begab,"
in Hirsch, Töppen, Strehlke, I, 615-616.

[283]Schütz, p. 62, maintains there were 250 Teutonic knights and
18,000 men excluding the infantry. Peter de Dusburg states there were
200 knights and 18,000 soldiers, Wigand von Marburg 300 knights and
10,000 soldiers, Cf. Hirsch, Töppen, Strehlke, I, 215; II, 463.
Guillaume de Wal, *Historie de l'Ordre Teutonique*, I (Paris, Rheims, 1784),
95, attempts to put the question into perspective: "Le continuateur de
Dusbourg s'exprime d'une maniere ambiguë; il paroît au premier coup-d'
oeil que le Grand Maître avoit 18 mille chevaux et une infanterie
indéterminée; on peut aussi entendre que le forces des croisés et du
Grand Maître montoient à 18 mille hommes de cavalerie, sans compter
l'infanterie, ce qui est le plus vraisemblable." This is a good example
of the problem of numbers, which in the Middle Ages are always suspect.

[284]For the dates involved see Hirsch, Töppen, Strehlke, II, 462,
fn. 50.

[285]Again as usual there is some discrepancy in the figures: Peter
de Dusburg and Nicolaus von Jeroschin claim that 6,000 Lithuanians were
baptized.

[286]Dobner, V, 431. The three volume *Chronicon Aulae regiae* was
compiled by Petrus von Zittau and Abbot Otto: Vol. 1, 1253-1316; Vol. 2,
1317-1334; Vol. 3, 1335-1337.

[287]Josef Emler, *Fontes rerum Bohemicarum*, V (Prague, 1893),
206. Pulkavia's *Bohemian Chronicle* was commissioned by Charles IV.

[288]Voigt, IV, 542-546.

[289]Three members of Albert's family belonged to the Teutonic
Order in the fourteenth century, Cf. Hirsch, Töppen, Strehlke, II, 157-8.

[290]Wigand von Marburg elaborates regarding the participants of
the expedition, but also does not give details pertaining to the action,
see Hirsch, Töppen, Strehlke, II, 490-492.

[291] Voigt, IV, 544.

[292] Stephan Katona, *Historia critica regum Hungariae,* II/9 (Budapest, 1790), 361. Johann von Thurócz chronicles the reign of King Louis of Hungary, 1342-1382.

[293] Voigt, V, 26-34; Johann Gottfried Arndt, *Liefländische Chronik,* II (Halle/Magdeburg, 1753), 98-99; Hirsch, Töppen, Strehlke, II, 72-74, 504-507.

[294] Voigt, V, 48-54; Hirsch, Töppen, Strehlke, II, 73-74; III, 76-77.

[295] Hirsch, Töppen, Strehlke, II, 508-514.

[296] Robert Michell and Nevill Forbes, trans., *The Chronicle of Novgorod 1016-1471,* Camden Society, 3rd Series, 25 (London, 1914), pp. 137-139, 149, 151.

[297] Busse, pp. 5-21.

[298] Arndt, p. XVI.

[299] Hirsch, Töppen, Strehlke, II, 159.

[300] Katona, III/10, 9.

[301] According to Hermann von Wartberge the expedition began in the fall of 1370, Cf. Hirsch, Töppen, Strehlke, II, 96-99; Wigand von Marburg places this campaign between November 1371 and April 1372, Cf. Hirsch, Töppen, Strehlke, II, 567-570. For another description see Voigt, V, 224-227.

[302] Hirsch, Töppen, Strehlke, II, 568.

[303] Hermann Maschek, "Die Geschichte des Pfarrers vom Kahlenberg," *ZfdA* 73 (1936), 43.

[304] Josef Feil, "Ueber die ältesten St. Georgsritter in Oesterreich oder die Gesellschaft der Tempelaise," *Oesterreichische Blätter für Literatur, Kunst, Geschichte, Geographie, Statistik und Naturkunde* 5 (1848), 222; Anton Victor Felgel, *Regesten aus dem k. und k. Haus-, Hof- und Staatsarchive in Wien,* vol. III/1 of *Quellen zur Geschichte der Stadt Wien,* ed. Anton Meyer (Vienna, 1897), No. 3025, p. 179; No. 3058, pp. 186-187.

[305] Johann Gustav Büsching, "Der heilige Graal und seine Hüter," in *Museum für altdeutsche Literatur und Kunst,* ed. Friedrich Heinrich von der Hagen, Bernhard Joseph Docen, and Johann Gustav Büsching, I (Berlin, 1809), 491-546.

[306] Maschek, pp. 43-46. For a description of this monastery and of the grail society which was designed for thirteen noble couples, see Ernst Schaus, "Das Kloster der Minne," *ZfdA* 33 (1894), 262-266. "Der Pfarrer vom Kahlenberg," printed about 1473, may have been composed by

Philipp Frankfürter. The hero is a cunning priest from a village near
Vienna at the time of Duke Otto, who plays crude and often filthy tricks
on the peasants for his own profit.

[307]Feil, p. 232.

[308]Hugh Clark, *A Concise History of Knighthood* (London, 1784), I,
175-211.

[309]Peter Heylyn, *The Historie of St. George*, 2nd ed. (London,
1633), pp. 278-279.

[310]Eugene L. Cox, *The Green Count of Savoy. Amadeus VI and
Transalpine Savoy in the Fourteenth Century* (Princeton, N. J., 1967),
pp. 78-79, 180-186, 359-362, 371-373.

[311]Pez, I, 536, 896, *Zwettler* and *Leoben* (from the birth of
Christ to 1343) *Chronicles*.

[312]Guglielmo and Albrigeti Cortusi, *Historia de novitatibus
Paduae et Lombardiae*, vol. VI of *Thesaurus antiquitatum et historiarum
Italiae, Patauii, Fori-julii et Istraiae*, ed. J. G. Graevius (Lugduni,
Batavorum, 1722), 36.

[313]Crysostomo Hanthaler, *Recensus diplomatico-genealogicus
Archivii Campililiensis*, II (Vienna, 1820), 157.

[314]Cortusi, pp. 55-56; Pez, I, 929, the *Leoben Chronicle* places
the date incorrectly in 1318; Italian sources are more reliable. Johann
Friedrich Lebret, *Fortsetzung der Algemeinen Welthistorie*, XLIII (Halle/
Salle, 1781), 239-243, 396-401.

[315]Cortusi, pp. 127-129.

[316]Jean Charles Leonard Sismondi, *History of the Italian Republics
in the Middle Ages* (London, 1895), p. 409.

[317]Ibid., p. 366.

[318]Primisser, *Peter Suchenwirt's Werke*, p. 252.

[319]Katona, II/9, 470. Again this is certainly an exaggeration.
Johann von Thurócz was writing to honor King Louis. Suchenwirt, too,
was following the customary practice of inflating the numbers of soldiers.

[320]Pez, I, 543, *Zwettler Chronicle*.

[321]Katona, III/10, 194.

[322]Ibid., pp. 195, 204.

[323]Ibid., p. 194.

[324]Dobner, V, 347.

[325] Pez, I, 916, the *Leoben Chronicle*.

[326] Ibid., pp. 1002-1003.

[327] Ibid., p. 1003.

[328] Ibid., pp. 484-485, 536, 921-923, the *Klosterneuburg, Zwettler,* and *Leoben Chronciles*.

[329] Friedrich von Kreußpeck must have been released early since he was in Italy in 1324.

[330] Pez, I, 924.

[331] Ibid., p. 537, the *Zwettler Chronicle*.

[332] Ibid., p. 411, the *Salzburg Chronicle*.

[333] Ibid., p. 538, the *Zwettler Chronicle*.

[334] Busse, pp. 5-21.

[335] Seemüller, *Österreichische Chronik*.

[336] Franz Kurz, *Oesterreich unter H. Albrecht dem Dritten* (Linz, 1827), II, 258-261.

[337] Seemüller, *Österreichische Chronik*, p. 232; Pez, I, 1161.

[338] Wolfgang Mohr, "Politische Dichtung," in *RL* III (Berlin, 1966), 181, claims that Suchenwirt has lost his sense of proportion in this poem, in other words, that a tax on wine is not suitable subject matter for poetry.

[339] Maurer, *Die Lieder Walthers...*, I, *Ðe religiösen und die politischen...*, pp. 21, 42.

LIST OF WORKS CONSULTED

ACADÉMIE INTERNATIONALE D'HÉRALDIQUE. *Vocabulaire-atlas héraldique en six langues*. Paris: Société du Grand Armorial de France, 1952.

ADAM-EVAN, Paul. "L'armorial universel du héraut Gelre (1370-1395)." *SAH* 75 (1961), 48-85; 76 (1962), 68-73; 77 (1963), 63-79; 78 (1964), 75-80; 79 (1965), 70-82; 81 (1967), 72-83; 82 (1968), 70-73.

_____. "Les fonctions militaires des hérauts d'armes." *SAH* 7 (1957), 2-33.

ADELUNG, Friedrich. *Altdeutsche Gedichte in Rom oder fortgesetzte Nachrichten von Heidelbergischen Handschriften in der Vatikanischen Bibliothek*. Königsberg: Friedrich Nicolovius, 1799.

ALPIN, Isabel. *Anglo-Norman Political Songs*. Oxford: Clarendon, 1953.

ANON. "Bruchstücke zur Geschichte des Tempelordens, zumahl in Oesterreich." *Archiv für Geographie, Historie, Staats- und Kriegskunst* 13 (1822), 753-755, 777-779, 787-789.

ANTHONY VON SIEGENFELD, Alfred. *Das Landeswappen der Steiermark*. Forschungen zur Verfassungs- und Verwaltungsgeschichte der Steiermark, 3. Graz: Verlags-Buchhandlung „Styria," 1900.

APPELT, Heinrich. "Die Entstehung des steirischen Landeswappens." In *Festschrift für Julius Franz Schütz*, ed. Berthold Sutter. Graz, Cologne: Hermann Böhlau, 1954, pp. 235-245.

ARNDT, Johann Gottfried. *Liefländische Chronik*. 2 vols. Halle/Magdeburg: Johann Justinus Gebauer, 1747-1753.

BACH, Adolf. *Die Werke des Verfassers der Schlacht bei Göllheim (Meister Zilies von Seine?)*. Rheinisches Archiv, 11. Bonn: L. Röhrscheid, 1930.

_____. "Zilies von Sayn." In *VL*. IV. Berlin: de Gruyter, 1953, 1144-1151.

BAECHTOLD, Jakob. *Geschichte der deutschen Litteratur in der Schweiz*. 1892; rpt. Frauenfeld: J. Huber, 1919.

BAESECKE, Georg. *Vor- und Frühgeschichte des deutschen Schrifttums*. Halle/Salle: Max Niemeyer, 1940.

BAHDER, Karl von. "Der König vom Odenwalde." *Germania* 23 (Vienna, 1878), 193-222.

BARACK, Karl August. *Die Handschriften der fürstlich-fürstenbergischen Hofbibliothek zu Donaueschingen*. Tübingen: H. Laupp, 1865.

BARNARD, Francis Pierrepont. *Mediaeval England*. Oxford: Clarendon, 1924.

BARTSCH, Karl. *Deutsche Liederdichter des zwölften bis vierzehnten Jahrhunderts.* 3rd ed. Stuttgart: G. J. Göschen, 1893.

_____. *Die altdeutschen Handschriften der Universitäts-Bibliothek in Heidelberg.* Heidelberg: Gustav Koester, 1887.

_____. *Die Schweizer Minnesänger.* Bibliothek älterer Schriftwerke der deutschen Schweiz, 6. Frauenfeld: J. Huber, 1886.

_____, ed. *Hugo von Montfort.* SLV, 143. Tübingen: L. F. Fues, 1879.

_____. "Leopold Hornburg." In *ALB*. XIII. Berlin: Duncker and Humblot, 1881, 147–148.

_____, ed. *Meleranz von den Pleier.* SLV, 60. Stuttgart: Auf Kosten des litterarischen Vereins, 1861.

BEBERMEYER, Gustav. "Herolddichtung (Wappendichtung)." In *RL*. 2nd ed. I. Berlin: Walter de Gruyter, 1958, 650–653.

BECHSTEIN, Reinhold, ed., *Heinrich's von Freiberg Tristan.* Deutsche Dichtungen des Mittelalters, 5. Leipzig: G. J. Göschen, 1877.

BECK, Edward. *Grundfragen der Wappenlehre und des Wappenrechts.* Veröffentlichungen der Pfälzischen Gesellschaft zur Förderung der Wissenschaften, 20. Speyer/aR: E. Jaeger, 1931.

BEELAERTS VAN BLOKLAND, Willem Adriaan. *Beyeren quondam Gelre, armorum. rex de Ruyris. Eene historische-heraldische studie.* 's-Gravenhage: n. publ., 1933.

BEHAGHEL, Otto, ed. *Heinrich von Veldecke. Eneide.* Heilbronn: Henninger, 1882; rpt. Hildesheim: Georg Olms, 1970.

BELL, Clair Hayden and Erwin G. GUDDE. *The Poems of Lupold Hornburg.* University of California Publications in Modern Philology, 27. Berkeley, Los Angeles: University of California Press, 1945.

BENNINGHOVEN, Friedrich. *Der Order der Schwertbrüder.* Cologne, Graz: Hermann Böhlau, 1965.

_____. "Zur Technik spätmittelalterlicher Feldzüge im Ostbaltikum." *Zeitschrift für Ostforschung* 19/4 (1970), 631–651.

BERCHEM, Egon von. "Die Herolde und ihre Beziehungen zum Wappenwesen, eine vorläufige Materialsammlung zur Geschichte des Heroldswesens." In *Beiträge zur Geschichte der Heraldik,* ed. Egon von Berchem, Donald Lindsay Galbreath, and Otto Hupp. Berlin: Verlag für Standesamtswesen, 1939, pp. 117–223.

_____. "Wapenboeck ou armorial de l'héraut Gelre, 1334 à 1372." *SAH* 44 (1930), 5–15, 106–112.

_____, Donald Lindsay GALBREATH, and Otto HUPP, eds. *Beiträge zur Geschichte der Heraldik.* Berlin: Verlag für Standesamtswesen, 1939.

_____. "Die Wappenbücher des deutschen Mittelalters." *SAH* 39 (1925), 17-30, 64-72, 97-107; 40 (1926), 23-33, 80-93, 114-124; 42 (1928), 32-40, 88-90; 34 (1929), 125-126.

BLOSEN, Hans. "Philologische Studien zu Suchenwirts ,Widertail'." (Staatsexamenarbeit, unpubl.). Wissenschaftliches Prüfungsamt der Universität Bonn, 1966.

_____. "Überlegungen zur Textüberlieferung und zur Textgestaltung bei einem Gedicht von Peter Suchenwirt." In *Probleme altgermanistischer Editionen*, ed. Hugo Kuhn, Karl Stackmann, and Dieter Wuttke. Forschungsberichte, 13. Wiesbaden: Franz Steiner, 1968.

BOEHMER, Johann Friedrich, ed. *Fontes rerum Germanicarum. Geschichtsquellen Deutschlands*. I. Stuttgart: J. G. Cotta, 1843.

BOERMA, Hermann Rudolph. "De liederen van hertog Jan van Brabant." *Tijdschrift voor nederlandsche Taal- en Letterkunde* 15 (1896), 220-238.

BOOR, Helmut de and Richard NEWALD. *Geschichte der deutschen Literatur.* 6 vols. Munich: C. H. Beck, 1949-1974.

BÖSS, Hugo. *Fischarts Bearbeitung lateinischer Quellen.* Prager Deutsche Studien, 28. Reichenberg i. B.: Franz Kraus, 1923.

BOUTELL, Charles. *Heraldry,* rev. by J. P. Brook-Little. London, New York: Frederick Warne, 1970.

BOUTON, Victor, ed. *Wapenboeck ou Armorial de 1334 à 1372 par Gelre, héraut d'armes.* 4 vols. Paris, Brussels: J. Olivier, 1881-1886.

Review: ANON. *Ler deutsche Herold* 22 (1891), 132-133.

BOYSSON, Richard de. *Études sur Bertrand de Born.* Paris: Alphonse Picard, 1902.

BRAULT, Gerard J. *Early Blazon. Heraldic Terminology in the Twelfth and Thirteenth Centuries with Special Reference to Arthurian Literature.* Oxford: Clarendon, 1972.

_____, ed. *Eight Thirteenth-Century Rolls of Arms in French and Anglo-Norman Blazon.* University Park, Penn.: Pennsylvania State University Press, 1973.

_____. "The Hatton-Dugdale Facsimile of the Caerlaverock Poem." *The Coat of Arms* 11 (1970), 77-80.

BRODFÜHRER, Eduard. "Hornburg, Lupold." In *VL.* II. Berlin: Walter de Gruyter, 1936, 488-491.

BUCH, Michael Richard, ed. *Ulrichs von Richental Chronik des Constanzer Concils 1414 bis 1418.* SLV, 158. Tübingen: H. Laupp, 1882.

BUCHER, Jakob. "Halbsuter." In *ADB*. X. Berlin: Duncker and Humblot, 1879, 405-406.

BÜSCHING, Johann Gustav. "Der heilige Graal und seine Hüter." In *Museum für altdeutsche Literatur und Kunst*, ed. Friedrich Heinrich von der Hagen, Bernhard Joseph Docen, and Johann Gustav Büsching. I. Berlin: Johann Friedrich Ungar, 1809, 491-546.

BULST, Walther, ed. *Martin Opitz: Das Anno-Lied*. 2nd ed. Heidelberg: Carl Winter, 1961.

BUSSE, Karl Heinrich von. "Peter Suchenwirt's Sagen über Livland." In *Mittheilungen aus dem Gebiete der Geschichte Liv-, Esth- und Kurland's*, ed. Gesellschaft für Geschichte und Altertumskunde der russischen Ostsee-Provinzen. III. Riga: Nicolai Kymmel, 1845, 5-21.

CARPZOV, Johann Benedict. *Neueröffneter Ehren-Tempel merckwürdiger Antiquitaeten des Marggraffthums Ober-Lausitz*. Leipzig: David Richter, 1719.

CHMEL, Joseph. *Regesta chronologico-diplomatica, Friderici IV. Romanorum regis (Imperatoris III.). Reichsregistraturbücher vom Jahre 1440-1493*. Vienna: Peter Rohrmann, 1838.

CLARK, Hugh. *A Concise History of Knighthood*. 2 vols. London: W. Strahan, 1784.

CLAUSS, Ludwig Ferdinand. "Die Totenklage der deutschen Minnesänger: Herkunft und Wesen ihrer Form." (Diss. unpubl.). Freiburg, 1921.

CORTUSI, Guglielmo and Albrigeti. *Historia de novitatibus Paduae et Lombardiae*. Vol. VI of *Thesaurus antiquitatum et historiarum Italiae, Patauii, Fori-julii et Istraiae*, ed. J. G. Graevius. Lugduni, Batavorum: Peter Van der Aa, 1722.

COX, Eugene L. *The Green Count of Savoy. Amadeus VI and Transalpine Savoy in the Fourteenth Century*. Princeton, N. J.: Princeton University Press, 1967.

COXE, William. *House of Austria*. I. London: H. G. Born, 1847.

CURTIUS, Ernst Robert. *Europäische Literatur und lateinisches Mittelalter*. Bern: A. Francke, 1948.

DAHLMANN, Friedrich Christoph. *Dahlmann-Waitz. Quellenkunde der deutschen Geschichte*. 9th ed. Ernst Baasch and Max von Bahrfeldt. Leipzig: K. F. Koehler, 1931.

DAVID, Lucas. *Preussische Chronik*. 2 vols. Königsberg: Georg Karl Haberland, 1812-1813.

DELAISSÉ, Léon M. J. *A Century of Dutch Manuscript Illumination*. Berkeley, Los Angeles: University of California Press, 1968.

DELBOUILLE, Maurice, ed., *Jacques Bretel. Le tournoi de Chauvency.*
Bibliothèque de la Faculté de Philosophie et Lettres de
l'Université de Liège, 49. Paris: E. Droz, 1932.

DENHOLM-YOUNG, Nöel. *History and Heraldry 1254 to 1310. A Study of
the Historical Value of the Rolls of Arms.* Oxford: Clarendon,
1965.

————. "The Song of Carlaverock and the Parliamentary Roll of Arms
as found in Cott. MS. Calig. A XVIII in the British Museum."
Proceedings of the British Academy 47 (1961), 252-262.

DIEZ, Friedrich. *Die Poesie der Troubadours.* 2nd ed. Karl Bartsch.
Leipzig: Johann Ambrosius Barth, 1883.

DOBLINGER, Max. "Die Herren von Walsee. Ein Beitrag zur österreichischen Adelsgeschichte." *Archiv für österreichische
Geschichte* 95 (1906), 235-578.

DOBNER, Gelasius. *Monumenta historica Boemiae.* III and IV. Prague:
Rosemüller Haeredum, 1774 and 1784.

DOCEN, Bernhard Joseph. "Beiträge zu einer Bibliothek der ältern
einheimischen Literatur." *Neue oberdeutsche allgemeine
Literatur-Zeitung* II/2 (Munich, 1810), 101-120.

————. "Die Schlacht bei Sempach. 1386. Von Peter Suchenwirt."
Sammlung für altdeutsche Literatur und Kunst I/1 (1812), 152-160.

————. "Versuch einer vollständigen Literatur der älteren Deutschen
Poesie, von den frühesten Zeiten bis zu Anfange des XVI. Jahrh.
Erste Abteilung." In *Museum für Altdeutsche Literatur und Kunst,*
ed. Friedrich Heinrich von der Hagen, Bernhard Joseph Docen, and
Johann Gustav Büsching. I. Berlin: Johann Friedrich Ungar,
1809, 126-237.

DUELLIUS, Raymund. *Excerptorum genealogico historicorum.* Leipzig:
Peter Conrad Monath, 1725.

ECKHART, Johann Georg von. *Historia genealogia principum Saxoniae
superioris.* Leipzig: Johann Friedrich Gleditsch, 1722.

EHRISMANN, Gustav. *Geschichte der deutschen Literatur bis zum Ausgang
des Mittelalters.* 4 vols. Munich: C. H. Beck, 1922-1935.

EICHHORN, Werner. "Die Chroniken der Schweiz im Spätmittelalter und
die Heraldik der Chronik des Ulrich v. Richental." *SAH* 85
(1971), 17-22.

EIS, Gerhard. "Deutschordensliteratur." In *RL.* 2nd ed. I. Berlin:
Walter de Gruyter, 1958, 244-251.

ELLIS, William Smith. *The Antiquities of Heraldry.* London: John
Russel Smith, 1869.

EMLER, Josef. *Fontes rerum Bohemicarum.* V. Prague: J. Otto, 1893.

ERLER, Georg. *Deutsche Geschichte von der Urzeit bis zum Ausgang des Mittelalters in den Erzählungen deutscher Geschichtsschreiber,* Vol. III, *Das deutsche Reich und das deutsche Volk in den letzten Jahrhunderten des Mittelalters.* Leipzig: Alphons Dürr, 1884.

EWALD, Wilhelm. *Rheinische Heraldik.* Düsseldorf: L. Schwann, 1937.

FANT, Erik Mikael. *Scriptores rerum Suecicarum medii aevi.* Upsala: Zeipel and Palmblad, 1818-1876.

FEIL, Josef. "Ueber die ältesten St. Georgsritter in Oesterreich oder die Gesellschaft der Tempelaise." *Oesterreichische Blätter für Literatur, Kunst, Geschichte, Geographie, Statistik und Naturkunde* 5 (1848), 217-218, 221-224, 227-228, 230-232, 241-242, 247-248.

FELGEL, Anton Victor. *Regesten aus dem k. und k. Haus-, Hof- und Staatsarchive in Wien.* Vol. III/1 of *Quellen zur Geschichte der Stadt Wien,* ed. Anton Mayer. Vienna: Verlag und Eigenthum des Alterthums-Verein zu Wien, 1897.

FERNIS, Hans-Georg. "Die Klage um den toten Herrn. Ein germanisches Motiv in höfischer Dichtung." *GRM* 25 (1937), 161-178.

_____. "Die politische Volksdichtung der deutschen Schweizer als Quelle für ihr völkisches und staatliches Bewußtsein vom 14.-16. Jahrhundert." *Deutsches Archiv für Landes- und Volksforschung* 2 (1938), 600-639.

FISCHER, Leopold. *Brevis notitia urbis Vindobonae.* Vienna: Johann Thomas Trattner, 1767.

FOX-DAVIES, Arthur C. *A Complete Guide to Heraldry,* rev. by J. P. Brook-Little, London: Thomas Nelson, 1969.

FRANCISQUE-MICHEL, ed. *Le Prince Noir poème du héraut d'armes Chandos. The Life and Feats of Arms of Edward the Black Prince by Chandos Herald.* London, Paris: J. G. Fotheringham, 1883.

FRANKLYN, Julian and John TANNER. *An Encyclopaedic Dictionary of Heraldry.* Oxford: Pergamon, 1970.

FREIBERGER, Felizitas. "Die geblümte Rede bei Peter Suchenwirt." (Diss. unpubl.). Vienna, 1913.

FREY, Ewald. *Die Temporalconjunctionen der deutschen Sprache in der Uebergangszeit vom Mhd. zum Nhd., besprochen im Anschluss an Peter Suchenwirt und Hugo von Montfort.* Berliner Beiträge zur germanischen und romanischen Philologie, Germanische Abteilung, 4. Berlin: C. Vogt, 1893.

FRIESS, Godfried Edmund. "Fünf unedierte Ehrenreden Peter Suchenwirts." *WSB* 88 (1877), 99-126.

FROELICH, Erasmus. *Genealogiae Sounekiorum comitum Celejae, et comitum de Heunburg specimina duo.* Vienna: Johann Thomas Trattner, 1755.

FURNEAUX, Henry, ed. *Cornelius Tacitus. De Germania.* Oxford: Clarendon, 1894.

GALBREATH, Donald Lindsay. *Handbüchlein der Heraldik.* 2nd ed. Lausanne: Spes, 1948.

_____. "La Suisse féodale d'après l'Armorial de Gelre." *SAH* 46 (1932), 1-5, 68-73, 124-128, 149-158.

GALLE, Arnold. "Wappenwesen und Heraldik bei Konrad von Würzburg. Zugleich ein Beitrag zur Chronologie seiner Werke." *ZfdA* 53 (1912), 209-258.

GANZ, Paul. *Geschichte der heraldischen Kunst der Schweiz im XII. und XIII. Jahrhundert.* Frauenfeld: J. Huber, 1899.

GASPAR, Camille and Frederik LYNA. *Les principaux manuscrits à peintures de la Bibliothèque Royale de Belgique.* I. Paris: Société française de reproductions de manuscrits à peintares, 1937.

GATFIELD, George. *Guide to Printed Books and Manuscripts relating to English and Foreign Heraldry and Genealogy.* London: Mitchell and Huges, 1892; rpt. Detroit: Gale Research Co., 1966.

GATTERER, Johann-Christoph. *Abriß der Heraldik.* Göttingen, Gotha: Johann Christian Dieterich, 1773.

GEBHARDT, Bruno. *Handbuch der deutschen Geschichte.* 9th ed. I. Stuttgart: Union, 1970.

GEISSAU, Anton Ferdinand von. *Historisches Tagebuch des durchlauchtigsten Erzhauses Oesterreich. Vom Jahre 994 bis 1780.* Vienna: in der Gräfferischen Buchhandlung, 1781.

GENT, Herta. *Die mittelhochdeutsche politische Lyrik.* Deutschkundliche Arbeiten A. 13. Breslau: Maruschke and Berendt, 1938.

GEREKE, Paul, ed. *Konrad von Würzburg. Engelhard.* 2nd ed. rev. by Ingo Reiffenstein. ATB, 17. Tübingen: Max Niemeyer, 1963.

GERVINUS, Georg Gottfried. *Geschichte der deutschen Dichtung.* 4th ed. II. Leipzig: Wilhelm Engelmann, 1853.

_____. *Handbuch der Geschichte der poetischen National-Literatur der Deutschen.* Leipzig: Wilhelm Engelmann, 1842.

GEUSAU, Anton von. *Geschlechtsfolge der Beherrscher Oesterreichs, baben- bergisch- habsburgisch- und lothringischen Stammens sic bis auf Kaiser Franz II.* Vienna: published by author, 1795.

GILLE, Hans. *Die historischen und politischen Gedichte Michel Beheims.* Palaestra, 96. Berlin: Mayer and Müller, 1910.

GOLLANCZ, Israel. *Ich Dene*. London: George W. Jones, 1921.

GOLTHER, Wolfgang, ed. *Tristan und Isolde und Flore und Blanscheflur*. Kürschners Deutsche National-Litteratur, 4. Berlin, Stuttgart: W. Spemann, n.d.

GOUGH, Henry and James PARKER. *A Glossary of Terms Used in Heraldry*. Oxford, London: James Parker, 1894; rpt. Detroit: Gale Research Co., 1966.

GRAFF, Eberhard Gottlieb. *Diutiska. Denkmäler deutscher Sprache und Literatur aus alten Handschriften zum ersten Male theils herausgegeben, theils nachgewiesen und beschrieben*. 3 vols. Stuttgart, Tübingen: J. G. Cotta, 1826-1829; rpt. Hildesheim, New York: Georg Olms, 1970.

GRAUTOFF, Ferdinand Heinrich, ed. *Chronik des Franciscaner Lesmeisters Detmar*. Hamburg: Friedrich Perthes, 1829.

GRIMM, Jacob and Wilhelm. *Deutsches Wörterbuch*. 32 vols. Leipzig: Deutsche Akademie der Wissenschaften zu Berlin, 1854-1960.

GRITZNER, Erich. "Ein Bericht über das Turnier der vier Lande zu Eisenach 1480." *Der deutsche Herold* 37 (1906), 67-68.

_____. "Heraldik." In *Grundriß der Geschichtswissenschaft*, ed. Aloys Meister. 2nd ed. I/4. Leipzig, Berlin: B. G. Tuebner, 1912.

GRITZNER, Maximilian. *Handbuch der heraldischen Terminologie in zwölf (germanischen und romanischen) Zungen*. Abtheilung B des Siebmacher'schen Wappenbuches. Nuremberg: Bauer and Raspe, 1890.

GRONER, Richard. *Wien wie es war*. 5th ed., rev. by Felix Czeike. Vienna, Munich: Fritz Molden, 1965.

GUDENUS, Valentin Ferdinand. *Codex diplomaticus anecdotorum*. III. Frankfurt, Leipzig: Ulrich Weiss, 1751.

GUTHRIE, William and John GRAY. *Allgemeine Weltgeschichte*, trans. C. G. Heyne et al. XV. Brünn: F. U. Schrämbls, 1788.

HAGEN, Friedrich Heinrich von der. "Graf Wilhelm von Holland aus der Berliner Handschrift von Gottfrieds Tristan." *Germania* 6 (Berlin, 1844), 251-271.

_____. "Klagegedicht auf Herzog Johannes von Brabant aus der Würzburger Handschrift." *Germania* 3 (Berlin, 1839), 116-130.

_____. *Minnesinger*. 4 vols. Leipzig: Johann Ambrosius Barth, 1838; rpt. Aalen: Otto Zeller, 1963.

_____, and Johann Gustav BÜSCHING, eds. *Deutsche Gedichte des Mittelalters*. I. Berlin: Realschulbuchhandlung, 1808.

_____. *Literarischer Grundriß zur Geschichte der deutschen Poesie von der ältesten Zeit bis in das sechzehnte Jahrhundert.* Berlin: Duncker and Humblot, 1812.

HAHN, Karl August, ed. *Ulrich von Zatzikhoven. Lanzelet.* Frankfurt/aM: Heinrich Ludwig Brönner, 1845.

HALTAUS, Carl, ed. *Liederbuch der Clara Hätzlerin.* Bibliothek des gesammten deutschen National-Literatur, 8. Quedlinburg, Leipzig, 1840; rpt. Deutsche Neudrucke, Reihe Texte des Mittelalters. Berlin: Walter de Gruyter, 1966.

HANTHALER, Chrysostomo. *Recensus diplomatico-genealogicus Archivii Campiliensis.* 2 vols. Vienna: Ferdinand Beck, 1819-1820.

HARRER, Paul. "Wien seine Häuser, Menschen und Kultur." 4 vols. (typed). Vienna Stadtarchiv, 1951-1955.

HAUPTMANN, Felix. *Wappenkunde.* Munich, Berlin: R. Oldenbourg, 1914.

HEINEMANN, Leopold. "Über Quellen, Entwicklung und Gestaltung der lyrischen Totenklagen deutscher Dichter bis zum Ausgang der mittel-hochdeutschen Zeit." (Diss. unpubl.). Marburg, 1923.

HELM, Karl. "Die Literatur des Deutschen Ordens im MA." *ZfdU* 30 (1916), 289-306, 363-370, 430-438.

_____. "Zu Suchenwirts Ehrenreden." *PBB* 62 (1938), 383-390.

_____, and Walther ZIESEMER. *Die Literatur des deutschen Ordens in Preußen.* Giessener Beiträge zur deutschen Philologie, 94. Giessen: W. Schmitz, 1951.

HENGSTL, M. Hereswitha. *Totenklage und Nachruf in der mittellateinischen Literatur seit dem Ausgang der Antike.* Würzburg: Richard Mayer, 1936.

HENRICI, Emil, ed. *Das deutsche Heldenbuch.* Kürschners Deutsche National-Litteratur, 7. Stuttgart: W. Spemann, 1890.

HERMANN, H. "Die St. Georgen-Ritter und ihre Besitzungen in Österreich, Kärnten und Steyer." *Neues Archiv für Geschichte, Staatenkunde, Literatur und Kunst* (Vienna, 1830), 501-504, 514-516.

HEWITT, Herbert James. *The Black Prince's Expedition of 1355-1357.* Manchester: Manchester University Press, 1958.

HEYLYN, Peter. *The Historie of St. George.* 2nd ed. London: Henry Seyle, 1633.

HIRSCH, Theodor, Max TÖPPEN, and Ernst STREHLKE, eds. *Scriptores rerum Prussicarum. Die Geschichtsquellen der preußischen Vorzeit bis zum Untergange der Ordensherrschaft.* 5 vols. Leipzig: S. Hirzel, 1861-1874.

HÖFLER, Otto. "Vorformen der Heraldik." *Genealogica et Heraldica* 10 (1970), 363-370.

_____. "Zur Herkunft der Heraldik." In *Festschrift für Hans Sedlmayr*, ed. Karl Oettingen and Mohammed Rassem. Munich: C. H. Beck, 1962, pp.134-200.

HOFFMANN VON FALLERSLEBEN, Heinrich. "Lieder Herzogs Jan I. von Brabant." *Germania* 3 (Vienna, 1858), 154-161.

HOHENECK, Johann Georg von. *Die Löbliche Herren Herren Stände, von Herren und Ritterstand in dem Erzhertzogthum Oesterreich ob der Ennß. Dero Familien abgestorben, und völlig erloschen oder Genealog- und Historische Beschreibung.* II and III. Passau: Gabriel Mangold, 1732 and 1747.

HORMAYR, Joseph von. *Tiroler Almanach auf das Jahr 1803.* Vienna: Andreas Gassler, 1803.

_____. *Wien, seine Geschicke [sic] und seine Denkwürdigkeiten.* Vienna: Franz Härter, 1823.

HOVERDEN, Johann Eduard Adrrian von. "Wie ist das Wort ‚Heraldik' zu erklären?" *Der deutsche Herold* 9 (1878), 14-15.

HUBATSCH, Walther. *Eckpfeiler Europas. Probleme des Preußenlandes in geschichtlicher Sicht.* Heidelberg: Quelle and Meyer, 1953.

_____. *Quellen zur Geschichte des Deutschen Ordens.* Göttingen, Frankfurt, Berlin: Musterschmidt, 1954.

HUBER, Alfons. *Geschichte Österreichs.* 5 vols. Gotha: Friedrich Andreas Perthes, 1885.

_____, and Alfons DOPSCH. *Österreichische Reichsgeschichte. Geschichte der Staatsbildung und des öffentlichen Rechts.* Vienna: 1900; rpt. Darmstadt: Scientia Verlag Aalen, 1968.

HUPP, Otto. *Die Wappenbücher des deutschen Mittelalters, I, Die Wappenbücher vom Alberg.* Berlin: Volksbund der deutschen Sippenkundlichen Vereine, 1937.

_____. *Wider die Schwarmgeister!* 3 vols. Munich: Max Kellerer, 1918-1927.

JACOBSOHN, Fritz. *Der Darstellungsstil der historischen Volkslieder des 14. und 15. Jahrhunderts und die Lieder von der Schlacht bei Sempach.* Rostock: Carl Hinstorff, 1915.

JÄGER-SUNSTENAU, Hanns. *General-Index zu den Siebmacher'schen Wappenbüchern 1605-1961.* Graz: Akademische Druck-u. Verlagsanstalt, 1964.

JANICKE, Oskar, ed. *Biterolf und Dietleib.* Deutsches Heldenbuch, 1. Berlin: Weidmann, 1866.

JANTZEN, Hermann. *Literaturdenkmäler des 14. und 15. Jahrhunderts.* Sammlung Göschen, 181. Leipzig: G. J. Göschen, 1903.

JEANROY, Alfred. *La poésie lyrique des troubadours.* 2 vols. Paris: H. Didier, 1934.

JOHANN VON VICTRING. *Das Buch gewisser Geschichten,* trans. Walter Friedensburg. Die Geschichtsschreiber der deutschen Vorzeit, 14. Jh., 8. Leipzig: Dyk, 1888.

JONES, Evan John. *Medieval Heraldry. Some Fourteenth Century Heraldic Works.* Cardiff: William Lewis, 1943.

JUNK, Victor, ed. *Rudolf von Ems. Willehalm von Orlens.* DTM, 2. Berlin: Weidmann, 1905.

KALLA, Anton. *Über die Haager Liederhandschrift, Nr. 721.* Prager deutsche Studien, 14. Prague: C. Bellmann, 1909.

KATONA, Stephan. *Historia critica regum Hungariae.* Budapest: Catharina Landerer Viduae, 1779-1817.

KELLER, Adelbert von, ed. *Karl Meinet.* SLV, 45. Tübingen: H. Laupp, 1858; rpt. Amsterdam: Rodopi, 1971.

KIESLICH, Günther. *Das „Historische Volkslied" als publizistische Erscheinung.* Studien zur Publizistik, 1. Münster: C. J. Fahle, 1958.

KITTEL, Erich. "Wappentheorien." *SAH Archivum Heraldicum (Schweiz),* 1971, Bulletin 2-3, 18-26, Bulletin, 4, 53-59.

KLEIN, Karen Wilk. *The Partisan Voice: A Study of the Political Lyric in France and Germany, 1180-1230.* Studies in General and Comparative Literature, 7. The Hague, Paris: Mouton, 1971.

KLEMME, Joseph. "Proben aus Gelre's Wappenbuch." *Jahrbuch Adler* 11 (1884), 159-168.

KLEMPERER, Victor. "Die Arten der historischen Dichtung." *DV LG* 1 (1923), 370-399.

KLOCKE, Friedrich von. "Die Knappen von den Wappen als Herolde und als Rittergenossen." *Genealogie und Heraldik* 2 (1950), 17-20.

KLUGE, Friedrich, and Alfred GÖTZE. *Etymologisches Wörterbuch der deutschen Sprache.* 14th ed. Berlin: Walter de Gruyter, 1948.

KOBERSTEIN, August. *Grundriß der Geschichte der deutschen National-literatur.* 5th ed., rev. by Karl Bartsch. I. Leipzig: F. C. W. Vogel, 1872.

―――. *Über die Sprache des österreichischen Dichters Peter Suchenwirt, I, Lautlehre.* Naumburg: C. A. Klaffenbach, 1828; II, *Quaestiones Suchenwirtianae, Deklination.* Naumburg: C. A.

Klaffenbach, 1842; III, *Über die Betonung mehrsilbiger Wörter in Suchenwirts Versen.* Naumburg: C. A. Klaffenbach, 1843; IV, *Abhandlung der Conjugation.* Naumburg: Heinrich Sieling, 1852.

_____. "Über die Sprache Suchenwirts." In *Kleinere Schriften,* ed. Jacob Grimm. V. Berlin: Ferdinand Dümmler, 1872, 45-50.

KOCH, Erduin Julius. *Kompendium der Deutschen Literatur-Geschichte von den ältesten Zeiten bis auf Lessings Tod.* II. Berlin: Verlag der Königl. Realschulbuchhandlung, 1798.

KOCHENDÖRFFER, Karl. "Zum Turnei von Nantheiz." *ZfdA* 28 (1884), 133-136.

KOISCHWITZ, Otto. *Der Theaterherold im deutschen Schauspiel des Mittelalters und der Reformationszeit.* Germanische Studien, 46. Berlin: Emil Ebering, 1926.

KOSSMANN, Ernst Ferdinand, ed. *Die Haager Liederhandschrift. Faksimile des Originals mit Einleitung und Transkription.* The Hague: Nijhoff, 1940.

KRATOCHWIL, Franz. "Der österreichische Didactiker Peter Suchenwirt, sein Leben und seine Werke." In *Jahresbericht des k.k. Ober-Gymnasiums in Krems am Schlusse des Schuljahres 1871.* Krems: Max Pammer, 1871, pp. 3-54.

_____. "Über den gegenwärtigen Stand der Suchenwirt-Handschriften." *Germania* 34 (1889), 203-244, 303-345, 431-487.

KROLLMANN, Christian, and Raymond BEAZLEY. *The Teutonic Order in Prussia,* trans. Ernst Horstmann. Elbling: Preußenverlag, 1938.

KRONES, Franz Xaver von. *Die Freien von Saneck und ihre Chronik als Grafen von Cilli.* Graz: Leuschner and Lubensky, 1883.

KURZ, Franz. *Oesterreich unter H. Albrecht dem Dritten.* 2 vols. Linz: Cajetan Haslinger, 1827.

_____. *Oesterreich unter H. Albrecht dem Lahmen.* Linz: Cajetan Haslinger, 1819.

_____. *Oesterreich unter Herzog Albrecht IV. nebst einer Uebersicht des Zustandes Oesterreichs während des vierzehnten Jahrhunderts.* 2 vols. Linz: Joseph Fink, 1830.

_____. *Oesterreich unter H. Rudolph dem Vierten.* Linz: Cajetan Haslinger, 1821.

LACHMANN, Karl, ed. *Wolfram von Eschenbach. Parzival.* 6th ed. Berlin, Leipzig, 1926; rpt. Berlin: Walter de Gruyter, 1965.

LAMPEL, Josef. *Regesten aus dem k. und k. Haus-, Hof- und Staatsarchive in Wien.* Vol. I/2 of *Quellen zur Geschichte der Stadt Wien,* ed. Anton Mayer. Vienna: Verlag und Eigenthum des Alterthums-

Vereines zu Wien, 1896.

LAMPRECHT, Karl Gotthard. *Teutsche Geschichte*. 4th ed. Berlin: R. Gaertner, 1911.

LANGLOIS, Charles Victor. *La société française au XIIIe siècle d'après dix romans d'aventure*. Paris: Hachette, 1904.

LASSBERG, Joseph von. *Lieder-Saal. Sammlung altteutscher Gedichte*. 4 vols. 1820-1825; rpt. Hildesheim: Goerg Olms, 1968.

LAUDAN, Hans. "Die Chronologie der Werke des Konrads von Würzburg." (Diss. unpubl.). Göttingen, 1906.

LEBRET, Johann Friedrich. *Fortsetzung der Algemeinen Welthistorie durch eine Gesellschaft von Gelehrten in Teutschland und England ausgefertiget*. XLIII. Halle/Salle: Johann Jacob Gebauer, 1781.

LEESENBERG, D. A. "Mitteilungen aus von Gelre's Wapenboek. I. Die Wappengedichte van Gelres." *Der deutsche Herold* 16 (1885), 3-5.

LEICHER, Richard. *Die Totenklage in der deutschen Epik von der ältesten Zeit bis zur Nibelungen-Klage*. Germanistische Abhandlungen, 58. Breslau: M. and H. Marcus, 1927.

LEITZMANN, Albert, ed. *Erec von Hartmann von Aue*. ATB, 39. Halle/Salle: Max Niemeyer, 1939.

LETTENHOVE, Kervyn de, ed. *Œuvres de Froissart publiées avec les variantes des divers manuscrits*. Brussels: Victor Devaux, 1867-1877.

LEVY, Emil. "Guillem Figueria." (Diss. unpubl.). Berlin, 1880.

LHOTSKY, Alphons. "Quellenkunde zur mittelalterlichen Geschichte Österreichs." *MIÖG* Supp. 19 (1963), 1-496.

_____, ed. *Thomas Ebendorfer. Chronica Austriae*. MGH, Scriptores rerum Germanicarum. NS XIII. Berlin, Zurich: Weidmann, 1967.

LICHTENSTEIN, Franz, ed. *Eilhart von Oberge*. Quellen und Forschungen zur Sprach- und Culturgeschichte der germanischen Völker, 19. Strassburg: Karl J. Trübner, 1877.

LICHNOWSKY, Edward Maria. *Geschichte des Hauses Habsburg*. 8 vols. Vienna: Schaumburg, 1836-1844.

LIEBENAU, Theodor von. *Das älteste Wappengedicht Teutschlands*. Luzern: n. publ., 1880.

_____. "Conrad's von Mure Clipearius Teutonicorum." *Anzeiger für schweizerische Geschichte* 3 (1880), 229.243.

_____. "Hans Halbsuter und die Schlacht zu Sempach." *Festzeitung für das Zentralschweizerische Schützenfest in Luzern, 7. bis*

14. Juli 1889. Luzern: Meyer, 1889, p. 40.

LILIENCRON, Rochus von. *Die historischen Volkslieder der Deutschen vom 13. bis 16. Jahrhundert.* I and II. Leipzig: F. C. W. Vogel, 1865 and 1866.

LINDNER, Theodor. *Deutsche Geschichte unter den Habsburgern und Luxemburgern (1273-1437).* I. Stuttgart: J. G. Cotta, 1890.

LISCH, Georg Christian Friedrich. *Jahrbücher des Vereins für meklenburgische Geschichte und Altertumskunde.* II and III. Schwerin: Verein für meklenburgische Geschichte und Altertumskunde, 1837 and 1838.

LOSERTH, Johann. *Die Königsaaler Geschichts-Quellen.* Fontes rerum Austriacarum, Scriptores VIII. Vienna: Karl Gerold, 1875.

LORENZ, Ottokar. *Deutsche Geschichte im 13. und 14. Jahrhundert.* Vienna: Wilhelm Braumüller, 1863.

_____. *Deutschlands Geschichtsquellen im Mittelalter seit der Mitte des dreizehnten Jahrhunderts.* 2 vols. Berlin: Wilhelm Hertz, 1886.

_____. "Die Sempacher Schlachtlieder." *Germania* 6 (Berlin, 1861), 161-186.

LÜPKE, Helmut. *Untersuchungen zur Geschichte des Templeordens im Gebiet der nordostdeutschen Kolonisation.* Bernburg: Otto Dornblüth, 1933.

MCDONALD, William C. *German Medieval Literary Patronage from Charlemagne to Maximilian I: A Critical Commentary with Special Emphasis on Imperial Promotion of Literature.* Amsterdam: Rodopi, 1973.

MARTIN, Ernst. "Johan I., Herzog von Brabant, 1267-1294." In *ADB.* XIV. Berlin: Duncker and Humblot, 1881, 148-149.

_____. "Mittelrheinische und Niederländische Gedichte in einer Berliner Hs." *ZfdA* 13 (1867), 348-377.

MASCHEK, Hermann. "Die Geschichte des Pfarrers vom Kahlenberg." *ZfdA* 73 (1936), 33-46.

MAURER, Friedrich, ed. *Der altdeutsche Physiologus.* ATB, 67. Tübingen: Max Niemeyer, 1967.

_____, ed. *Die Lieder Walthers von der Vogelwiede, I. Die religiösen und die politischen Lieder.* 3rd ed. ATB, 47. Tübingen: Max Niemeyer, 1967.

_____, ed. *Die Lieder Walthers von der Vogelweide, II, Die Liebeslieder.* 3rd ed. ATB, 47. Tübingen: Max Niemeyer, 1969.

MAYR, Norbert. *Dié Reiselieder und Reisen Oswalds von Wolkenstein.* Schlern-Schriften, 215. Innsbruck: Wagner, 1961.

MEGISER, Hieronymus. *Annales Carinthiae.* 2 vols. Leipzig: Abraham Lamberg, 1612.

MENHARDT, Hermann. "Hirzelin." In *VL.* II. Berlin: Walter de Gruyter. 1936, 466-467.

_____. *Verzeichnis der altdeutschen literarischen Handschriften der österreichischen Nationalbibliothek.* III. Berlin: Akademie Verlag, 1961.

MENKEN, Johann Burchard. *Historia vitae Imp. Sigismundi.* Scriptores rerum Germanicarum praecipve Saxonicarum. I. Leipzig: n. publ., 1728.

MERZ, Walther, and Friedrich HEGI, eds. *Die Wappenrolle von Zürich.* Zurich, Leipzig: Orell Fussli, 1930.

MESS, Friedrich, ed. *Heinrich von Ofterdingen. Wartburgkrieg und verwandte Dichtungen.* Weimar: Hermann Böhlau, 1963.

MICHELL, Robert, and Nevill FORBES, trans. *The Chronicle of Novgorod 1016-1471.* Camden Society, 3rd Series, 25. London: C. E. Maurice, 1914.

MOHR, Wolfgang, and Werner KOHLSCHMIDT. "Politische Dichtung." In *RL.* 2nd ed. III. Berlin: Walter de Gruyter, 1966, 157-200.

MÜLLER, Kuno. "Hans Halbsuter." In *NDB.* VII. Berlin: Duncker and Humblot, 1966, 535.

MÜLLER, Richard. "Wiens höfisches und bürgerliches Leben im ausgehenden Mittelalter." In *Geschichte der Stadt Wien,* ed. Albert Starzer. III/2. Vienna: Adolf Holzhausen, 1907, 626-757.

_____. "Wiens räumliche Entwicklung und topographische Benennungen vom Ende des XIII. bis zum Beginne des XVI. Jahrhunderts." In *Geschichte der Stadt Wien,* ed. Heinrich Zimmermann. II/1. Vienna: Adolf Holzhausen, 1900, 108-283.

MÜLLER, Ulrich, ed. *Politische Lyrik des deutschen Mittelalters. Texte I. Von Friedrich II. bis Ludwig dem Bayern.* GAG, 68. Göppingen: Alfred Kümmerle, 1972.

_____, ed. *Politische Lyrik des deutschen Mittelalters. Texte II. Von Heinrich von Mügeln bis Michel Beheim. Von Karl IV, bis Friedrich III.* GAG, 84. Göppingen: Alfred Kümmerle, 1974.

_____. *Untersuchungen zur politischen Lyrik des deutschen Mittelalters.* GAG, 55/56. Göppingen: Alfred Kümmerle, 1974.

NICKEL, Helmut. "Der mittelalterliche Reiterschild des Abendlandes." (Diss. unpubl.). Berlin, 1958.

NICKEL, Wilhelm. *Sirventes und Spruchdichtung*. Palaestra, 63. Berlin: Mayer and Müller, 1907.

NICOLAS, Nicholas Harris, ed. *The Siege of Carlaverock*. London: J. B. Nichols, 1928.

NIEWÖHNER, Heinrich. "Suchenwirt-Handschriften." *ZfdA* 68 (1931), 273-4.

PAETOW, Louis John. *A Guide to the Study of Medieval History*. New York: F. S. Crofts, 1931.

PANKRAZ VON FREYBERG, Maximilian. *Sammlung historischer Schriften und Urkunden*. 5 vols. Stuttgart, Tübingen: J. G. Cotta, 1827-1836.

PEZ, Hieronymus, ed. *Scriptores rerum Austriacarum*. 3 vols. Leipzig, Regensburg: Johann Friedrich Gleditsch, 1721-1745.

PFAFF, Friedrich. *Die große Heidelberger Liederhandschrift*. Heidelberg: Carl Winter, 1903.

PFEIFFER, Franz, ed. *Wirnt von Gravenberg. Wigalois*. Dichtungen des deutschen Mittelalters, 6. Leipzig: G. J. Göschen, 1847.

_____. "Über Konrad von Würzburg." *Germania* 12 (Vienna, 1867), 1-48.

PÖLZL, Julius. "Der gegenwärtige Stand der Suchenwirt-Hss." *Blätter des Vereines für Landeskunde von Niederösterreich* 24 (1890), 184-185.

POPE, Mildred K., and Eleanor C. LODGE. *Life of the Black Prince by the Herald of Sir John Chandos*. Oxford: Clarendon, 1910.

POSSE, Otto. *Heraldik und Spragistik der Wettiner*. Leipzig: Giesecke and Devrien, 1893.

POTTHAST, August. *Bibliotheca historica medii aevi. Wegweiser durch die Geschichtswerke des europäischen Mittelalters bis 1500*. 2 vols. Berlin: W. Weber, 1896.

PREUENHUEBER, Valentin. *Annales Styrenses samt dessen übrigen Historisch- und Genealogischen Schriften*. Nuremberg: Johann Adam Schmidt, 1740.

PRIMISSER, Alois. "Der Wiener Dichter, Peter Suchenwirth." *Archiv für Geographie, Historie, Staats- und Kriegskunst* 13 (1822), 188-191, 218-221.

_____. "Nachricht von einer neuentdeckten Handschrift mit deutschen Gedichten aus dem vierzehnten Jahrhundert, verfaßt von Peter Suchenwirt, aus Oesterreich." *Jahrbücher der Literatur* 15 (1821), Anzeigeblatt 10-51.

_____. "Ottokars von Horneck Reimchronik." *Jahrbücher der Literatur* 15 (1822), 227-246.

_____, ed. *Peter Suchenwirt's Werke aus dem vierzehnten Jahrhunderte. Ein beytrag zur Zeit- und Sittengeschichte.* Vienna: J. B. Wallishausser, 1827; rpt. Vienna: H. Geyer, 1961.

Review: ANON. *Göttingische gelehrte Anzeigen* 85 (1827), 841-848.

PRINET, Max. "Armoiries françaises et allemandes décrites dans un ancien role d'armes anglais." *Moyen Age* 34 (1923), 223-256.

_____. "L'Armorial de France, composé à la fin du XIIIe s. ou au commencement du XIVe s." *Moten Age* 31 (1920), 1-49.

_____. "Les armoiries françaises dan de Tournoi de Nantes de Conrad de Wurtzbourg." *Moyen Age* 32 (1921), 223-232.

RANKE, Friedrich. "Von der ritterlichen zur bürgerlichen Dichtung. 1230-1430." In *Annalen der deutschen Literatur,* ed. Heinz Otto Burger. Stuttgart: J. B. Metzler, 1952, pp. 179-253.

RAUCH, Adrian. *Rerum Austriacarum scriptores.* 3 vols. Vienna: Joseph Stahel, 1793-1794.

REGEL, Karl. "Ein Fragment einer unbekannten Handschrift von Gelres Wapenboeck." *Tijdschrift voor nederlandsche Taal -en Letterkunde* 5 (1885), 17-48.

Register of Edward, The Black Prince. Great Britain Public Record Office. London: H. M. Stationery Office, 1930-1933.

RENESSE, Théodore de. *Dictionnaire des figures héraldiques.* Brussels: Societé Belge de Librairie, 1892-1903.

REUSCHEL, Helga. "Werner von Hohenberg." In *VL*. IV. Berlin: Walter de Gruyter, 1953, 926-928.

REUSCHEL, Karl. "Historisches Lied." In *RL*. I. Berlin: Walter de Gruyter, 1925/26, 510-512.

RIETSTAP, Johannes Baptist. *Armorial général, précédé d'un dictionnaire des termes du blason.* 2nd ed. 2 vols. Berlin: J.A. Stargardt, 1934.

RIQUER, Martin de. "La littérature provençale à la cour d'Alphonse II d'Aragon." *Cahiers de civilisation médiévale X^e-XIIe siècles* 2 (1959), 177-201.

ROBENS, Arnold. *Elementarwerkchen der Wapenkunde.* Düsseldorf, Aachen: n. publ., 1790.

ROCHOLZ, Ernst Ludwig. "Die Homberger Gaugrafen des Frick- und Sisgaues." *Argovia, Jahresschrift der historischen Gesellschaft des Kantons Aargau* 16 (1885).

ROETHE, Gustav. "Rosenplüt." In *ADB*. XXIX. Berlin: Duncker and Humblot, 1889, 222-232.

_____. "Sayn: Zilies (Cäcilius)." In *ALB*. XXX. Berlin: Duncker and Humblot, 1890, 464.

RÖGGEL, Joseph. "Goswins Chronik von Marienberg." *Beiträge zur Geschichte, Statistik, Naturkunde und Kunst von Tirol und Vorarlberg* 1 (1825), 67-265.

ROQUES, Mario, ed. *Les romans de Chrétien de Troyes, III, Le chevalier de la charrete.* Les classiques Français du moyen age, 86. Paris: Honoré Champion, 1969.

ROSENFELD, Hans Friedrich. "Suchenwirt, Peter." In *VL*. IV. Berlin: Walter de Gruyter, 1953, 301-315.

ROSENFELD, Hellmut. "Gelre." In *VL*. V. Berlin: Walter de Gruyter, 1955, 251-252.

_____. "Holland, Johann." In *VL*. II and V. Berlin: Walter de Gruyter, 1936, 479, and 1955, 420-422.

_____. "Konrad von Mure." In *VL*. V. Berlin: Walter de Gruyter, 1955, 561-565.

_____. "Nordische Schilddichtung und mittelalterliche Wappendichtung." *ZfdPh* 61 (1939), 232-269.

ROSENHAGEN, Gustav. "Johann von Brabant, Herzog." In *VL*. II. Berlin: Walter de Gruyter, 1936, 587-588.

RÜCKERT, Heinrich, ed. *Der Wälsche Gast des Thomasin von Zirclaria.* Bibliothek der gesammten deutschen National-Literatur, 30. Quedlinburg, Leipzig, 1852; Deutsche Neudrucke, Reihe Texte des Mittelalters. Berlin: Walter de Gruyter, 1965.

RUPPRICH, Hans. "Das Wiener Schrifttum des ausgehenden Mittelalters." *WSB* 228 (1954), 3-190.

_____. *Vom späten Mittelalter bis zum Barock. Das ausgehende Mittelalter, Humanismus und Renaissance 1370-1520.* Vol. IV/1 of *Geschichte der deutschen Literatur,* ed. Helmut de Boor and Richard Newald. Munich: C. H. Beck, 1970.

RYE, Reginald Arthur. *Catalogue of the Manuscripts and Autograph Letters in the University Library...with a Description of the Manuscript Life of Edward, Prince of Wales, the Black Prince by Chandos the Herald.* London: University of London Press, 1921.

SACKEN, Eduard von. *Heraldik.* 7th ed. rev. by Moriz von Weittenhiller. Leipzig: J. J. Weber, 1906.

SALMEN, Walter. *Der fahrende Musiker im europäischen Mittelalter.* Die Musik im alten und neuen Europa, 4. Kassel: Hinnenthal, 1960.

SALMON, Thomas. *A New Historical Account of St. George.* London: Nath. Dancer, 1704.

SAN-MARTE (pseud. of Albert Schulz). "Das Wappen Wolframs von Eschenbach."
Germania 3 (Berlin, 1839), 20-25.

_____. *Zur Waffenkunde des älteren deutschen Mittelalters.* Quedlinburg,
Leipzig: Gottfried Basse, 1867.

SARRAZIN, Gregor. *Wigamur, eine litterarhistorische Untersuchung.* Quellen
und Forschungen, 35. Strassburg: Karl J. Trübner, 1879.

SCHAUS, Ernst. "Das Kloster der Minne." *ZfdA* 38 (1894), 361-368.

SCHELER, August, ed. *Lits et contes de Baudouin de Condé et de son fils
Jean de Condé.* Brussels: Victor Devaux, 1866.

SCHLATTER, Gustav. "Zu Halbsuters Sempacherlied und seiner Erzählung
von der That Winkelrieds." *Anzeiger für Schweizerische
Geschichte,* NS 1 (1870-1873), 14-15.

SCHNEIDER, Fedor. "Studien zu Johannes von Victring." *Neues Archiv der
Gesellschaft für ältere deutsche Geschichtskunde* 29 (1904), 397-442.

SCHNEIDER, Hermann. "Spruchdichtung, mittelhochdeutsche." In *RL.*
III. Berlin: Walter de Gruyter, 1928/1929, 237-292.

SCHOLL, Gottlob Heinrich Friedrich, ed. *Diu Crône von Heinrich von
dem Türlin.* SLV, 27. Tübingen: H. Laupp, 1852.

SCHONACH, Ludwig. "Zu Peter Suchenwirt." *AfdA* 36 (1913), 199.

SCHOTTKY, Julius Max. "Herzog Albrechts III. von Österreich Kreutzzug
gegen die heidnischen Preussen." *Archiv für Geographie,
Historie, Staats- und Kriegskunst* 13 (1822), 444-447.

_____. "Ueber Heinrich Teychner, einen Wiener Spruchdichter des 14ten
Jahrhunderts." *Jahrbücher der Literatur* 11 (1818), Anzeigeblatt
26-40.

SCHRAMM, Percy Ernst. *Herrschaftszeichen und Staatssymbolik; Beiträge
zu ihrer Geschichte vom dritten bis zum sechzehnten Jahrhundert.*
Schriften der MGH, 13/I-III. Stuttgart: Hiersemann, 1954-1956.

SCHRÖDER, Edward, ed. *Kleinere Dichtungen Konrads von Würzburg, II,
Der Schwanritter, Das Turnier von Nantes.* 3rd ed. Berlin:
Weidmann, 1959.

_____, ed. *Konrad von Würzburg. Die goldene Schmiede.* Göttingen:
Vandenhoeck Ruprecht, 1926.

_____. "Studien zu Konrad von Würzburg." In *Nachrichten von der
Königlichen Gesellschaft der Wissenschaften zu Göttingen, Phil.-
Hist. Kl.* Göttingen: Dieterich, 1912, 1-47, and 1917, 96-129.

SCHULTZ, Alwin. *Höfisches Leben zur Zeit der Minnesinger.* 2nd ed.
2 vols. Leipzig: S. Hirzel, 1889.

SCHULTZE, Johannes. *Die Mark Brandenburg, II, Die Mark unter Herrschaft*

der Wittelsbacher und Luxemburger (1319-1415).   Berlin: Duncker
and Humblot, 1961.

SCHÜTZ, Kaspar. *Historia rerum Prussicarum.*   2nd ed.   Leipzig: G.
Knoff, 1599.

SEEMANN, Erich. "Historisches Lied." In *RL.* 2nd. ed. I. Berlin:
Walter de Gruyter, 1958, 666-669.

SEEMÜLLER, Joseph. "Chronologie der Gedichte Suchenwirts." *ZfdA* 41
(1897), 193-223.

_____. "Deutsche Poesie vom Ende des XIII. bis in den Beginn des XVI.
Jahrhunderts." In *Geschichte der Stadt Wien,* ed. Albert Starzer.
III/1. Vienna: Adolf Holzhausen, 1907, 1-81.

_____, ed. *Österreichische Chronik von den 95 Herrschaften.*   MGH,
Deutsche Chroniken, VI. Hannover, Leipzig: Hahn, 1909.

_____, ed. *Ottokars Österreichische Leimchronik.*   MGH, Deutsche
Chroniken V/1,2. Hannover: Hahn, 1890-1893.

_____, ed. *Seifried Helbling.*   Halle/Salle: Buchhandlung des
Waisenhauses, 1886.

SENCKENBERG, Heinrich Christian. *Collectanea manuscripta de judicus
Westphalius.*   Regensburg: Johannes Henricus David Goebel, 1762.

SEYLER, Gustav A. *Geschichte der Heraldik.*   Abtheilung A des Siebmacher'
schen Wappenbuches. Nuremberg: Bauer and Raspe, 1885; rpt.
Neustadt a.d. Aisch: Degener.

SIEBENKEES, Johann Christian. *Erläuterungen der Heraldik als ein
Commentar über Herrn...Gatterers Abriss dieser Wissenschaft.*
Nuremberg: Adam Gottlieb Schneider, 1789.

SIEBMACHER, Johann. *Allgemeines grosses und vollständiges Wappenbuch.*
6 vols. Nuremberg: Gabriel Nicolaus Raspe, 1772.

_____. *J. Siebmacher's grosses und allgemeines Wappenbuch in
Verbindung mit Mehreren neu herausgegeben und mit historischen,
genealogischen und heraldischen Notizen begleitet von Dr. Otto
Titan von Hefner.* 8 vols. Nuremberg: Gabriel Nichlaus Raspe,
1856-1936.

_____. *New Wapenbuch: darinnen dess H. Rom. Reichs teutscher hoher
potentaten, fürsten, herren, und adelspersonen auch anderer
ständt und stätte wapen in der zahl über 3320.*   Nuremberg:
published by author, 1605.

SINGER, Samuel. *Die mittelalterliche Literatur der deutschen Schweiz.*
Frauenfeld, Leipzig: J. Huber, 1930.

SISMONDI, Jean Charles Leonard. *History of the Italian Republics in the
Middle Ages.*   London: Routledge, 1895.

SPIESS, Philipp Ernst. *Archivische Nebenarbeiten und Nachrichten vermischten Inhalts mit Urkunden.* 2 vols. Halle/Salle: Johann Jacob Gebauer, 1783.

SPRINGER, Hermann. *Das altprovenzalische Klagelied.* Berliner Beiträge zur germanischen und romanischen Philologie, 7. Romanische Abteilung, 2. Berlin: C. Vogt, 1896.

STAMMLER, Wolfgang. "Holland, Johann." In *VL.* II. Berlin: Walter de Gruyter, 1936, 479.

STAUB, Franz. *Die ältesten Kaufbücher (1368-1388).* Vol. III/1 of *Quellen zur Geschichte der Stadt Wien,* ed. Anton Mayer. Viénna: Verlag und Eigenthum des Alterthums-Vereines zu Wien, 1898.

_____. *Gewerbuch B (1373-1419)--Verbotbuch (1373-1399).* Vol. III/2 of *Quellen zur Geschichte der Stadt Wien,* ed. Anton Mayer. Vienna: Verlag und Eigenthum des Alterthums-Vereines zu Wien, 1911.

STEYERER, Anton. *Commentarii pro historia Alberti II.' Lucis Austriae, cognomento sapientis scripti.* Leipzig: Thomas Fritsch, 1725.

STRAUCH, Philipp, ed. *Jansen Enikels Werke.* MGH, Deutsche Chroniken, III. Hannover, Leipzig: Hahn, 1900.

STRNAD, Alfred. "Herzog Albrecht III. von Österreich (1365-1395). Ein Beitrag zur Geschichte Österreichs im späten Mittelalter." (Diss. unpubl.). Vienna, 1961.

STRÖHL, Hugo Gerhard. *Leutsche Wappenrolle.* Stuttgart: Julius Hoffmann, 1897.

_____. *Heraldischer Atlas: eine Sammlung von heraldischen Muster- blättern für Künstler, Gewerbetreibende, sowie für Freunde der Wappenkunde.* Stuttgart: Julius Hoffmann, 1909.

_____. *Oesterreichisch-ungarische Wappenrolle.* 2nd ed. Vienna: Anton Schroll, 1895.

STURTEVANT, Albert Morey. "Zur Sprache des Peter von Suchenwirt. ,Der Widertail'." *MLN* 25 (1910), 47-51.

TALVJ (pseud. of Therese Robinson). *Volkslieder der Serben.* 2nd ed. 2 vols. Leipzig: F. U. Brockhaus, 1853.

THIERL, Heinrich Gustav. "Zur Symbolik der Abzeichen alter Ritterorden." *Jahrbuch Adler,* NS 13 (1903), 83-103.

TIMPSON, Geroge F. "Heraldry in Wolfram's Parzival." *The Coat of Arms* 4 (1957), 179-281.

TOISCHER, Wendelin. "Die altdeutschen Bearbeitungen der pseudo- aristotelischen Secreta-secretorum." In *Programm, Prag-Neustadt Staatsobergymnasium.* Prague: Rohlizek, 1884.

TUMLER, P. Marian. *Ler deutsche Orden im Werden, Wachsen und Wirken bis 1400 mit einem Abriß der Geschichte des Ordens von 1400 bis zur neuesten Zeit.* Vienna: Panorama, 1954.

UHL, Wilhelm. "Peter Suchenwirt." In *ADB.* XXXVII. Berlin: Duncker and Humblot, 1894, 77-780.

UHLIRZ, Karl. "Quellen und Geschichtschreibung." In *Geschichte der Stadt Wien,* ed. Heinrich Zimmermann. II/1. Vienna: Adolf Holzhausen, 1900, 35-107.

_____, and Mathilde. *Handbuch der Geschichte Österreich-Ungarns.* 2nd ed. I. Graz, Vienna, Cologne: Hermann Böhlau, 1963.

ULMENSTEIN, Christian Ulrich von. *Über Ursprung und Entstehung des Wappenwesens.* In *Forschungen zum deutschen Fecht,* ed. Franz Beyerle, Herbert Meyer, and Karl Rauch. I/2. Weimar: Hermann Böhlau, 1935.

VANCSA, Max. "Politische Geschichte der Stadt Wien (1283-1522)." In *Geschichte der Stadt Wien,* ed. Albert Starzer. II/2. Vienna: Adolf Holzhausen, 1905, 499-591.

VAN D'ELDEN, Stephanie Cain. "Peter Suchenwirt and Heraldic Poetry." (Diss. unpubl.). Minneapolis, Minnesota, 1974.

VETTER, Ferinand, ed. *Lehrhafte Litteratur des 14. und 15. Jahrhunderts.* Kürchners Deutsche National-Litteratur, 12. Berlin, Stuttgart: W. Spemann, 1889.

VOIGT, Johannes. *Codex diplomaticus Prussicus. Urkunden-Sammlung zur ältern Geschichte Preussens.* 4 vols. 1853; rpt. Osnabrück: Otto Zeller, 1965.

_____. *Geschichte Preussens von den ältesten Zeiten bis zum Untergange der Herrschaft des Deutschen Ordens.* IV and V. Königsberg: Gebrüder Bornträger, 1830 and 1832.

WACKERNAGEL, Wilhelm. "Konrad von Würzburg aus Würzburg oder aus Basel?" *Germania* 3 (Vienna, 1858), 257-266.

WAGNER, Anthony Richard. *Heralds and Heraldry in the Middle Ages.* London: Oxford University Press, 1939.

_____. *Heralds of England. A History of the Office and College of Arms.* London: H. M. Stationery Office, 1967.

_____. *Historic Heraldry of Britain.* London: Oxford University Press, 1939.

WAL, Guillaume de. *Historie de l'Ordre Teutonique.* 8 vols. Paris, Rheims: n. publ., 1784-1790.

WANDRUSZKA, Adam. *Las Haus Habsburg.* Stuttgart: Friedrich Vorwerk, 1956.

Wappenfibel Handbuch der Heraldik. Ed. "Herold" Verein für Heraldik, Genealogie und verwandte Wissenschaften. 16th ed. Neustadt a.d. Aisch: Degener, 1970.

WARTON, Thomas. *History of English Poetry*. London: 1774; rpt. New York, London: Johnson Reprint Corp., 1968.

WEBER, Karl Julius. *Das Ritterwesen und die Templer, Johanniter und Marianer oder Deutsch-Ordens-Ritter*. 2nd ed. 3 vols. Stuttgart: Hallberg, 1849.

WEBER, Otfried. *Peter Suchenwirt: Studien über sein Wesen und Werk*. Deutsches Werden, 11. Greifswald: L. Bamberg, 1937.

WEDEN, Fritz. *Das Spätmittelalter (vom Interregnum bis 1500)*. Vol. III of *Quellenkunde der deutschen Geschichte im Mittelalter (bis zum Ende des 15. Jahrhunderts)*, ed. Karl Jacob. Sammlung Göschen, 284. Berlin: Walter de Gruyter, 1952.

WEISKE, Julius, ed. *Der Sachsenspiegel (Landrecht)*. 5th ed. Leipzig: O. R. Reisland, 1876.

WESLE, Carl, ed. *Das Rolandslied des Pfaffen Konrad*. 2nd ed. ATB, 69. Tübingen: Max Niemeyer, 1967.

WIESSNER, Hermann, ed. *Die Kärntner Geschichtsquellen 1326-1335*. Vol. IX of *Monumenta historica Iucatus Carinthiae*, ed. Geschichtsverein für Kärnten. Klagenfurt: Verlag des Geschichtsvereines für Kärnten, 1965.

WINKEL, Jan te. "Neue Bruchstücke des Gedichtes von der Böhmenschlacht." *PBB* 19 (1894), 486-494.

WINTER, Ernst Karl. *Rudolph Ⅳ. von Österreich*. 2 vols. Vienna: Reinhold, Gsur, 1934-1936.

WIRSUNG, Marx. *Wann und umb wellicher ursachen willen das loblich Ritterspil des turniers erdacht und zum ersten geübet worden ist*. Augsburg: n. publ., 1518.

WISSGRILL, Franz Karl. *Schauplatz des landsässigen Nieder-Oesterreichischen Adels*. II. Vienna: Franz Seizer, 1795.

WOLF, Werner, ed. *Albrechts von Scharfenberg Jüngerer Titurel*. DTM, 45. Berlin: Akademie-Verlag, 1955.

WOLFF, Ludwig, ed. *Hartmann von Aue*. *Iwein*. 7th ed. Berlin: Walter de Gruyter, 1968.

WRIGHT, Thomas, ed. *Political Poems and Songs relating to English History, composed during the period from the Accession of ELW. III. to that of RIC. III*. Rerum Britannicarum medii aevi, Scriptores, XIV/1. London, 1859; rpt. London: Kraus Reprint Ltd., 1965.

_____. *The Political Songs of England, from the Reign of John to that of Edward II.* Bibliotheca Curiosa, 33. Edinburgh: privately printed, 1884.

_____, ed. *The Roll of Arms of the Princes, Barons, and Knights who attended King Edward I. to the Siege of Caerlaverock, in 1300.* London: John Hotten, 1864.

WÜRDINGER, Joseph. "Friedrich von Lochen, Landeshauptmann in der Mark Brandenburg." *MSB* 1 (1874), 373-416.

WURMBRAND-STUPPACH, Johann Wilhelm. *Collectanea genealogico-historica ex Archivo in Clytorum Austria.* Vienna: Johann Baptist Schöonwetter, 1705.

ZACHER, Julius. "Handschrften im Haag." *ZfdA* 1 (1841), 209-269.

ZAPPE, Alfred. *Grundriß der Heraldik.* Limburg a.L.: C.A. Starke, 1968.

ZIPS, Manfred. "Das Wappenwesen in der mittelhochdeutschen Epik bis 1250." (Diss. unpubl.). Vienna, 1966.

_____. "Einige Zeugnisse aus der mittelhochdeutschen Epik zur Beziehung zwischen dem ritterlichen Helden und seinem Wappensymbol." *Jahrbuch der Heraldisch-Genealogischen Gesellschaft „Adler"* 8.3. (1971/73), 155-182.

_____. "Tristan und die Ebersymbolik." *PBB* 94 (Tübingen, 1972), 134-152.

ZWIERZINA, Konrad. "Lupold Hornburgs Gedichte." In *Festschrift des k.k. Erzherzog Rainer-Real-Gymnasiums im II. Gemeinde-Bezirke in Wien.* Vienna: Carl Fromme, 1914, 115-136.

SELECTED INDEX

WIENER ARBEITEN
ZUR GERMANISCHEN ALTERTUMSKUNDE
UND PHILOLOGIE

Verlag Karl M. Halosar

1040 Wien, Margaretenstraße 35
Tel. 56 13 53